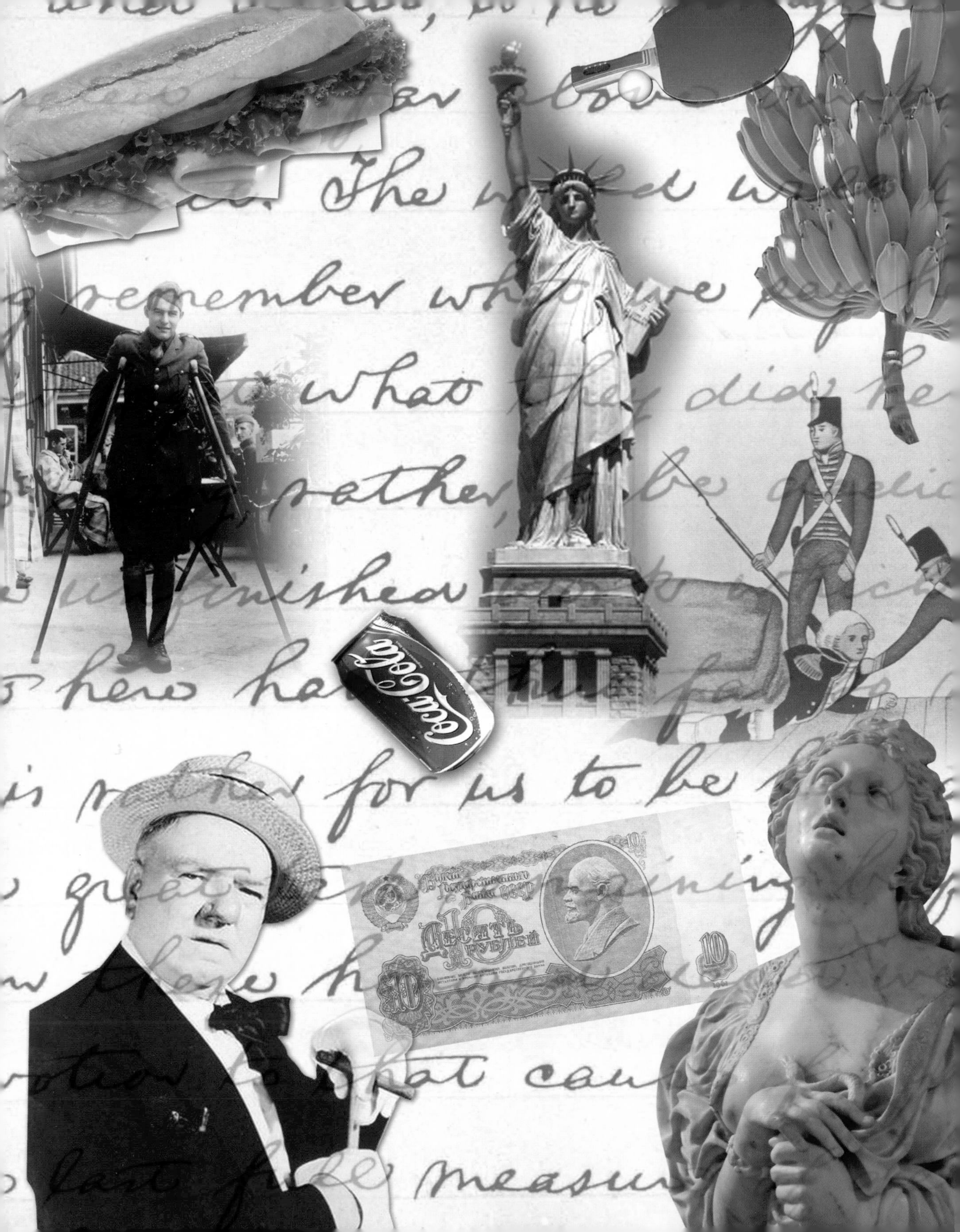

The world will

remember who we are

what they did

rather

finished

hero ha

for us to be

great

measur

Hundreds of "Facts" You Thought Were True, But Aren't

David Diefendorf

With a Foreword by James Randi

STERLING

New York / London

www.sterlingpublishing.com

Produced by The Reference Works, Inc.

STERLING and the distinctive Sterling logo are registered trademarks of
Sterling Publishing Co., Inc.

Library of Congress Cataloging-in-Publication Data Available

4   6   8   10   9   7   5

Published by Sterling Publishing Co., Inc.
387 Park Avenue South, New York, NY 10016
© 2007 by The Reference Works, Inc.
Distributed in Canada by Sterling Publishing
c/o Canadian Manda Group, 165 Dufferin Street
Toronto, Ontario, Canada M6K 3H6
Distributed in the United Kingdom by GMC Distribution Services
Castle Place, 166 High Street, Lewes, East Sussex, England BN7 1XU
Distributed in Australia by Capricorn Link (Australia) Pty. Ltd.
P.O. Box 704, Windsor, NSW 2756, Australia

Interior design by Raquel Shapira
Illustrations by Nicholas Meola

Sterling ISBN-13: 978-1-4027-3791-6
        ISBN-10: 1-4027-3791-2

For information about custom editions, special sales, or premium
and corporate purchases, please contact Sterling Special Sales
Department at 800-805-5489 or specialsales@sterlingpub.com.

DEDICATION

We dedicate this book to Cliff Clavin, the obnoxious but lovable know-it-all from the TV show *Cheers*, played inimitably by John Ratzenberger. A relentless and sometimes barely tolerated dispenser of trivia, half-truths, and "little-known facts," Cliff is a living monument to thinly veiled ignorance and closely cherished misinformation.

and dead who struggled

ated it... two or

detract. The world will

remember what we say here

forget what they did here

living, rather to be dedica

unfinished work which

here have thus far so n

rather for us to be here d

great task remaining bef

these honored dead t

tion to that cause for

last full measure of dev

Contents

Author's Note

Otherwise known as a preface, the author's note is probably the least-read part of any book, with the possible exception of the copyright page. But in this instance I would ask the reader to hang in there for a while. This book has a few idiosyncrasies that should be mentioned at the outset, and some of them need to be explained.

Amazing…But False! is the book's title, but let's not take it too literally. It jokingly alludes, of course, to the old cliché "amazing but true." But the amazing part is not always the misconception itself. In some instances what is most amazing is the truth that debunks the myth, and in others what is most amazing is that a particularly odd or unlikely notion ever became widely accepted in the first place…and is still widely believed today.

We all live with misconceptions, whether we know it or not. They proliferate like viruses, touching on every aspect of our daily lives. Some were taught to us in school (infinitives should not be split; Marie Antoinette said "Let them eat cake"; the Emancipation Proclamation freed the slaves; the Wright brothers invented the airplane). Some are creations of movies and the media (women burned their bras; if arrested you are allowed only one phone call; Lassie was played by female dogs; lemmings commit mass suicide).

In the world of falsehoods, misquotes attributed to famous people abound, as do misusages in written and spoken English ("presently" for "right now"; "reticent" for "reluctant"). Juicy rumors are passed along by teens and college students (Catherine the Great died having sex with a horse; Walt Disney had his head frozen; Mister Rogers was a Navy SEAL). People often make assumptions just because they seem logical (paper is better than plastic; the Immaculate Conception is about the birth of Jesus; white wine always comes from white grapes). And some notions are passed along without question or

hesitation from one generation to the next (reading in low light will hurt your eyes; poison ivy gets worse when you scratch it; cold weather causes colds).

Whatever the origin of popular misconceptions, it's wise to remember that truths and falsehoods are relative and multi-layered. They evolve and mutate with the times, the circumstances, and the people who pass them along. In perusing other books of this kind, for instance, I have discovered in some cases that the debunkers turned out to be wrong. And I have no doubt that some of the notions proclaimed as true in this book will also, at some point in the not-too-distant future, be proved erroneous or at least questionable.

To belabor this point a bit further, I should say that the proliferation of inadvertent misinformation, deliberate disinformation, and information that has simply outlived its fifteen minutes of usefulness has given rise to a mood of skepticism regarding *all* claims to veracity. We are living in a time when truth seems to have a short shelf life. People have come to mistrust any fact, belief, or tenet—be it in science, history, religion, medicine, politics, whatever—because although it may be a viable certainty for now, just wait a few months or a few years: there's a good chance it will eventually be deemed obsolete.

Once a respected "science," phrenology was proved to be about as scientific as reading tea leaves. After Darwin, people spread the word that humans were "descended from apes," but Darwin himself never said any such thing. Pluto used to be a planet, and today it's not. A few decades ago doctors would laugh out loud at the notion that ulcers are caused by bacteria, but now we (and they) know they are. Over the years, eggs have been deemed good for you, then bad for you, then good for you, etc. And when some British pranksters admitted fabricating a few crop circles, people came to assume (unjustifiably) that all crop circles were hoaxes.

Depending on the subject matter, the tone of the writing in this book may vary from solemn to comedic, semi-poetic to ploddingly prosaic, modest to smug. Speaking of smug, when one undertakes the task of debunking commonly accepted myths, it's hard not to sound, at times, like a shameless know-it-all. But in the hope of scoring a few points for author humility, I should mention that a large percentage of the revelations uncovered in this book were as surprising to me as I hope they will be—entertainingly so—to you.

On the subject of sources, the reader should know that I used anything and everything available: books, periodicals, scholars, librarians, and the wealth of information available via search engines and multiple Internet links. The material for each topic was confirmed by numerous sources and represents what I believe to be a fair and reasonable consensus regarding what is true, what is false, and what lies somewhere in between. Since this is a pop reference tome, I didn't want to scare readers away with lots of footnotes and a lengthy bibliography. If the reader wants to explore a topic further, my advice (as a friend puts it) is to "google and google."

In case you hadn't noticed, this book is dedicated to Cliff Clavin, the lovable but irritating know-it-all from the TV show *Cheers*. He had a way of dispensing "little-known facts" to his friend Norm and anyone else at the bar who cared to (reluctantly) listen. Cliff took pride in surprising his bar-mates with new and fascinating information, but he unwittingly (and pompously, at that) conveyed not the enlightened truth but misinformation of a hilariously distorted ilk. For example, "It's a little-known fact that the tan became popular in what is known as the Bronze Age" or "Everyone in the Swiss Army owns a Swiss Army knife. That's why no one messes with Switzerland."

In the domain of misinformation, at least, the Clavin Syndrome will not affect readers who want to impress friends and acquaintances with "little-known facts" from this book. But to avoid being compared with another side of Clavin—namely, the obnoxious know-it-all—a few suggestions are in order.

First, when a particular misconception happens to come up in conversation, you should of course feel free to dispense one or two choice tidbits of debunkery (usually prefaced by something like "I'll bet you didn't know…"). But be careful not to insult someone by contradicting what he or she has just said. If you get past this hurdle, the new and surprising info may be greeted with appreciation, if not wonderment. Be cautioned, however, that if you keep up this wiser-than-thou behavior too relentlessly, you may reach what might be called the "CSP" (Clavin Saturation Point). The tip-off would come when the oohs and aahs are replaced by silence, blank stares, scowls, eye-rolling, or the phrase "There you go again." In other words, if you want to avoid morphing into the likes of Cliff Clavin, think "less is more." And above all, have fun.

David Diefendorf
Winooski, Vermont
September 2006

Foreword

by James Randi

In his remarkable book of 1843, *Extraordinary Popular Delusions & the Madness of Crowds*, author Charles Mackay described in detail a variety of strange ideas and obsessions that had seized the people of his time. He began:

In reading the history of nations, we find that, like individuals, they have their whims and their peculiarities; their seasons of excitement and recklessness, when they care not what they do. We find that whole communities suddenly fix their minds upon one object, and go mad in its pursuit; that millions of people become simultaneously impressed with one delusion, and run after it, till their attention is caught by some new folly more captivating than the first. We see one nation suddenly seized, from its highest to its lowest members, with a fierce desire of military glory; another as suddenly becoming crazed upon a religious scruple, and neither of them recovering its senses until it has shed rivers of blood and sowed a harvest of groans and tears, to be reaped by its posterity.

For generations, Mackay's readers have chortled at the naivete of those who chose to accept so many bizarre notions, and who in many cases were very willing to invest money and trust in them—much to their subsequent sorrow. The book you hold in your hand deals with somewhat similar subjects—claims, ideas, notions, reports, news items, and downright scams. Those who laughed at the dupes of generations long gone described by Mackay will see here how a very modern populace can fall as easily and as hard for this sort of misinformation, even though we now have the Internet and other technical advantages that should keep us from falling head-long into irrational convictions.

There are rascals out there who have a variety of reasons for wanting to deceive us. Some want to sell us spurious products or services. Others literally want to steal from us, by one means or another. And some want to gain access to our private lives. However, a great deal of misinformation is created and disseminated by pranksters, those who want to create some excitement so that they can stand back and be amused at those of us who should've been a little more alert by checking out sources.

Today, more than ever, we find perpetual motion machines, "free energy" schemes, and strange little devices that we're told to place at strategic spots around internal-combustion engines in order to obtain better performance and economy, sold via mail order and even through in-person public lectures. Sometimes we even get to see videos that appear to establish the validity of these claimed inventions, though you'd think we should be a bit smarter than to accept "special effects" that any teenager can now create on a computer screen by means of easily available software programs. Apparently, we aren't, as *Amazing...But False!* shows us.

At our office headquarters in Fort Lauderdale, Florida, we can show you a huge library that long ago overflowed its shelves and continued on into the hall outside. At least sixty percent of this collection is sheer nonsense. Every sort of crackpot idea, every possible conspiracy theory, all sorts of "scientific" theories are represented here. We maintain this library for reference purposes of students, researchers, the media, and just-curious people who want to have a better view of how easily we can be deceived—and how easily we deceive ourselves. Publishers adore what we call "woo-woo" books, because they know they can sell several printings of them, public taste being what it is. As soon as a would-be author shows up in an editor's doorway and outlines a ridiculous, impossible idea, you can almost hear the trees begin to fall in nearby forests in preparation for the paper that will be wasted—again—on yet another silly book. In this office, at least, we know the contents of our library, and we warn readers well in advance that they should be very careful about accepting what they find on our shelves as true.

Except for my books, of course ...

I recall that many years ago, during the time that I did my late-night radio show out of New York City, I was invited to attend the opening—on Broadway—of the "Believe It or Not" museum containing many of the original artifacts that belonged to that cartoonist-turned-columnist, Robert Ripley, and upon which he based many of his highly popular illustrated articles describing various wonders of nature and of Man. Now, some of these were obviously spurious, and I suppose that we were expected to filter those out as amusements rather than actual discoveries. As with many of those who began with good intentions, Ripley tended, in his later articles, to rather overexaggerate. This might have been due to a shortage of material; I can't say. In any case, I was willing to tour the facility and form an opinion. I did. As I exited, I was met by a crowd of media people who were doubtless anxious to hear what the Great Skeptic might have to say. "So what did you think of the exhibit, Mr. Randi?" asked a chap who stuck a microphone in my face. I put my hand to my chin in a contemplative mode, paused for a few seconds, and gave him a short quotation that evidently delighted him: "Not!"

There is always a place in our lives for fantasy, and no one enjoys that luxury more than I. After all, for half a century I made my living traveling the world as a professional magician, and a magician deals in that commodity every moment that he's on stage. The art, of course, lies in recognizing reality and carefully separating it from fiction. Professionals, certainly, know how that's done. Years ago, I toured the U.S. and several foreign markets as part of the Alice Cooper rock show—my job was to chop his head off with a guillotine every night—without actually doing him any harm. It worked, for three months, and during that period of time I had the opportunity of seeing a unique phenomenon. Alice and I were always the last to leave the dressing room to begin the show, because I had to equip him with two hand-held mechanisms that enabled him to throw long flames from his fingertips. These were semi-dangerous devices that he'd only take into his hands at the very last moment. When the stage manager would poke his head in the door and announce, "Two minutes!" I could watch Vincent Furnier—that's Alice Cooper's original name—rapidly and magically change from a reasonably normal young man into the showbiz monster that his audience expected him to be. He adopted the character by simply putting it on like a pullover. His walk, his facial expression, his entire demeanor changed—and a moment later as he would totter Frankenstein Monsterlike into the spotlight, Vincent would become Alice. Two hours later, when he retired from the stage dressed in white satin tails and top hat, he became Vincent as soon as he hit the lights of the dressing room. I always admired that in him, his ability to step into fantasy and then shed it so easily. It's a talent we might all try to acquire.

We raptly watch *Star Wars*, but we don't really believe we're seeing space warriors firing ray-guns at one another. *Gone with the Wind* charms us, but we know we're still in the twenty-first century and we didn't watch Atlanta burning. Engrossed in *Moby Dick*, we can empathize with Ahab, but we're still aware that we're reading fiction. Why, then, do so many of us suspend our judgment so that we can be scammed by people who would sell us felt insoles with embedded magnets, merchandisers who will prescribe a gel-stick with no active ingredients in it that we rub on our foreheads because we were told that headaches can be thus relieved, or a guru who says that if we take his course, we'll be able to fly just by thinking deeply about it? It's time to come under the lights of the dressing room and return to the real world.

In summary: Enjoy the fantasy, the fun, the stories—but make sure that there's a clear, sharp line drawn on the floor so that you can step back behind that mark and reembrace reality. To do otherwise is to embrace madness.

Enjoy this book and accept the many surprises that will be found here. Or, if you can't manage to do that, please resolve that at least you'll give it a really good try ....

—James Randi
President, the James Randi Educational Foundation
www.randi.org
Fort Lauderdale, Florida
September 2006

Famous Firsts

The First Automobile Was Built by Daimler and Benz

We elsewhere establish that Henry Ford did not (contrary to popular belief, at least in some quarters) invent the automobile. That the first automobile is said to be the work of Daimler and Benz is what the history books claim, but is it true? Karl Benz and Gottlieb Daimler were certainly the first to produce a practical gasoline-driven automobile in

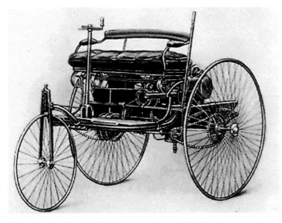

Daimler replaced the steam engine with his improved gasoline-powered four-stroke internal combustion engine. Above, the first gas-powered Benz automobile, 1885.

1885, based on the internal combustion engine, which was invented by Daimler and Nikolas Otto in 1875. But theirs was not the first. Before gasoline and the internal combustion engine, there was steam, and in the mid-seventeenth century—more than two hundred years before Daimler and Benz—a Belgian named Ferdinand Verbiest and a fellow Jesuit missionary, Philipe-Marie Grimaldi, built and operated a small steam-driven automobile while they were working in Peking, China. The machine was only two feet long and putt-putted along at about four miles an hour, but on its first test run in 1671, it ran for some two hours. The device was looked upon as a novelty (even by the Chinese) and no further work was done on it.

About a century later, in 1765, a French inventor named Nicolas-Joseph Cugnot invented a more practical steam-driven vehicle which many regard as the first true automobile. Afterward, steam-driven models were produced every now and then, but none were considered commercially viable. A few years later, in the 1870s, a German mechanic named Siegfried Marcus built

Gottlieb Daimler (1834–1900), born in the town of Schorndorf, near Stuttgart, Germany.

a very primitive gas-powered engine and attached it to a handcart, making what some consider a kind of milestone.

In 1885, Daimler powered a vehicle with his newly developed four-stroke internal combustion engine. And on November 10, 1885, Daimler's son Paul drove the first practical gasoline-driven automobile from Cannstatt, Germany, to Untertürkheim and back—marking the beginning of the automotive age.

But wait—didn't Siegfried Marcus beat them by ten years? Well, perhaps. It later became clear that Marcus had fudged some of his notes and his vehicle may not have been running prior to Paul Daimler's historic jaunt. In any case, Marcus's machine was impractical—it had to be lifted off the ground in order to start—and lurched around with virtually no control of either speed or direction until the engine failed, and then the engine had to be virtually rebuilt. (See also "Henry Ford Invented the Car, Its Engine, and the Assembly Line.")

Baseball Was Invented by Abner Doubleday in Cooperstown, New York

The Baseball Hall of Fame was founded in Cooperstown, New York, but our national pastime was not. Nor was it invented by Abner Doubleday, who was given the honor mistakenly by a panel of executives from a sporting goods company. Baseball's origin can be traced to a British game called "rounders," which evolved into an American version called "townball." It was in 1845, when Alexander Cartwright of Hoboken, New Jersey, introduced a new set of rules, not previously included in earlier editions of townball (including three strikes to a batter, three outs to an inning, tags and force-outs, and an umpire), that the game of baseball was born. Cartwright also assembled the first baseball team, called the Knickerbocker Baseball Club.

The first game of baseball was played on a field in Hoboken named Elysian Fields. (For lovers of the game, the phrase couldn't be more apt: in ancient Greek mythology, Elysian Fields is synonymous with paradise.) Once the new sport caught on, baseball clubs and inner-city games became commonplace. The first professional team, the Cincinnati Red Stockings (now the Reds), was founded in 1869.

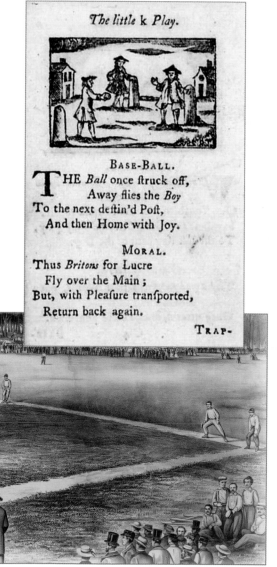

The little k Play.

BASE-BALL.

THE *Ball* once ftruck off,
Away flies the *Boy*
To the next deftin'd Poft,
And then Home with Joy.

MORAL.

Thus *Britons* for Lucre
Fly over the Main;
But, with Pleafure tranfported,
Return back again.

TRAP-

Right: Nursery rhyme describing the rules of "base-ball," from *A Little Pretty Pocket-Book,* by John Newbery, first known reference to the game and first appearance of the word *base-ball* in print. Below: Painting of the Elysian Fields in Hoboken, New Jersey.

The Bagpipe Was Invented in Scotland

Although associated with Scotland since it was introduced to that country in the early 1400s, the bagpipe did not originate there. Various forms of pipes with a bag attached have been written about in ancient scriptures and depicted in the art of ancient Egypt, Persia, Greece, and Rome. Bagpipes were seen throughout Europe from 900 to 1500, and they were introduced to the British Isles by the Romans in the early Middle Ages. But they didn't find a permanent home—or become a national symbol—until they reached the shores of Scotland in the fifteenth century.

Various forms of bagpipes are found in Spain, Italy, France, and Scandinavia. Incidentally, the proper term for the instrument is "bagpipe" (singular)—not "bagpipes" (plural). The pipe essential for the instrument to work is the intake pipe through which the player blows air into the bag. The three other pipes that are commonly seen sticking out of the bag are the (aptly named) drone pipes, which provide the bass background. Ardent bagpipe players are convinced these drone pipes are also essential; why, one couldn't say.

Bauernhochzeit in einem Dorf bei Samokov (translation: *A Peasant Wedding in a Village near Samokov*), painted by Nikola Obrasopissez in 1892.

Darwin Invented the Theory of Evolution continued opposite page

The theory that living things evolve over many generations, gradually changing and making improvements along the way, was proposed long before Charles Darwin. The idea had occurred to the ancient Greeks, and for centuries it was reiterated by European philosophers, naturalists, and breeders of pets and farm animals who selectively bred species to retain desirable traits. Even average observers with a grain of imagination could compare a man with a monkey and put two and two together. Darwin's contribution was not

Alexander Graham Bell Invented the Telephone

As in the case of the lightbulb, the steamboat, the automobile, and other world-changing inventions, invention of the telephone definitely cannot be attributed entirely to any single inventor. The list of inventors who deserve honorable mention includes Antonio Meucci, Charles Bourseul, Johann

Alexander Graham Bell (1847–1922) speaking into a prototype of the telephone in 1876.

Philipp Reis, Innocenzo Manzetti, Elisha Gray, Emile Berliner, and even Thomas Edison. Bell got the credit due to a number of factors: he happened to be in the right place at the right time; he selected the right theories from a host of ideas floating around at the time; and he was astute in defending himself in the many lawsuits brought by other inventors claiming credit.

Bullfighting Was Invented in Spain

Although bullfighting is a modern-day institution in Spain and other Hispanic countries, some archaeologists conjecture that it began with Neanderthals living in Europe more than 25,000 years ago. Later on, within the purview of recorded history, acrobatics involving bulls can be traced to Knossos, Greece, where such events were depicted in wall paintings dating from 2000 BCE. Bullfighting is also associated with ancient

Rome, where contests between humans and animals served as opening acts for the gladiators.

After the Moors of North Africa conquered the Visigoths of Europe in the eighth century, bullfighting began to evolve into its modern form. Accounts from the period describe men on horses killing bulls, as well as men on the ground with capes who aided in positioning the bulls.

● ● ● ● ● ●

the theory itself but the preponderance of data he laboriously accumulated during his expedition to the Galápagos Islands, in support of natural selection, as put forth in his classic opus, *On the Origin of Species* (which is, incidentally, often incorrectly referred to as simply *The Origin of the Species*).

Opposite: Charles Darwin (1809–1892).
Left: Waved Albatross from the Galápagos Islands.

Edison Invented the Lightbulb

A prolific inventor of countless gadgets we all use today (if not in their original form), Edison got the credit for inventing the lightbulb in 1879. The fact is that while Edison perfected it and made it both practical and popular, others did the inventing. Between 1800 and Edison's day, a whole slew of scientists and inventors were working on the invention of electric light—among them Sir Humphrey Davy, J. W. Starr, Joseph Swan, Charles Francis Brush, Moses Farmer, William Sawyer, Albon Man, Hiram Maxim, and St. George Lane-Fox. Joseph Swan, a partner of Starr's (who died young), was the most successful, and he patented a bulb before Edison got around to it.

After a legal dispute, in which the U.S. Patent Office upheld Swan's patent, Edison and Swan teamed up via a kind of entrepreneurial shotgun marriage, resulting in the Edison & Swan United Company, called "Ediswan." Edison later bought out Swan, and the rest is history. But Edison also invented a myriad of contraptions—switches, sockets, cords, etc.—that made electricity home-friendly, and for that alone he deserves to be considered the "father of the Electric Age."

Thomas Alva Edison (1847–1931) did not invent the lightbulb, but he perfected it and made it eminently practical.

Euclid Invented Geometry

Called the "father of geometry," Euclid was more of an adoptive father than a biological one. Most of what we know as Euclidean geometry was gathered from other sources, which are now untraceable. Like the Brothers Grimm, who did not write their famous tales but brought them together under one cover, Euclid was a great compiler of the mathematical knowledge of his time. His text, called *Elements,* composed of thirteen books, was the first systematic discussion of geometry in history and amounted to a mathematical milestone.

Euclid (circa 325–265 BCE), Greek mathematician, lived in Alexandria, Egypt.

Golf Was Invented in Scotland

When and where the game of golf was invented has been debated for a long time. Early forms of the game were played not only in England and Scotland but also in ancient Rome, France, Holland, Flanders, Belgium, and even such far-flung lands as China and Laos. Golf got its name from *kolf* (meaning "club"), a game similar to golf that was played in thirteenth-century Holland. Kolf, which used clubs and counted the number of times the ball was struck, made its way to Scotland in the 1400s. The Scots added the hole—perhaps the key and crowning ingredient—and continued to make refinements until the game evolved into what it is today.

Henry Ford Invented the Car, Its Engine, and the Assembly Line

The first automobile ran on steam, and its invention is often credited to a Frenchman named Nicolas-Joseph Cugnot in 1769, about a century before Henry Ford was born. The origins of the internal combustion engine that now powers our cars stretch back centuries, but it was the German inventors Karl Benz (of Mercedes-Benz) and Gottlieb Daimler, working in the late 1880s, who put together the engine and the automobile that most resemble the versions we know today. The assembly line was introduced by Ransom Olds (of Oldsmobile) in 1902. Henry Ford added a conveyor belt to the assembly line, and by doing so he was able to assemble a car (the Model T) whose cost was within the budget of the average American. In other words, he built them so cheaply that almost anyone could "afford a Ford," but invent the car he did not. (See also "The First Automobile Was Built by Daimler and Benz.")

Ford assembly line, circa 1913.

The Goose Step Was Invented by the Nazis

The stiff-legged marching style known as the goose step, which makes flesh-and-blood soldiers look like wind-up toys, was used long before the Nazis (whose stiff-armed salute was a kind of matching gesture).

The goose step made its first appearance in the 1600s when Prussian generals deemed it an apt expression of both warlike arrogance and fine-tuned discipline. The marching style was adopted by the Russians throughout the twentieth century, and it is still used by a number of countries in the Middle East and by the current regime in North Korea.

North Korean soldiers goose-stepping.

The Guillotine Was Invented by Dr. Guillotin; It Caused Instant Death

As a member of the French National Assembly, Dr. J. I. Guillotin proposed the machine that bears his name (the *e* was added later). The device was designed and built, however, by Antoine Lewis. In proposing the idea, Dr. Guillotin's original intent was to make executions more "humane" by doing away with the often blunt and fallible axe. The guillotine may have been a bit more humane for those executed, but for horrified onlookers, "humane" was not the first word that came to mind. Incidentally, the head-chopping machine was not an original idea. Similar devices had been used for centuries in England, Scotland, Ireland, Germany, Italy, Switzerland, and Persia.

Gruesome as it sounds, witnesses to guillotine executions during the French Revolution claimed they saw severed heads blinking, moving their eyes, frowning, smiling, responding to the sound of their own names, and even trying to talk. How could such eerie anecdotes be true, since the guillotine is supposed to cause instant death?

In one horrid account, a French scientist slated for execution asked an assistant to count the number of times the scientist blinked his eyes after being guillotined. The assistant counted at least fifteen blinks, about one per second. In a more recent account from the 1980s, a man told of being in a car accident during which his friend

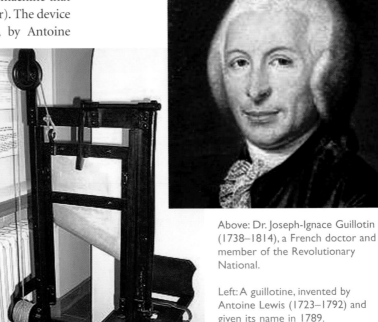

Above: Dr. Joseph-Ignace Guillotin (1738–1814), a French doctor and member of the Revolutionary National.

Left: A guillotine, invented by Antoine Lewis (1723–1792) and given its name in 1789.

was beheaded. The man claimed that over a period of about fifteen seconds he saw his friend's eyes move and his mouth open and close. The friend also made facial expressions that showed shock, confusion, horror, and grief.

A present-day consensus appears to confirm these morbid accounts. The scientific supposition is that a head remains conscious for up to fifteen seconds after being severed from the body. Phosphates stored in cerebral enzymes keep the brain alive and aware for that short period of time, and then death is brought on by the lack of oxygen and other nutrients no longer delivered through the bloodstream.

Edison Invented Motion Pictures

In the few moments Thomas Edison wasn't inventing something else, he was supposedly inventing motion pictures—or so many people have come to believe. In reality, motion pictures combine a number of technologies that were the brainchild of different people. First, William George Horner, an Englishman, invented the zoetrope in 1833. It's little more than a slotted cylinder that has images placed opposite the slots, showing a sequence of movements. Spinning the cylinder (commercially marketed as the "wheel of life") makes the images on the opposite inner wall appear to come alive.

The second innovation is credited to San Franciscan Eadweard Muybridge, a photographer who created (and patented in 1879) photographing an object in motion through a quick sequence of still photographs. Maybridge developed the system to help California governor Leland Stanford win a bet that a galloping horse lifts all four legs off the ground.

Meanwhile, in France, the Lumière brothers, Auguste and Louis, were developing a mechanism for projecting images onto a screen by shining light through acetate film. The brothers created a sensation in 1895, when their films of onrushing trains sent the audiences scurrying in panic. Back in 1887, Thomas Edison had directed his assistant William Kennedy Dickson to use all these technologies to create "moving pictures." It took Dickson and the Edison team two years of arduous (and secretive) work to come up with the "Kinetograph"—a motion picture camera that used 35mm film and created movies with sound. Two years later, Edison patented a device—the Kinetoscope—for viewing the films. Edison's accomplishments in the development of motion pictures were considerable and undeniable, but in the final analysis, he built his film technology on the work of others.

George Eastman Invented Photography

Photography, in one form or another, has been around for centuries. Like most technologies, it doesn't have a single "inventor."

The ancient Greeks and Chinese described the basic principles behind photography back in the fourth and fifth centuries. But it wasn't until the sixteenth century that Renaissance artists discovered that the use of a *camera obscura* ("dark chamber")—a box in which a light-reflected image is projected from a small hole onto the back surface— could create a perfect miniature reproduction of a scene.

The next quantum leap in photography's history occurred in 1826, when Joseph Nicéphore Niépce took the first permanent photograph. He and Louis Daguerre had collaborated on a technology in which a sheet of polished pewter—coated with silver salts and exposed to mercury vapor to make it light-sensitive—was placed in the back of the *camera obscura*, where the image was registered. Unfortunately, daguerreotypes, even in their later, more sophisticated days, took up to twenty hours to develop, making it difficult to photograph much of anything other than inanimate objects.

In 1841, William Henry Fox Talbot contributed the photographic negative, enabling unlimited prints, or copies, to be made of the same photograph. Later innovators found various ways to reduce development time, eventually making it possible to photograph people.

George Eastman's claim to fame is the modern camera—small, portable, and loaded with a thin roll of plastic film pre-coated with the requisite chemicals. Eastman called his camera—introduced in July of 1888—the "Kodak," hence the company known as Eastman Kodak.

The Egyptians Invented Paper

Actually, it was papyrus they invented, sometime in the third or fourth millennium BCE. Paper didn't come along until the second century CE, and it didn't come into wide use in the Western world until the sixteenth century.

In ancient times, papyrus was used throughout Egypt, Palestine, Syria, and southern Europe—and it was, in fact, very similar to paper, so much so that our word "paper" derives from papyrus. Making papyrus required thinly slicing the stem of a papyrus plant (native to Egypt and surrounding areas), placing the strips side by side, beating them and flattening them, and then drying them in the sun. The resulting product could then be further flattened and polished with rounded stones.

Papyrus was the only game in town until the second century BCE, when King Eumenes II of Pergamon (modern-day Turkey) invented parchment. At the time, Eumenes was in the process of creating a glorious, all-encompassing library of human knowledge—and naturally, this required a lot of papyrus. Eumenes invented a modern method of cleaning, polishing, and stretching animal skins to create a thin, durable writing material. Parchment was used almost exclusively in Europe through the Middle Ages, until long after the invention of paper.

Why didn't the Europeans catch on sooner? Maybe because paper was invented in China. Recent excavations suggest that rudimentary methods of papermaking were probably in use in China by the second century BCE. But according to ancient records, "true" paper was the contribution of Ts'ai Lun, a Chinese court official, who in 105 CE offered his new papermaking formula as a gift to Emperor Ho-Ti. His recipe utilized various "waste" materials, such as tree bark, hemp by-products, rags, and fishnets—basically, any cellulose-containing plant substance. Ts'ai Lun's method called for beating these fibers and mixing them with water; the resulting paste was spread onto a coarse cloth, allowed to drain, and dried. The outcome of this process, more or less, was modern-day paper.

The Chinese kept their secret until around 600 CE, when paper finally spread to other parts of East Asia. But it was at the Battle of Talas in 751 CE in Samarkand (a city on the Silk Route to Europe) that the foundation was laid for future European papermaking. There a group of Chinese papermakers were captured, and their technology was then disseminated throughout the Middle East. Finally, in 1151, the first European paper mill was constructed in Valencia, Spain. This paved the way for similar mills throughout Europe, which culminated in a wave of improvements in papermaking methods.

Remarkably, though, despite all the eventual European and American innovations that evolved during the industrial era—ushering in our current age of fast, cheap paper—the fundamentals of the papermaking craft today are identical to those employed in ancient China.

Ping-Pong Was Invented in China

It's a favorite sport in China, and the name definitely sounds Chinese, but Ping-Pong was invented in England in the 1880s. Formerly (and formally) known as table tennis, the game later acquired the name Ping-Pong because of the sound the ball makes when hitting the paddles and table. Although the name was widely used beforehand, "Ping-Pong" was trademarked in 1901 by a company that made sports equipment, and the name was later sold to Parker Brothers. By the way, the game is called Ping Pang Qiu in China and Takkyu in Japan.

Marconi Invented the Radio

The radio is one of those devices that have many fathers. Its operating principles were laid out as early as 1864 by the Scottish physicist James Clerk Maxwell, and the first laboratory experiments were conducted by the German physicist Heinrich Hertz (whose name is prominently echoed in the radio-broadcasting term "megahertz"). Guglielmo Marconi conducted a series of successful experiments in Bologna, Italy, in 1895, and as a result he was granted a British patent in 1896 for "wireless telegraphy" or "radio" (from the Latin for "radiation"). But the closest thing to what we think of as the modern radio was introduced in 1906, when the first vacuum tube, the "vacuum rectifier" (called the "audion") was invented by an American engineer, Lee De Forest.

Guglielmo Marconi (1874–1937) (left) invented the radio based on the physics of Heinrich Rudolf Hertz (1857–1894) (right).

Mercedes-Benz Was Founded by Mercedes and Benz

Synonymous with class and quality in the world of cars, the Mercedes-Benz was named after two persons, but not in the way you might think. Mercedes was the daughter of Emil Jellinek, an Austrian employed by the Daimler car company who used his daughter's name for an engine and several racing cars. The other half of the name comes from Karl Benz, an auto manufacturer whose company merged with Daimler in 1926, forming the brand name Mercedes-Benz. The name Daimler surfaced again in 1998, when the company merged with an American company to form Daimler-Chrysler.

The Earl of Sandwich Invented the Sandwich

There's a difference between inventing something and having one's name affixed to it. It's no secret that the sandwich was around long before John Montagu, the fourth Earl of Sandwich, but it didn't have a name—at least in merry England—until 1762. So how did the English earl happen to lend his aristocratic moniker to the hand-held meal? The earl loved to play cards so much that he wanted to find a way to eat and keep playing without getting his hands sticky, so he put a piece of meat between two slices of bread and chomped away,

Centuries before Montagu was born, Arabs were stuffing meats into pita bread and medieval European peasants working in fields were eating meals that combined bread and cheese. Ancient Jews ate sandwiches of nuts and fruit placed between matzo during the Passover feast to represent the mortar used by their ancestors in Egypt when (supposedly) building the pyramids.

It's ironic that the Earl of Sandwich is remembered for something he didn't do but not for the things he actually did do. Montagu's other accomplishments included keeping the

holding the sandwich in one hand while playing cards with the other. Since the earl was a high-profile kind of guy (the Hawaiian Islands once bore his name as well), "sandwich" became the permanently popular name for the utensil-free meal.

British fleet in European waters during the American Revolution (contributing to Britain's loss). He was also known for taking more than the acceptable amount of bribes, perhaps using his position as First Lord of the Admiralty to excuse himself.

Robert Fulton Invented the Steamboat

In 1807, Robert Fulton was the first to make the steamboat (the *Clermont*, below) a successful and profitable venture, but he was not the inventor. Two decades earlier, in 1787, John Fitch had produced a large steamboat that carried passengers between Trenton and Philadelphia.

Three years before that, James Rumsey demonstrated a cruder version of a steamboat on the Potomac River, and ideas for steamboats had been floating around since Denis Papin first thought up the notion in 1690.

The Telescope Was Invented by Galileo

Credit for assembling the first telescope (in 1608) is usually given to Dutch optician Hans Lippershey, although a few others may have been involved. Galileo (right) heard about the invention and promptly cobbled together his own version.

He was the first to use a telescope to gaze at the moon and stars, laying the foundation for modern astronomy. Galileo also named the device, using the Italian word *telescopio*, from which we get "telescope."

Sudoku Puzzles Were Invented in Japan

It is true that these familiar logic puzzles, consisting of numbers in a grid, have a Japanese name. But the puzzles themselves were invented in the 1970s by an American—Howard Garns, a retired architect from Indianapolis. Originally called Number Place puzzles, they were published by Dell in a magazine for children. In the 1980s, the puzzles were "rediscovered" by the Japanese puzzle publisher Nikoli, where they were renamed Suuji Wa Dokushin Ni Kagiru ("the numbers must occur only once"). Realizing that the name was cumbersome, to say the least, the publisher abbreviated the name to Sudoku. The puzzles took root in Japan, and by 2005 they had conquered the world, rivaling crossword puzzles in popularity.

				9	8	7	6	
9			7			4		
7		2		4				
5							3	
8		1				2		6
	3							7
				2			5	3
		4			3			1
	7	5	8	6				

For solution, see page 256. In Sudoku, every row, column, and 3x3 box on the 9x9 grid must contain only one instance of the digits 1 through 9. There can be no repeats. In the example above, in the upper left-hand box, since the numbers 9, 7, and 2 are already given, the digits 1, 3, 4, 5, 6, and 8 must be filled in. The location of these digits in the grid would be based on the numbers given in the other boxes in the entire grid.

The Wright Brothers Invented the Airplane and Were the First to Fly

This is a complicated one for several reasons. First, the Wrights had a tough time securing their place in American and aviation history. Being outside the inner circle of the scientific community of their day, and being retiring young men on the laconic side (to put it mildly), and operating in places far removed from the centers of technology, they were dismissed by the media and by the academic and scientific communities.

Operating out of a remote (albeit successful)

them, largely by rival Glenn Curtis, who discerned that the brothers' hypersensitivity was a weakness and exploited it. The Wrights became embroiled in Curtis's suits, and that slowed down their technical experimentation and the improvement that the nascent technology needed. Meanwhile Curtis himself was surpassing the Wrights in developing the technology and the business of aviation. The Wrights were also insulted by the Smithsonian Institution's reluctance to acknowledge their accomplishment,

The Wright brothers' first flight on December 17, 1903. The airplane "flew" for 120 feet and remained in the air for just 12 seconds. The famous photograph (taken by a neighbor coast guard seaman) was responsible for the fame of the Wright brothers.

bicycle business in Dayton, Ohio, and conducting aeronautical tests on the desolate sand dunes of North Carolina, it's a miracle they showed up on the radar screen at all. Had that famous photograph of the first flight, with Orville lying flat on the bottom wing and Wilbur running alongside, not been taken and circulated, their achievement might have been ignored entirely.

Second, the Wrights were very sensitive about getting credit—so much so that they took personal umbrage at the various lawsuits that were thrown at

because in their view they had beaten a chief rival, Samuel P. Langley, Secretary of the Smithsonian. As a result of this dispute, the *Kitty Hawk* was not exhibited at the Smithsonian at first, and the Wrights maintained a secrecy that thwarted efforts to credit them properly.

Finally, in the world of aviation at the turn of the twentieth century, "flying" meant controlled, unassisted, powered, non-gliding flight as well as the ability to take off from a standstill and land. Others had achieved some aspects of that combination.

For example, impressive gliding was accomplished most notably by the German Otto Lilienthal. Uncontrolled flight was achieved by Clément Ader, considered by some aviation historians as the first person to genuinely fly. He performed the feat on October 9, 1890, more than a decade before the Wrights, though without any ability to turn or control elevation. Then there was Hiram Maxim, who demonstrated the potential of his winged steam-driven machine to achieve flight but for some reason failed to demonstrate it actually flying.

What distinguished the Wrights' flight of December 17, 1903, at Kill Devil Hills, North Carolina, were two factors, both of which turn out to be possibly not true. First, they appeared to have mastered the problem of controlling flight, which they did through a system of "wing warping," in which the pilot contorted the wings. But wing warping was totally impractical and could at best shift the flight of the aircraft by a few degrees. Though they improved the system and ultimately were able to control flight quite well with wing warping, the ailerons and control surfaces that had been developed by Henry Farman became the preferred system of control, even for the Wrights.

Also, the Wright brothers' flights may not have been unassisted. They frequently used a system in which a weight was dropped from the top of a derrick, pulling a cord that propelled the airplane to take-off speed. The question is, was this the case on that cold December day? In the famous photograph of the first flight, one can clearly see the track and the small rail car on which the plane was perched as it took off. The photo shows the track going off to the rear and then off the edge of the photo. It is along this track that the cord would have run, from the derrick to the front of the track and from there to the cart holding the plane. In the Wrights' diaries and letters, much is made of the fact that Wilbur ran alongside the plane holding the wing up so that it would not drag in the sand, but that he was careful not to push the aircraft along. The text leaves open the possibility that the launching mechanism was still used—and that would make this an *assisted* flight, not the much sought-after unassisted flight.

If the Wright brothers were not the first to fly, they still deserve credit for being the first to apply the principles of flight-test engineering to the problem of flight by building (though not inventing) a wind tunnel and carefully measuring the effect of moving air on different wing shapes. The Wrights were the first to accurately measure the lift for wing designs that would be the ones most used in the early years of flight, and they were the first to fly with a full understanding of why and how flight was achieved at all.

Brothers Wilbur (1867–1912) (top) and Orville Wright (1871–1948) (bottom). They may not have been the first to achieve flight, but they made many critical scientific discoveries during their aeronautical careers.

History

The 182 People Who Defended the Alamo in 1836 All Died Fighting the Mexicans

They all died, but not all of them died in battle. The small band of Texans who defended the Alamo from the onslaught of 6,000 Mexicans fought bravely, it's true, and the episode marks a heroic milestone in American history. But several of the Alamo defenders, including none other than Davy Crockett, survived the battle and were taken captive by General Manuel Castrillón, who led the Mexican troops into the Alamo once the walls were breached. Castrillón was apparently impressed by the bravery of the Texans and argued to his commanding officer, General Antonio de Santa Anna, that the prisoners be spared. Santa Anna would have none of it, however, and they were all summarily executed.

Several myths have arisen about the stand at the Alamo—that the defenders were expecting reinforcements to arrive and help them; that commander William Travis drew a line in the sand with his sword and challenged the people there to cross the line and join him in defending the fortified mission or else leave; and that the survivors (including Crockett) were discovered cowering under a bed. There were no significant reinforcements to be found at the time; the Travis story was first told some forty years after the fact by someone who had heard it from someone who had heard it from someone who was there.

The discussion between Santa Anna and Castrillón gives every indication that every one of the defenders of the Alamo, including Crockett and the few other survivors of the battle, had conducted themselves honorably.

Left to right: Antonio López de Santa Anna (1794–1876); William Travis (1809–1836); Davy Crockett (1786–1836). Below: The Alamo in San Antonio, Texas.

Anarchism Advocates Societal Chaos

Throughout American history, anarchism has been associated with violence, suspicion, and misunderstanding. Anarchists in Chicago were said to have incited the deadly Haymarket Square riot of 1886; President McKinley was assassinated by an anarchist in 1901; and the prosecution in 1920 of accused murderers Sacco and Vanzetti, both anarchists, precipitated a storm of controversy around the world. But as a political philosophy with many and varied interpretations, anarchism is hardly the bastion of evil that its reputation would suggest. Loosely speaking, anarchism disapproves of government and social class. It does not, as is widely believed, advocate chaos, nihilism, or Marxian revolution. Rather, it promotes a kind of utopian dream, a harmonious society composed of peaceful citizens who help each other out and are collectively unencumbered by governmental and societal coercion.

The Bikini Was Invented in the Twentieth Century

If by "bikini" you mean a scanty two-piece swimsuit, then the bikini was invented somewhere in ancient Greece or Rome, as depicted on frescoes and vases from a few decades BCE.

The first bikini to be so named (representing a departure from other, more modest, midriff-baring two-piece swimsuits) was invented in 1946 by two Frenchmen, Jacques Heim and Louis Réard. At the time, the U.S. Army was testing nukes on the Bikini Atoll. In hopes of making the new swimsuit's arrival on the scene equally explosive, fashionistas adopted the name "bikini." Subsequent variations on the theme include the monokini, tankini, string bikini, thong, slingshot, minimini, teardrop, and micro.

Mosaic, Villa del Casale, near Piazza Amerina, Sicily, Italy.

Atomic Bombs Convinced the Japanese to Surrender

The explanation (the *official* explanation) for dropping atomic bombs on Japan in August of 1945 goes as follows: the decision to do so saved countless lives by shortening the war and preventing a more prolonged and costly invasion of Japan. What is missing from this familiar scenario is the generally agreed-upon observation that Japan had been defeated militarily by June of 1945, two months before the bombings. Also, some experts contend that Japan had been trying to surrender for months and the U.S. government knew it, but the two sides couldn't agree on the precise terms. According to postwar government surveys, including strategic analyses and testimonials from military and government personnel on both sides, it is now recognized that the bombings of Hiroshima and Nagasaki were unnecessary as a means for ending the war. Whether or not the U.S. government knew that to be true at the time, and whether or not there may have been ulterior motives for dropping the bombs (such as keeping Russia out of Japan), is a matter of continued speculation and controversy.

Abortion Was Illegal until *Roe v. Wade*

Women have been having abortions in the United States ever since colonial times. Only at certain times and in certain places has the practice been illegal. As long as pregnancies were terminated before the fourth month, abortions could be performed legally in most states well into the mid to late 1800s. By the 1870s, records show that one out of five pregnancies was terminated by abortion. At about the same time, thanks to a vigorous campaign by the recently founded American Medical Association, a number of states began to pass laws prohibiting abortion. By the turn of the century, it was outlawed just about everywhere due in part to Victorian prudishness and misogyny.

The practice continued to be widespread but was necessarily clandestine. By the 1950s, a gathering number of voices called for antiabortion laws to be repealed. By the 1960s, a survey showed that 87 percent of doctors favored liberalization of abortion laws, reversing the trend begun by the medical community a century before. During the same period, a number of states moved to alter or do away with antiabortion laws in the name of women's rights.

This liberalizing trend, though opposed by a host of dedicated adversaries—from the Catholic Church to Christian fundamentalists and secular moralists—culminated in 1973 with *Roe v. Wade*. The Supreme Court ruled that women, as part of their constitutional right to privacy, could choose to terminate a pregnancy during the months before the fetus could survive outside the womb. The ruling managed to cancel a host of state antiabortion laws and, ironically, returned the country to the same legal standards regarding abortion that were in place during the time of Washington and Jefferson.

Columbus Set Out to Prove the World Was Round

Elementary schools have often taught that Columbus began his voyage in 1492 to confirm that the world was round. Why? Supposedly because most Europeans of his time believed the earth was flat, and Columbus was eager to prove them wrong. The fact is, almost every educated person of that time, including most sailors, believed the world was round. So why did Columbus undertake his risky adventure?

The reason was more economic than exploratory. He wanted to find a faster route to the Far East in order to facilitate trade. Even if the Americas weren't in his way, however, Columbus would never have reached the destination he'd hoped for by traveling west. Spain and the Orient are too far apart. He and his crew would have died of starvation while still at sea.

The "First World War" Was the First World War

If you define "world war" as an armed conflict between a number of major powers on several continents, then what we call the First World War may be more like the seventh, eighth, or ninth. For example, the series of invasions that preceded the creation of the thirteenth-century Mongol Empire took place across much of Europe and Asia, stretching from present-day Japan, Vietnam, and China to such western climes as Mesopotamia, Persia, the Balkans, Russia, and Hungary. Lasting from the late 1500s to the mid-1600s, the Dutch-Portuguese War embraced such far-flung territories as Brazil, Europe, much of Africa and India, Indonesia, and the vast oceans surrounding them. The Seven Years' War, which took place in the mid-1700s, was dubbed the first world war by Winston Churchill. It stretched from North America to most of Europe and all the way to India. Other major conflicts regarded by historians as world wars include the War of the Grand Alliance (1688–97),

the War of the Spanish Succession (1701–14), the War of the Austrian Succession (1740–48), the French Revolutionary Wars (1792–1802), and the Napoleonic Wars (1803–15).

So why is it given such a grandiose name as World War I? Possibly because it was a global military conflict that left millions dead and reshaped the modern world. It caused the disintegration of four empires: the Austro-Hungarian, German, Ottoman, and Russian, and created new states such as Czechoslovakia, Poland, and Yugoslavia. Ultimately, World War I marked a decisive break with the old world order that had emerged after the Napoleonic Wars.

The Cow Was the First Animal To Be Domesticated

Because of its versatility as both a work animal and a food source, the cow was often assumed to have been the first animal to be domesticated. Other animals—sheep, horses, pigs, camels, dogs, chickens, and

animals were already domesticated way back in prehistoric times.

Three factors suggest that dogs may have been first. For one thing, dogs have been present in virtu-

geese—have also competed (so to speak) for the honor. Sheep, for example, were once thought to be the first because the book of Genesis refers to Abel as a "keeper of sheep" (and what can be more "first" than Genesis, right?). Actually, it is very difficult for us to determine for sure which animal was numero uno, from our faraway perspective, because most of these

ally every human society since the beginning of recorded history. Second, dogs were first to be accepted into family homes. And third, dogs were the only animal that could assist hunters, suggesting that they have been human companions since the time when humankind was still in its hunter-gatherer stage, before the dawn of agriculture.

The Chicago Fire Was Started by Mrs. O'Leary's Cow

The myth is that the Great Chicago Fire of October 8, 1871, was started by Mrs. O'Leary's cow kicking over a lantern in the barn. The fire virtually leveled Chicago, killing 250 people and destroying almost every house in the city. One of the few left standing was, paradoxically, the one owned by Mrs. O'Leary. A board of inquiry for the Chicago Fire Department determined that the fire definitely started behind the O'Leary home—where their barn had been standing—but the board was unable to pinpoint the exact cause.

All kinds of rumors and gossip spread for years. For example: Mrs. O'Leary was doing the unpardonable by smoking in the barn in the middle of the night; or Mr. O'Leary was having a rendezvous with a neighbor woman in the barn; or the jealous husband of a woman with whom Mr. O'Leary was having an affair set the fire as revenge ... and so on. The story that blamed the fire on Mrs. O'Leary's cow first appeared in a newspaper account by Michael Ahern, and it became the prototype for whatever theory the imaginations of gossips all over the country could concoct. Not until Ahern was near death in 1927—more than 50 years later—did he confess that he had fabricated the entire story.

The fire of 1871, by John R. Chapin, from *Harper's Weekly*.

A "Harem" Means a Place for Wives and Concubines; the Eunuchs That Served in the Harems Were Sexless

In the Arabic tradition, a harem is a part of the household forbidden to males—a kind of sanctuary for the female sex. It may include wives (up to four under Islamic law) and concubines, but it also may include mothers, sisters, daughters, aunts, nieces, grandmothers, in-laws, guests, and servants.

Eunuchs have appeared throughout history in roles ranging from slave to high-ranking official. But stereotypically we think of eunuchs (literally, "guardians of the bed") as slaves doing the bidding of some alpha male who wants to protect his harem from intruders. Castrated males would hardly be foxes in the chicken coop, right? Or would they? Supposedly, males castrated after puberty are capable of erections and intercourse. Some sources even contend that Roman women

Shopping in the Harem, by Austrian Rudolf Swoboda (1859–1914).

preferred eunuchs as bed partners not only because there was no danger of pregnancy but also because of their superior staying power.

The *Hindenburg* Blew Up on Its Maiden Voyage, over Lakehurst, New Jersey, on May 6, 1937

There are a number of widely held myths and misconceptions about the *Hindenburg* disaster.

- The disaster did not occur on the airship's maiden voyage; people who think that are confusing it with the *Titanic*, which did sink on its maiden voyage. By the time of the disaster on May 6, the *Hindenburg* had made ten round trips across the Atlantic without a mishap.

- The *Hindenburg* did not explode—it burst into flames. Had it exploded, the ship would have been destroyed in a matter of seconds, leaving the frame scattered in pieces over Lakehurst airfield. Instead, the wreckage shows the frame to be mangled but intact.

- The *Hindenburg* was not the first large airship to regularly cross the Atlantic. Its predecessor, the *Graf Zeppelin*, had made over one-hundred-forty crossings between 1928 and 1937, without mishap. The *Graf Zeppelin* had used hydrogen, which was more buoyant than helium and cheaper to produce.

- Again, had the *Hindenburg* exploded, the remains of the ship would have crashed to the ground immediately and there would have been no survivors. In fact, the passenger gondola "landed" and sixty-one of the ninety-seven people aboard were pulled out alive. A few died later from burns sustained in the course of their escape, and the reason for these burns provides a clue to the entire disaster: the burn victims were showered with aluminum dust, the highly flammable substance that covered their skin. It was this covering that burned, causing the destruction of the airship—not the hydrogen (which burned upward and away from the ship).

- The official explanations of both the German and American courts of inquiry—that a hydrogen leak had been ignited by static electricity—now seem to have been cover-ups. The Germans had sought to blame America for withholding its newly discovered helium stores, and Americans were seeking to curtail German air flights over U.S. territory, which would have been accomplished by ending the airship business.

- Neither did the *Hindenburg* disaster actually put an end to the airship industry. A secret report by an independent investigator, engineer Otto Beyersdorff, submitted to the Zeppelin Company in June 1937, correctly identified the cause of the fire as the highly combustive mixture of iron oxide and cellulose acetate (a combination that is virtually the same as rocket fuel) in the outer skin,

The LZ 129 *Hindenburg* in flames over Lakehurst Naval Air Station, Lakehurst, New Jersey, May 6, 1937.

covered by a layer of powdered aluminum (added to give the hull a silvery sheen, but also very flammable). The company made the necessary design changes and completed construction on the *Graf Zeppelin II*, though it was never put into commercial service. The *Graf Zeppelin II* was used for military missions until both it and its predecessor were dismantled in 1940 for their duralumin (a lightweight aluminum alloy) and steel, needed for other aircraft.

The French and Indian War Was Fought between the French and the Indians

Who else? Actually, this war for territorial supremacy in North America got its name from the coalition of French-Americans and Native Americans (Algonquin and Huron) who joined forces against the British. To make matters more confusing, the British side included not only British soldiers but American settlers and some Native Americans (mainly Iroquois) as well.

Called the French and Indian War from the perspective of North America, this conflict was actually part of the Seven Years' War (1756–63), which ranged from North America to most of Europe and all the way to India and other colonial outposts around the globe. So extensive was the theater of the

Death of General Wolfe (1770), by Benjamin West.

Seven Years' War, in fact, that Winston Churchill dubbed it the real "First World War."

Lava Killed the People of Pompeii

In Italy on August 24, 79 CE, the volcano known as Mount Vesuvius erupted, and many citizens of nearby Pompeii were killed. It is commonly assumed that lava from the colossal volcano is what caused the deaths of thousands. If this had been the case, there would be no excavation, and the famous molds of corpses and various objects that exist today would have been impossible.

For the most part, it was not the lava that killed those trapped by the eruption but the noxious fumes and ashes. Most people died from the fumes and were then covered by the ashes and cinders that coated the entire city. When the ashes and other substances were drenched in water, they hardened and formed a kind of plaster of Paris, which resulted in the preservation of artifacts and corpses.

Pompeii had actually experienced a devastating earthquake sixteen years before in 63 CE. Rebuilding was still taking place when Vesuvius erupted. Many have thought that all of the city's inhabitants were killed, but it is estimated that only about 2,000 of the 20,000 citizens perished. And although history focuses on the dramatic eruption, the earthquake did far more damage to the city of Pompeii.

Vesuvius Erupting (1826), by Johann Christian Claussen Dahl.

Lincoln Freed the Slaves with the Emancipation Proclamation

Lincoln was no fan of slavery, to be sure. But his primary aim in delivering the Emancipation Proclamation was not to free the slaves but to save the Union. How? By threatening to free all the slaves in those states that did not rejoin the Union. Also, the document applied only to slaves in the secessionist South. It did not apply to slaves remaining in the four slave states that were still in the Union. What's more, the Emancipation Proclamation had no legal authority to end slavery; it only stated the federal government's policy on the issue. Slavery as a lawful institution was not terminated until the Thirteenth Amendment was ratified in 1865.

The statue of Abraham Lincoln, located inside the Lincoln Memorial in Washington, D.C., looking eastward toward the Reflecting Pool outside and the Washington Monument. Inside the memorial, on the north wall, are the inscriptions of the Gettysburg Address and Lincoln's second inaugural address, two of his better-known speeches.

Lindbergh Was the First to Fly across the Atlantic

Between 1919 and 1927 (the year Lindbergh made his famous flight from New York to Paris), approximately eighty people flew across the Atlantic. They included American naval officers, British RAF fliers, Spanish and Portuguese military officers, and the crews and passengers (plus a stowaway or two) of British and German dirigibles. Lindbergh's distinction was that he was the first flier to make the transatlantic trip alone.

Mussolini Made the Trains Run on Time

This myth is often invoked to suggest that bad things, such as tyranny and fascist dictators, have their good side—in this case, promptness and efficiency. It's true that some improvements were made in the Italian railway system after World War I, but most of them were already in place before Mussolini came to power in 1922. Also, there is no evidence to

suggest that the trains ran any more efficiently during the fascist era than at any other time in Italian history.

A veteran conductor on the Florence-Venice run once related that, in the years following the war, the Italian railroad placed a higher priority on punctuality over safety, resulting in a horrendous series of crashes—all to live down the reputation of being unconcerned with being on time.

Machiavelli Was a Schemer Who Promoted Dirty Politics

In the world of politics, "Machiavellian" has become synonymous with "ruthlessly corrupt and conniving." But the fact is that Niccolò Machiavelli (1469–1527), who flourished during the Italian Renaissance, was a pretty good guy. He was a gentleman and a scholar—and a statesman, diplomat, musician, poet, and playwright. Detractors contend that Machiavelli advocated

cruelty, tyranny, and other inhumane practices. But in his 1513 treatise, *The Prince*, he simply pointed out that politicians who lie, steal, and cheat may have compellingly advantageous reasons to act that way. He never said that such bad behavior should be cultivated, and his own life was a model of integrity and patriotism. Machiavelli's philosophy can perhaps best be summed up in these words from *The Prince*: "It must be understood that a prince ... cannot observe all of those virtues for which men are reputed good, because it is often necessary to act against mercy, against faith, against humanity, against frankness, against religion, in order to preserve the state."

Nero Fiddled While Rome Burned

This popular notion is actually impossible, if only because the violin, or fiddle, wasn't invented until more than one thousand years after the burning of Rome in 64 CE. It is true that Nero studied the lyre and was musically inclined, but according to the historian Tacitus, Nero was at his villa in Antium when the fire began, about thirty-five miles away from Rome.

It has been supposed that Nero started the fire because he wanted to rebuild Rome, a desire that he made well known at the time. Although he did use the nine-day fire that consumed most of the city as an excuse to rebuild Rome in the Greek fashion and on a magnificent scale, there is no evidence to support the claim that he had anything to do with starting the fire. He responded to the crisis responsibly by opening shelters for the homeless and increasing the amount of food brought in from the provinces.

More American Soldiers Were Killed in World Wars I and II Than in the Civil War

The number of deaths in the American Civil War—more than 600,000—actually exceeded that of both World War I and World War II. Of course, the two world wars elicit a certain horror that the Civil War doesn't; technological "advances" such as chemical warfare and nuclear weaponry tend to make them seem more destructive than wars of centuries past. Ironically, though, modern medical technology is a primary reason for the reduced casualties of twentieth-century wars—more than two out of three of the fallen Civil War soldiers did not die in combat but succumbed to old-fashioned diseases and infections.

Paul Revere Rode Alone

Paul Revere was a patriot who did lots of horse-back riding for the revolutionary cause, but on the night mentioned in Longfellow's famous poem (April 18, 1775), he did not ride alone to warn the people of "Concord town." He had started with two others, William Dawes and Samuel Prescott. On their way from Lexington to Concord, the three were spotted by the British, and Revere was captured and held overnight. Dawes retreated to Lexington, and Prescott managed to get away by leaping over a fence. Prescott continued his ride to Concord, where he warned the citizens about the British. Revere was released the next day, but he had to walk home because the British kept his horse. With these historical facts in mind, the poem should probably have read: "Listen my children, and you shall hear/ Of the midnight ride of Samuel Prescott," but that would spoil the rhyme.

Portrait of Paul Revere, silversmith (circa 1768–70), by John Singleton Copley.

You Can't Be Punished Twice for a Single Crime

You can if the single criminal act violated both federal and state law. The Fifth Amendment to the U.S. Constitution prohibits double jeopardy in federal cases. But in 1922, the U.S. Supreme Court held that someone could be tried in federal court for a federal offense and then in state court for violating a state statute. That's why criminal attorneys who ask for immunity for their clients admitting to criminal acts specify that they request immunity from both federal and state prosecution.

You Can't Be President If You Were Not Born in the United States

This question was discussed during the few milliseconds people thought the newly elected governor of California, Arnold Schwarzenegger, might be presidential timber. A citizen of the United States who is an American citizen by virtue of his or her birth is eligible to be president, even if he or she was born outside the country (such as the child of an American diplomat living abroad). It is people who become citizens through naturalization who are excluded from the presidency. This was clarified by Congress in 1790 and again in 1855. So that an American citizen who is vacationing or traveling outside the United States, or is stationed overseas in the military or the diplomatic corps, is still eligible to run for the presidency.

The Pilgrims Landed at Plymouth Rock

The *Mayflower*'s first stop in North America was Provincetown on Cape Cod, where a small landing party went ashore. Not finding a ready source of fresh water, the ship ventured on toward the vicinity of present-day Plymouth. There is no mention of the rock in written records from the time of the landing in 1620, and there are no references of any kind about a rock until more than a century later. The first mention of any rock was made by John Faunce in 1741, but he was then in his eighties and had not been born until twenty-six years after the Plymouth landing. The historical sanctity of Plymouth Rock did not take hold until the bicentennial celebration of the landing, in 1820.

Historians discussing the rock tend to use words like "hearsay," "supposedly," "allegedly," "myth," and "legend." But what's most important, of course, is not where the Pilgrims landed but the fact that they landed at all.

The Embarkation of the Pilgrims at Delft Haven, Holland, July 22, 1620 (1843), by Robert W. Weir.

The Attack on Pearl Harbor Was a Complete Surprise

Over the years, this notion, as well as its opposite, have been hotly debated. The trail of evidence, the various angles of speculation, and the supposedly final claims one way or the other are so complex and protracted that one could write an entire book on the subject—and dozens of authors have done just that. For our purposes, let's keep it brief. Here are a few points that serve to fuel the debate.

• Some claim that an eight-step plan aiming to provoke Japan into war with the U.S. was submitted to FDR, and he implemented each step over the course of 1941.

• Not all classified documents relating to Pearl Harbor and the circumstances that prevailed before and after the attack have been declassified, even at this late date.

USS *Arizona* burning, December 7, 1941; it burned for two days after the initial attack. 1,177 of those on board lost their lives.

• Much intelligence had been gathered (decoded transmissions, intercepted correspondences, etc.) that some claim would have made it impossible for America's top leadership not to know what was coming.

• Some sources insist that, although FDR publicly voiced his determination to stay out of the war, he privately felt compelled to have the U.S. participate—and an attack on Pearl Harbor would galvanize the American public into going to war.

• At the Japanese military academy, the final examination for many years prior to 1941 had consisted of just one question: "How would you mount an attack on the U.S. Naval Base at Pearl Harbor?" This did not go unnoticed in American military circles but was just not acted upon.

The Pyramids Were Built by Slaves

In movies about ancient Egypt, legions of starving, thirsty slaves—many of them shackled Hebrews—are forced to do backbreaking work under the unforgiving sun, while sadistic overseers drive them to exhaustion and lash them unmercifully until their sweaty, sunburned backs are striped with gashes and welts or they keel over and die.

But in the case of the pyramids, a wide gulf separates the movies (and many a grammar-school textbook) from historical fact. For one thing, most of the pyramids were built long before the Hebrews entered the history books. Secondly, those who built them were not slaves but (as recent excavations of their homes indicate) solid Egyptian citizens who were well fed and well paid. Many of them were farmers who worked on the pyramids during flood season, when the waters of the Nile covered their fields. For the most part, the laborers were well treated, and many of them actually looked forward to their seasonal stint. To invoke a comparison from recent history, you could say that the building of the pyramids was not all that different from our WPA projects of the 1930s.

Incidentally, people living nowadays have a distorted picture in their mind's eye of what a pyramid looked like in ancient Egypt. They were not the simple heaps of stone that their modern-day ruins would suggest. Each pyramid was quite literally a tomb fit for a king (or, in this case, a pharaoh). Rather than the progression of stony steps that survive today, pyramids were covered with a smooth "skin" of precious materials. The bottom third was made of white marble, the middle third was coated with topaz-like gemstones, and the top third was plated with slabs of gold. The sight must have been quite spectacular.

The Pyramids of Giza.

Teddy Roosevelt Led the Rough Riders up San Juan Hill

In 1898, during the Spanish-American War, future president Theodore Roosevelt organized the First Regiment of U.S. Cavalry Volunteers and gave them the nickname "Rough Riders." However, their commander was not Roosevelt but Colonel Leonard Wood. Roosevelt was second in command.

Many details concerning the American assault on Cuba during the war were misconstrued. The Rough Riders did not actually "ride" at all. Rather, they were forced to walk during their entire stay in Cuba because their horses had been left behind in Florida. (The regiment sardonically renamed itself "Wood's Weary Walkers.") Although the charge up San Juan Hill has gone down in history as a prime example of American gallantry, as well as a factor that contributed immensely to his celebrity, Roosevelt himself was probably not even present at the battle. Contemporary accounts have it that he served in a supporting role from his position on nearby Kettle Hill.

Theodore Roosevelt and the Rough Riders atop San Juan Heights in 1898.

San Francisco Was Devastated by the 1906 Earthquake

The majority—perhaps up to ninety percent—of the destruction occurred only in the aftermath of the quake. Tellingly, most San Franciscans actually refer to the disaster as the 1906 San Francisco Fire.

The earthquake itself, which struck the town on the morning of April 18, 1906, did cause a great deal of damage. But the far worse problem was that it began an unstoppable domino effect of fiery destruction. Huge conflagrations broke out throughout the city, the result of toppled stoves and chimneys, fallen electrical wires, broken gas lines, and even arson. Ruptured water mains meant efforts to put out the fires were mostly unsuccessful, and the dynamite used to create firebreaks actually worsened the situation. Finally, seawater pumped in from the bay brought the blazes under control.

At the time, fearing negative publicity (and failing to count the large immigrant population of

Chinatown), the city reported only several hundred dead. But recent analysis suggests that over 3,000 probably perished, and 225,000—out of a population of 410,000—were left homeless.

American Indians Devised and Promoted the Scalping of Settlers

While scalping is most often associated with American Indians, historical evidence has revealed that the practice has taken place in Europe and other locales throughout history. It's possible that among Native Americans scalping either evolved from the ritual of cutting off various body parts as trophies during warfare, or it may have been introduced, or at least encouraged by—Europeans.

Scalping didn't actually become a common occurrence in the New World until after European settlers had arrived. The newcomers exploited the ritual and paid high bounties for scalps of Indians and Europeans alike. During the time that European countries were battling each other in America, white Europeans began scalping other whites.

So while it is possible that the early American Indians had some ritual resembling scalping before the settlers came to North America, it was not until they started getting paid for scalps that the practice really took off.

Incidentally, in the early 1700s, Europeans began to use killer dogs as instruments of warfare against the Indians. While it was illegal to use dogs to bait bears and bulls, it was considered completely moral and legal to use them to bait Indians.

Presidents Are Treated Much More Harshly These Days

Some of the most revered presidents in U.S. history, including George Washington, were greatly criticized by the American people during their terms. Thomas Jefferson was called a coward and an atheist, and Ulysses Grant was ridiculed as a crook and a drunkard.

Washington became wrapped up in political debate surrounding the emergence of political parties in the early 1790s. When he issued the Proclamation of Neutrality during the outbreak of war between Britain and France, Republicans called for his impeachment. Lincoln was treated no less kindly.

In more recent times, Nixon was denounced by a number of partisan groups, and when Watergate came along he was excoriated from all sides. Reagan, Clinton, and George W. Bush took plenty of heat from the time they were governors until the end of their presidencies.

President-bashing has long been a popular public pastime in American history. Presidents today experience it no more (and probably no less) than did the leaders of yesteryear.

Thanksgiving Is a Pilgrim Holiday Tradition

The famous "first Thanksgiving" was indeed celebrated by the Pilgrims in 1621, when William Bradley, governor of the fledgling Puritan Plymouth community, invited Indians to join in a three-day festival.

Throughout the next two centuries, similar feasts would occur sporadically, often as a celebration of success in battle or after an especially good harvest. In 1789, President George Washington issued a proclamation to make Thanksgiving a national holiday, but the idea didn't catch on. The holiday was not regularly observed until October 3, 1863, during the Civil War. President Abraham Lincoln (responding to pleas from Sarah Josepha Hale in *Godey's Lady's Book* for the observance of the "Pilgrim" celebration) proclaimed the fourth Thursday of November "a day of thanksgiving and praise to our beneficent Father who dwelleth in the heavens," and it's been celebrated as such ever since.

The only exception occurred during the years 1939 and 1940, when FDR moved it to the third Thursday of November in order to accommodate merchants and give them more time to get the commercial ball rolling between Thanksgiving and Christmas.

The Old West Was a Violent, Lawless Place

The notion that the frontier towns of the Old West—the settlements that sprang up in the second half of the nineteenth century west of the Mississippi River—were violent places in which street duels, murder, and all sorts of other mayhem were the daily fare is simply not true. Most of the people who headed out west were Civil War veterans, which meant they were armed and not about to be pushed around. The few cases on record of gunslingers entering a town and terrorizing the public all end the same way—with the miscreants hanging from tree branches, usually at the hands of hundreds of townspeople.

The exploits of the celebrated gunmen of the Old West—Wyatt Earp, Bat Masterson, and the James Gang—were wildly exaggerated, sometimes by dime novelists and sensational journalists, and sometimes by the towns themselves, which were trying to drum up some tourism and shake off the uncouth image of the frontier town.

While it is true that men routinely wore sidearms (Mark Twain writes that he carried a holster just to avoid being perceived as a dandy), the murder and robbery rates were far lower then than they are today virtually anywhere in the U.S. Rape and violence against women were virtually unknown; cursing or spitting in front of a woman could result in a prison sentence or even a hanging. Remember that in a small town in the middle of the prairie, everyone knows everyone and there's really no place to hide.

Yet the image of the cowboy as the rough, individualist driver of cattle through hostile territory has some basis insofar as great cattle drives were conducted through hostile Indian territory (often in violation of treaties) under the guidance of settlers.

The story of William Bonney—born Henry McCarty in New York City, but better known as "Billy the Kid"—is typical: Billy was part of a territorial war among ranchers, known as the Lincoln County War, that got out of hand and that ended with his being hanged in 1881. While the details of that war are certainly interesting, nearly none of the legends about Billy the Kid—including the one about the wrong man being shot and buried in his grave—have any basis in fact.

Bottom: A town in the Old West. Right: The only known photograph of Billy the Kid.

Women Burned Their Bras in Protest during the Sixties

The image of feminists in the sixties and seventies burning their bras in protest is a media creation that has no basis in fact. It was most likely invoked as a catchy but improbable echo of draft-card burning by Vietnam War protesters of the late sixties.

The closest thing to bra burning on record occurred at the 1968 Miss America Pageant, where radical feminists were photographed hurling bras, girdles, cosmetics, and high-heeled shoes into a

"Battling" Bella Abzug (1920–1998), congresswoman and leader of the women's rights movement.

"freedom trash can." None of the items, however, was set on fire.

More People Have Been Killed by War Than by Their Own Government

In the twentieth century alone, wars resulted in more than 40 million deaths. But the number of mass murders of citizens by their fellow citizens or by their own governments, according to various estimates, amounts to nearly 200 million—five times the number of people killed by war. Among governments, the worst offenders were the Soviet Union, China, Germany, Turkey, Cambodia, Pakistan, Yugoslavia, Mexico, and Rwanda.

The Big Three in twentieth-century genocide: Adolf Hitler, Joseph Stalin, and Mao Zedong.

In the Past, People Died Much Younger

In the days of the Roman Empire, the average life expectancy was about thirty-five years. The term "average" is misleading, however, because it takes into account the legions of deaths due to infant and child mortality. Between ancient times and the twentieth century, young people died from diseases that are rarely fatal today, thanks to the relatively recent advances in public health, nutrition, and medical care.

In the old days, a person who made it to age forty had an average (there's that word again) of twenty years left to live. But many people born in centuries past lived into their eighties and nineties, and a few lived even longer. With fewer medicines available, longevity was determined more by heredity than it is today, so that families who had a "family reputation" for long life had a little something extra to bring to a marriage.

George Burns (1896–1996) (left) died at age 100; Elizabeth Bolden (1890–2006) (right) died at age 116; she is the eighth oldest person in recorded history.

AMAZING... BUT FALSE!

Religion and the Bible

The Christmas Tree Has Always Been a Christian Tradition

The quick and easy explanation for the Christmas tree is that it is part of an ancient pagan tradition that predates Christianity. Pagans used the winter solstice in December as an occasion to celebrate rebirth and renewal. Because evergreen boughs stay green all year, they served as a reminder that spring was on the way.

Ancient pagan traditions aside, however, it is generally acknowledged that the Christmas tree as we know it today got its start in Germany in the 1500s, when Christians brought trees into their homes and decorated

them with ornaments and lights. In England, it wasn't until a few hundred years later that Christmas trees became de rigueur, largely because an admiring populace followed the example of Queen Victoria and her German relatives.

The Christmas tree was a late-blooming phenomenon in America, too. Although common among German immigrants in Pennsylvania for some time, the decorated trees didn't catch on with the public at large until the mid to late 1800s.

The Christmas tree at Rockefeller Center, New York City. The enormous tree looms over the famous skating rink below.

Ship Captains Can Perform Weddings

Although ship captains sometimes perform weddings in the movies, it is not permitted aboard a U.S. ship—unless the captain also happens to be a priest, rabbi, minister, judge, justice of the peace, or notary public—and the odds of that are pretty slim. In fact, some U.S. maritime regulations expressly forbid ship captains to conduct wedding ceremonies. Although the same holds for most other countries, there are a few exceptions. Captains of Japanese ships can marry couples at sea, and captains on some Atlantic cruise ships are licensed, independent of their naval credentials, to tie the knot for vacationing couples.

Catholic Priests Cannot Be Married

Catholic priests are not allowed to get married after they are ordained, but in some branches of Catholicism, such as the Eastern Orthodox Church, they may be ordained after being married. It was actually not until the Second Lateran Council, in 1139, that celibacy was deemed mandatory for all priests and other Roman Catholic clerics. Since that time the norm has been upheld. In the centuries previous to that, priests were allowed to decide for themselves about their own sexual conduct and would marry if they so desired. Today, the celibacy requirement persists, and the debate continues.

The Fish Is a Christian Symbol Because the Apostles Are Called "Fishers of Men"

This well-known symbol, composed of two simple arcs that meet at one end (the head) and cross at the other (the tail), has been around for millennia—long before the advent of Christianity. For ancient pagans the fish symbol represented fertility in the form of a "great mother." Originally depicted vertically, the symbol referred to the female womb and/or vulva, a fact that may horrify some devout Christians and fascinate readers of *The DaVinci Code*.

So how did the symbol become associated with Christianity? Appearing here and there throughout the Roman Empire, the symbol was adopted by early Christians during the days of religious persecution. They used it as a secret code to identify fellow believers. Some claim the fish was associated with Christ because his disciples were "fishers of men" or because of the many miracles (such as the miracle of the loaves and fishes) that Jesus performed with fish. Others link the fish to baptism ("born in water") or to a similarity in the pronunciation of the Hebrew words for "Christ" and "fish."

One often-repeated explanation for the link between Christianity and the fish symbol is more cryptic. It involves *ichthus*, the Greek word for "fish," used as an acronym. Each letter of ichthus stands for a word in a Greek phrase meaning "Jesus Christ, Son of God, Savior." How's that again? Spelled out, it goes like so: *i* (*Iesous*, "Jesus"), *ch* (*Christos*, "Christ"), *th* (*theou*, "God"), *u* (*huios*, "son"), *s* (*soter*, "savior"). This explanation sounds a bit concocted, and it may fall into the category of an after-the-fact rationalization. So why the fish symbol for Christ? No one knows for sure.

The Star of David Was Always a Jewish Symbol

Also known as the Magen David, or Mogen David ("shield of David"), the six-pointed star is an ancient symbol, but it was not associated specifically with Judaism until the 1600s, and it was not adopted by Zionists until 1897. Six-pointed stars are found in many societies in virtually every epoch of history. Betsy Ross

once suggested that the stars on the American flag be six-pointed because of the ease with which that shape can be created from a square patch of cloth. The idea was rejected, not because of the association of the symbol with Judaism but because of its association with European aristocracy.

The symbol appears on the walls of the ancient synagogue of Capernaeum, as does the swastika. And the star appears frequently on Christian church lintels and in Christian religious paintings throughout the Middle Ages. Why was it chosen, and why has it become so identified with the Jewish people? No one knows for sure, but one theory is that rabbinic literature says that God protected David "from six sides" and the six sides correspond to the six points of the star, now familiarly known as the Star of David.

Delilah Cut Off Samson's Hair

According to the Bible, Samson's hair was shaved off, not clipped off. And it was another man, not Delilah, who did the deed while Samson slept in Delilah's lap. Even so, it was Delilah who plotted his undoing. She nagged him repeatedly to reveal the source of his strength so she could betray him to his enemies in exchange for silver. (Why he didn't see this coming, based on her repeatedly treacherous behavior, is hard to fathom.) Once Samson's hair was gone, and with it his strength, his enemies gouged out his eyes. In Samson's case, love was blind—figuratively at first and then literally.

Incidentally, the explanation for Samson losing his strength when his hair was cut is not that there was some magical property inherent in his locks. Samson was a Nazarite, which means he had taken a vow to abstain from certain pleasures of life, such as eating meat, drinking wine, and the cutting of hair. Allowing his hair to be cut constituted breaking his vow, for which he was punished (perhaps more severely than any other Nazarite) with the loss of his strength.

Easter Is All about the Resurrection of Christ

If it's all about Jesus, then what's the Easter Bunny about? And what's with all those parades and bonnets and Easter eggs?

Easter began as an ancient pagan holiday celebrating spring, fertility, and rebirth. Since its timing roughly coincided with Passover and the Resurrection, the proselytizing Christian church incorporated the lore and festivities of the pagan holiday for its own purposes in order to make Christianity more acceptable to the pagans.

Easter got its name from the Saxon fertility goddess Eastre, whose sacred animal was the hare, another symbol of fertility. The Easter Bunny as such first made its appearance a few centuries ago in Germany, where the so-called *Oschter Haws* laid colored eggs in nests to the delight of children on Easter morning. When Germans immigrated to Pennsylvania, they brought the tradition with them, and the *Oschter Haws* became the Easter Bunny.

The Easter parade is not a pagan but a Christian tradition. After being baptized, early Christians wore new clothes to symbolize their rebirth into a life with Christ. Led by marchers carrying candles and crucifixes, medieval churchgoers would walk through the town in large groups after Easter Mass. Today these processions, combined with showy new clothes, survive as Easter parades.

The "Immaculate Conception" Refers to the Birth of Jesus

The Immaculate Conception must be all about the birth of Jesus, right? After all, what could be more immaculate than a virgin birth? But this is a common *mis*-Conception (sorry about that) that even many Catholics still harbor.

The Immaculate Conception, as laid down by Catholic dogma, refers to the conception of Mary, not Jesus. It's confusing, because Mary was conceived in the usual way—that is, biologically. So

what's so immaculate about that? At the time of her conception, Mary was protected by God from the stain of original sin. Her soul remained sinless and stainless, hence "immaculate."

So unlike the conception that preceded the Virgin Birth, the Immaculate Conception does not refer to conception without the union of man and woman—it means conception without the "original" sin that all humans inherited from Adam.

Jesus Christ Was Born on December 25 and Spoke Hebrew

No one knows which day of the year—or even which month or season of the year—Jesus was born. In the year 336, the Church of Rome adopted December 25 as the day to honor Christ's birth. Why that date? Because it was the same as a popular pagan holiday—namely, *Natalis Solis Invicti*, which celebrated the birth of the sun (and its rebirth after the winter solstice). By commandeering that already happy birthday, Christian proselytizers hoped to win lots of converts. They did, of course, and along with the pagan holiday came most of the trappings we now associate with Christmas: gift-giving, lights, fir trees, Yule logs, tempting foods, and festive merrymaking.

Four languages were floating around Palestine at the time of Jesus: Latin, Greek, Hebrew, and Aramaic. Latin and Greek were spoken to a limited extent by officials and educators. Hebrew, once the principal language of the Jews, was no longer commonly spoken in Jesus's day, but it was used liturgically in synagogues (just as Latin was used in the Catholic Church until recently). Jesus knew some Hebrew, but the language he spoke on an everyday basis was Aramaic, the main language of his contemporaries. Aramaic, however, was not used in writing the Bible, except for an occasional quote. The Old Testament was written in Hebrew, the New Testament in Greek.

Christo Redentor (Christ the Redeemer) in Rio de Janeiro, Brazil.

Most Muslims Are Arabs

Muslims in the Middle East get a lot of attention, and many of them are Arabs. But Arabs make up only about 15 percent of the world's Muslim population. In fact, the majority

of Muslims live east of Pakistan, and more live in Indonesia than in any other single country. Of the 1.2 billion Muslims worldwide (one out of five people on the planet), about 69 percent live in Asia, 27 percent in Africa, less than 3 percent in Europe, and less than .5 percent in the United States. Even so, the number of Muslims in the U.S. has been estimated at about 2.8 million, roughly equal to the population of Chicago.

The Mark of Cain Was a Punishment Meted Out to Cain for Killing His Brother

Quite the contrary, the mark referred to in Genesis 4:15 was not a punishment but a means of protecting Cain from being punished by others for his sin. This is clearly the intent of the text—"And the Lord said unto him, Therefore whoever slayeth Cain, vengeance will be taken on him sevenfold. And the Lord set a mark upon Cain, lest any finding him should kill him." —but over time, the mark was itself regarded as a punishment: a stain that forever reminded Cain and everyone who met him that he had committed the grievous sin of murdering his brother. What the mark looked like is not clear. From antiquity to the medieval period, the mark was imagined to be a scar on the forehead, which was visible and striking but also unsightly and shaming. Other sources have suggested that the mark was not inflicted on Cain's person at all but was a natural sign (like the rainbow that was the sign of God's covenant with Noah) serving as a reminder of the Lord's protection of Cain. What that sign might have looked like is not spelled out, but it would have to be something widely observable—and it would have to have some symbolic significance to indicate God's acceptance of Cain's plea for forgiveness. Any suggestions?

One of the Popes Was a Woman

The first story about a woman pope—namely, Pope Joan—appeared in the 1200s. She must have been very good at keeping a secret—at least until she got pregnant and, accidentally and rather indiscreetly (while trying to mount a horse), went into labor in front of a crowd and gave birth to a child. The crowd became angry, dragged her through the streets, and stoned her to death. Apparently the onlookers had little tolerance for whelping papal male-impersonators.

Although the story seems never to die, there are a number of reasons not to believe it. For one thing, the first mention of the female pope didn't occur until centuries after she was supposed to have reigned. Secondly, no gaps in the rather meticulous historical records of papal succession allow any elbow room into which to squeeze a lady pope. Thirdly, common sense dictates that such a secret would not only be hard for Pope Joan to keep but also be even harder for the legions of proximate faithful to cover up. On the other hand, to name a more recent example, there is the remarkable case of jazz musician Billy Tipton. A woman posing as a man, Tipton fooled band leaders, fellow musicians, and even his several wives for decades. No one knew his (her) secret until he (she) met his (her) maker.

Saint Patrick Was Irish

Not only was he not Irish, he hated and feared the Irish—for a while, anyway. Why? Born in 386 somewhere on the island of Great Britain, Patrick was rudely abducted at age sixteen by a band of Irish hooligans, marauders, or (possibly) pirates. He was taken to Ireland and sold into slavery, where he spent six years tending sheep and yearning to escape. He did, finally, and returned to the Emerald Isle later on as a shepherd of souls—i.e., a Christian missionary who aimed to convert all the Irish. He succeeded, more or less, becoming the patron saint of his accidentally adopted homeland. Patrick died in 461—on March 17, which happens to be St. Patrick's Day. What a coincidence!

Statue of St. Patrick at The Hill of Tara, County Meath, Ireland.

Popes Have Never Had Children

In the first sixteen centuries of the papacy, more than a dozen of the holy fathers were also biological fathers. Some had children before they became popes. Some sired illegitimate offspring while serving as popes. And one or two of the Holy Roman patriarchs were, it seems, promiscuous, if not wantonly licentious. In an odd twist on the tradition of producing a royal "heir to the throne," a few of the illegitimate sons of popes became popes themselves.

The Puritans Celebrated Christmas

One would think that all Christians, especially those as devout as the seventeenth-century Puritans, would embrace Christmas as their holiest holiday. But not only did the Massachusetts Puritans eschew Christmas, they regarded it as diabolically anti-Christian and even outlawed it between 1659 and 1681. During those years, no one was allowed to take Christmas Day off from work, and anyone caught celebrating the holiday was subject to a fine. Although the law was lifted in 1681, Puritans continued to frown on Christmas until well into the 1800s, viewing the holiday ("holy day") as, well, unholy.

Why were the Puritans such party-poopers? For one thing, they didn't care for Roman Catholics, and it was the Catholics who had (somewhat arbitrarily) assigned the date of December 25 to the birth of Christ back in fourth-century Rome. By that time, or so the Puritans believed, the Catholic Church had become corrupt and alienated from Christ's teaching. Also, December 25 had been chosen by the Church because it happened to coincide with a popular pagan holiday celebrating the birth of the sun. The Puritans viewed the raucous merrymaking associated with the holiday to be sacrilegious and "impure," which is one of the reasons they were called Puritans.

The Puritans Were Puritanical

They took a hard line on lots of things, but when it came to sex, the New England Puritans were not prudes. They considered sex a gift from God, as long as it took place prayerfully and within marriage. In fact, if a spouse was not delivering an adequate amount of sex unto his or her partner, the church authorities would get together and offer serious counsel, and in some cases they would mete out some form of punishment to the withholder. Their pro-sex philosophy only went so far, however: any sex outside of marriage was considered a grievous sin, and adultery was punishable by death.

Engraving showing Puritans, artist and date unknown.

Salem Witches Were Burned at the Stake

First of all, what did these "witches" do that aroused the suspicions of their fellow townspeople in seventeenth-century Salem, Massachusetts? Most of the accused—who had previously been regarded as ordinary folks—were suddenly gripped by seizures, hallucinations, hysterical blindness and deafness, and other bizarre behaviors that prompted many of their God-fearing neighbors to believe they were possessed.

Examination of a Witch (1853), by Tompkins H. Matteson.

The events that ensued were the Salem witch trials of 1692 (not a proud year for Massachusetts). Some one hundred fifty people (and two dogs) had been arrested, thirty-one were tried, and twenty were put to death, but none were burned at the stake. Of the twenty put to death, nineteen were hanged and one (an old man) was crushed by a form of torture called *peine fort et dure* (stones were piled on his body over the course of two days) because he refused to enter a plea.

All this is pretty gruesome, but when compared with the witch-hunting that went on in Europe for more than two centuries, what happened in Salem sounds almost mild. In England, France, and elsewhere throughout Europe, it is estimated that some 500,000 people were burned at the stake because they were accused of heresy or of practicing witchcraft.

The Salem witches, by the way, were all pardoned twenty years after their executions—one of the more memorable instances of "too little too late."

The Vatican Is in Rome, Italy

It might seem that way, since the city of Rome surrounds the Vatican. But politically and territorially Vatican City is an island unto itself, somewhat like Washington, D.C., only not quite. The official Italian name is *Stato Della Città del Vaticano*, which translates as "the State of Vatican City." This home of the pope and the papacy (and the seat of government for the Roman Catholic Church) is actually no less than an independent country—and at a little over one hundred acres it's the smallest one in the world. The Vatican has its own citizenry, police, diplomatic corps, currency, postage stamps, and flag.

Vatican City is a sovereign microstate whose territory consists of a landlocked, almost completely walled enclave within the city of Rome. It is actually all that remains of the former Papal States, which from 756 to 1870 also included Rome and most of central Italy. This tiny, independent nation was created in 1929 by the Lateran treaties. Its head of government is, of course, the pope. The secretary of state (the President of the Pontifical Commission for the Vatican City State) and the governor round out the governing body of Vatican City. These, like all other officials, are appointed by the pope and can be dismissed at his pleasure. Although the pope's official residence is the Apostolic Palace, and Vatican City is considered to be the governmental capital of the Catholic Church, the principal ecclesiastical seat of the Holy See is actually located in Rome itself at the Basilica of St. John Lateran.

The 790 citizens who call Vatican City home consist mainly of clergy, including high dignitaries, priests, nuns, and the Swiss Guard. Citizenship is conditional upon their employment at the Vatican. When their employment is terminated, so is their citizenship. But no one leaves the Vatican without a country. In the event that one loses his citizenship of both Vatican City and his native land, one automatically becomes an Italian citizen.

St. Peter's Basilica (*Basilica di San Pietro*) on St. Peter's Square (*Piazza San Pietro*), Vatican City.

Handel's *Messiah* Was Meant To Be Played at Christmas and "The Christmas Song" Was Composed at Christmas Time

George Frideric Handel's great oratorio *Messiah* was composed during the summer of 1741 and had absolutely nothing to do with the Christmas season. Based on the Biblical libretto written by Charles Jennens, it was first performed in April of 1742 in Dublin during a benefit for a hospital as well as for prisoners who were in jail for debt. Also, the actual title of the work is simply *Messiah*, and not *The Messiah*, as is often supposed.

Surprisingly, what can be considered Handel's greatest work took only twenty-four days to complete. Handel (above) conducted *Messiah* many times, and because he often altered the arrangement to suit each particular performance, there is no single "authentic" version of the work. Mozart also rearranged the music and translated the lyrics into German.

The story of another familiar composition associated with Christmas is equally surprising. "The Christmas Song"—"Chestnuts roasting on an open fire/Jack Frost nipping at your nose"—was composed by Mel Tormé and Bob Wells while they were in Florida during a sweltering heat wave in the summer of 1944. In an effort to find relief from the heat, Tormé and Wells started thinking "cool thoughts," and the two of them composed the words and music in less than an hour. It went on to become a major hit for Tormé and, of course, for Nat King Cole.

The Philistines Were a Barbaric, Godless People

Not according to the archaeological record. It is true that the Philistines were a particularly warlike nation—they were the principal seafaring traders of the Mediterranean in antiquity—they had more to protect; hence they had more reason to solve their problems militarily. But the pottery and artifacts that remain from that culture indicate a high level of sophistication and a refined religious sensibility—with maturely developed moral and spiritual values. Today, Philistia is considered a notable example of high Mycenaean culture.

So how did the term "philistine" become linked with boorishness and lack of culture? The association dates back to the seventeenth century, during a period of turmoil in Germany. In one particularly violent encounter between students and the German militia in the city of Jena, a student was killed by a soldier. At the funeral, the pastor delivering the eulogy called the soldiers "Philistines," and thereafter the term became associated with everything coarse and uncivilized.

The Scopes Trial Upheld the Teaching of Evolution

Also known as the "monkey trial," the 1925 trial of John Thomas Scopes in Dayton, Tennessee, centered on the accusation that Scopes violated the Butler Act, a bill that outlawed teaching evolution in Tennessee public schools. The common misconception is that the trial was actually resolved in Scopes's favor and that, as a result, the teaching of the theory of evolution became legal in Tennessee. In fact, Scopes was found guilty and fined $100. The Butler Act was not repealed in Tennessee until 1967. A year later, in 1968, the United States Supreme Court declared that similar laws in other states were unconstitutional.

Despite the actual outcome of the trial, the hoopla that surrounded the incident made the public aware of the evolution issue and began the series of debates and protests that led to the Supreme Court decision. Yet, in most people's minds, the Scopes trial settled the issue for good. How wrong recent history has shown that to be!

Noah's Flood Was Pure Mythology Transposed to the Bible

The story of Noah's Flood has had more lives than the proverbial cat—passing in and out of the realm of the real, it seems, with each decade. For centuries, pilgrims have climbed Mount Ararat, the putative resting place of the Ark (though a careful reading indicates that it was a mountain in the Province of Ararat), claiming to have found or seen remnants, but none have been convincing.

In 1872, a bank clerk named George Smith deciphered some cuneiform tablets (brought to the British Museum from the Middle East by the explorer Sir Henry Layard two decades earlier) and pieced together the Gilgamesh Epic, an ancient Babylonian tale that seemed to be the source (the mythical source) for the Noah story in the Bible.

In the late nineteenth century, lists of ancient Sumerian kings were unearthed from 4,000 years ago that describe them as having reigned "before the flood," indicating that a flood actually took place in ancient history. Then the world was electrified by the news that British archaeologist Sir Leonard Woolley had discovered an eleven-foot layer of silt—clearly the remnants of a major flood—in the

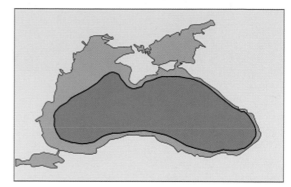
The Black Sea (light blue) and the lake it once was (dark).

area around Ur of Chaldees in Sumer. This, Woolley claimed, was proof that the Flood had taken place. But careful follow-up and diggings elsewhere showed that flooding of the plains around the twin rivers was common and happened at many different times. The Flood was once again relegated to the world of fable.

Then, in 1993, two Columbia University geologists, William Ryan and Walter Pitman, found evidence that a great flooding of the basin of the Black Sea had indeed taken place around 5,600 BCE, when the Mediterranean rose and broke through the Bosporus Strait. Analysis of the bed of the Black Sea (using the underwater submarine technology of famous *Titanic* explorer Robert Ballard) shows that prior to 7,600 years ago, the Black Sea was a fresh-water lake fed by the Danube and the Don. It was much smaller than the Black Sea is today, with many settlements on its shores.

Then, as the polar ice caps melted and the Mediterranean rose, the sea broke through the Bosporus and inundated the area with salty sea water. The torrents that poured through from the Bosporus would have been the equivalent of ten Niagara Falls, according to Ryan and Pitman, and would have been a cataclysmic event for what was then human civilization in the low-lying region—more a flood than a great rain…a distinction which is also reflected by a more accurate reading of the Biblical text.

So welcome back, Noah, to the world of the real!

From *Nuremberg Chronicle* b, by Hartmann Schedel. Painting by Albrecht Dürer (first published in 1493).

Joan of Arc Was a French Peasant Burned at the Stake by the French

Above: Statue of Joan of Arc from a parish church. At right: Statue of Joan of Arc in the Place des Pyramides, Paris, France, by Emmanuel Frémiet, 1874.

First of all, Joan of Arc was not French. She was born in Domrémy, located in the independent duchy of Bar, a part of Lorraine—and Lorraine was not annexed to France until 1776. Joan's family, although perhaps peasants in the technical sense (they were landowners who made their living primarily by farming), were actually financially comfortable, and among Domrémy's most prominent citizens.

According to Joan, she was directed by the archangel Michael only to "go to France if you must," perhaps suggesting that she did not want to have anything to do with France at the time.

The political situation in France was essentially one of civil war. France was not only at war with England (this was the latter part of the Hundred Years' War) but also with themselves: Burgundy, once part of France, was now an enemy, siding with England in the fight for control of the French throne. Many areas of the duchy of Bar were dominated by Burgundian loyalists; hence Joan's hesitancy to heed Michael's orders.

Joan of Arc was only seventeen when she led the French army against English and Burgundian forces. During the siege of Orléans, Joan defeated the enemy and the siege was lifted after a brief nine days. This battle was a defining moment in the war. After a few more victories, Charles VII was crowned King of France, settling all disputes over the succession.

During her life, Joan was admired by commoners and royalty alike in France (once they got over their initial skepticism). So why would they have burned her at the stake, especially after she had led them to victory? The real story, predictably, is that her execution was political: captured by the Burgundians in 1430, she was sold to the English, who were bent on making her look insane in order to discredit France's victory and, by implication, Charles VII's claim to the throne. So after an inquisition-style trial—filled with highly suspicious maneuvering on the part of the prosecution—Joan was convicted of witchcraft and heresy. She was burned at the stake at Rouen on May 30, 1431, at the age of nineteen.

And wouldn't you know it—after all that to-do, England's plan didn't work. Charles VII retained his position, and France remained free. Not only that, but Joan's martyrdom only added to the legend surrounding her courageous victories. Joan's reputation increased steadily over the years until she became a venerated national hero and finally, in 1920, a saint.

"Cleanliness Is Next to Godliness" and "Spare the Rod, Spoil the Child" Are Old Biblical Maxims

The "cleanliness" phrase is not from the Bible, though people seem certain it is. John Wesley, one of the founders of Methodism in the eighteenth century, used it in one of his sermons. Wesley was actually quoting a proverb from the famous "ladder to saintliness" by Phinehas ben-Yair, a Hebrew sage from the second century. Wesley's sermon "On Dress" was based on a passage from the New Testament. He accurately used quotation marks when he stated, " 'cleanliness is, indeed, next to godliness.' "

In Proverbs, a reader can find the Biblical advice for raising children as, "He that spareth his rod hateth his son: but he that loveth him chasteneth him betimes," and "Foolishness is bound in the heart of a child; but the rod of correction shall drive it far from him." The poet Menander said, "The man who has never been flogged has never been taught." English poet Samuel Butler was the one to actually write "Then spare the rod and spoil the child" in *Hudibras* in 1664.

The popular maxim "God helps him who helps himself" is a quote from the Bible and probably has its origins in the writings of the Greek sage Aesop. The actual words in "Hercules and the Wagoner" are "Help when you pray or prayer is vain." Or, in another translation, "… never more pray to me for help, until you have done your best to help yourself, or depend upon it you will henceforth pray in vain."

Another biblical-sounding phrase, with its religious intonation and a reference to angels, is that of British poet Alexander Pope, who wrote "Fools rush in where angels fear to tread" in his *An Essay on Criticism* in 1711.

It's also worth mentioning that the Ten Commandments sections of the Bible (the list appears twice) do not enjoin the broad act of killing but specifically refer to murder. "Thou shalt not murder" would be the proper translation, as opposed to "Thou shalt not put another human being to death." Many people are put to death in one way or another in the course of the Bible story without their killers being counted among the sinners.

Gambling Is Forbidden by the Bible

You may or may not believe gambling is a bad idea, and there are certainly plenty of laws against it just about everywhere you look, but nowhere in the Bible does it say gambling is wrong or sinful. In fact, a number of model citizens in the Bible are depicted as "casting lots," and gambling is never specifically condemned by the Almighty. Later commentaries regarded gambling as at best simply a waste of time and unproductive, and at worst a form of stealing—taking money from someone unfairly.

A related misconception commonly held is that the Bible says "money is the root of all evil." The actual quote, by the Apostle Paul in the book of Timothy, is that "the love of money is the root of all evil." Apparently, money itself isn't so bad; it's greed and an obsession with money that are deplorable.

"Original Sin" Refers to Sexual Appetite

Original sin, although not directly referred to in the Bible, applies to man's first act of disobedience and actually has absolutely nothing to do with sex. Over the course of centuries, original sin has evolved into a complex religious doctrine that (sometimes controversially) involves the transmission of guilt at birth to all humankind.

So is original sin Adam's fault? It is often supposed that Adam was the first to defy God by eating an apple from the forbidden tree. But not only was it not an "apple," it was actually Eve who ate the "forbidden fruit," according to Genesis 3:6. Although Eve convinced Adam to eat the fruit as well, it was only *his* disobedience that counted (Eve was just an overgrown rib, after all) and henceforth brought all kinds of evils into the world.

The Bible Contains Coded Messages Predicting the Future

According to Michael Drosnin's best-selling book *The Bible Code,* anyone can read the future in the Bible by simply applying a proven mathematical code. Using what mathematicians call the "skip code" on the Torah, Drosnin claims that he found prophecies about various assassinations, including those of President John F. Kennedy, Robert Kennedy, and Israeli Prime Minister Yitzhak Rabin. He even found prophecies about the Oklahoma City bombing and the rise of Hitler. The skip code works by beginning with any letter in the Bible, skipping a chosen number of letters and writing down the next letter, then skipping the same number of letters and writing down the next letter, and so on. You can choose any number of letters to skip until you find recognizable words and phrases.

Although this may seem like an intriguing way of fortune-telling for many people, especially since many of the predictions Drosnin found were true, it is important to bear in mind that many of the events had already happened when Drosnin "predicted" them. And Drosnin had to skip 4,771 letters at a time in order to find the name "Rabin."

Also, many of Drosnin's predictions are so broad (he found messages using his method that predicted the end of the world in 2000 CE, or in 2006, or after 2006, or never), they are guaranteed to come true.

The Hebrew language usually omits short-sounding vowels, so they must be added in later. Hebrew names can be written in many different ways, increasing chances of success with the code. One important problem is what to do with spaces between words—in antiquity, there were no spaces between words, but Drosnin elects to count the spaces ... if they yield a meaningful "prophecy."

According to Professor Brendan McKay, the code will work on any book. McKay applied Drosnin's code to *Moby Dick* and also found prophecies for the assassinations of Prime Minister Rabin, John F. Kennedy, and Martin Luther King, Jr.

Drosnin wasn't the first to use the skip code to predict the future. Masters of the twelfth-century Jewish mystical movement, the Kabbalah, also applied the code to Genesis and found hidden messages.

Buddhists Worship the Buddha

Obviously, the Buddha is the central figure of Buddhism, and it's true that most schools revere him as a great teacher and a model of spiritual wisdom and goodness. What form this reverence takes will depend on which school you're talking about, and there are a few sects that do see him as almost godlike.

By and large, though, Buddhists don't really "worship" anything. The religion is nontheistic; the Buddha refused to answer questions about the existence or non-existence of God. He saw that

as not only outside his purview but also irrelevant to the spiritual process he taught—which, in modern-day terms, could be described as a system of psychological exercises, including meditation. The focus of the Buddhist has always been on connecting not with a deity but with the self.

In a sense, all this makes Buddhism less a religion than a method—and that, in fact, is the way most Buddhists think of it.

Three Wise Men Visited Baby Jesus

The story of the birth of Jesus can be found in the second chapter of the book of Matthew. Wise men are said to have visited the newborn babe, but they are described only as "wise men from the east." (The Bible asserts that they were not from Judea.) No specific number of men is mentioned.

The idea that there were three Wise Men probably stems from the fact that three gifts—gold, frankincense, and myrrh—are specified in the biblical text, and for visual depictions it made sense to have one Wise Man holding each kind of gift. But according to some Greek traditions, there were twelve Wise Men, and other sources suggest as many as fourteen.

The Wise Men are usually depicted as having ridden to the scene on camels, but nothing in the Bible supports this; most scholars think they probably walked. And they almost certainly didn't come to the manger.

The confusion may stem from the fact that shepherds are described as having visited the family there. The Bible says specifically that the Wise Men visited Jesus at the "house of the child." The same passage later refers to Jesus as a "young child" at the time of the Wise Men's visit,

One depiction of the Three Wise Men visiting baby Jesus. *Adoration of the Magi,* painted by Albrecht Dürer in 1594.

implying that he was no longer an infant by then. This is further suggested by Herod's subsequent directive that all children under the age of two be killed, which happened immediately after the Wise Men's visit. If Jesus had still been an infant, presumably Herod would have simply ordered all infants killed.

Nor were the Wise Men guided by a star—at least not for the whole journey. The Wise Men first headed to Jerusalem—in the opposite direction of the star—and asked King Herod where the baby was. Herod redirected them south to Bethlehem, at which point the star helped them find their way.

The Wise Men weren't kings, either, as is commonly believed. In Greek the Wise Men are called *magoi* or *magi*, meaning "sorcerers" or "sages"; they were Zoroastrian priests, as well as learned astrologers (a calling highly respected at the time).

The Wise Men weren't thought of as kings until the second century, when African church leader Tertullian referred to them as *fere regis* or "almost kings." Not until the sixth century were the men given names—Gaspar, Balthazar, and Melchior.

Lady Godiva (1890), by Jules Lefebvre.

People

Captain Bligh Was a Sadistic Disciplinarian

Fodder for a number of Hollywood movies, the mutiny that actually took place on the HMAV *Bounty* in 1789 did not happen as depicted on the silver screen. In each film version, Captain William Bligh was portrayed as a despicable villain, most notably by Charles Laughton in the 1935 film *Mutiny on the Bounty*. The fact is that the real Captain Bligh was not such a bad guy. He was competent, considerate, and quite kind toward his crew.

So why the mutiny? The *Bounty* was on a mis-

punished, but others managed to avoid the long arm (in this case, the very long arm) of the law and lived out their days in Eden.

A similar case occurred in 1611 when Henry Hudson's crew mutinied and set him adrift in a small boat in Hudson Bay. The mutineers were caught and tried—but they were exonerated because the court martial determined that Hudson's decision to forge on in search of a Northwest Passage was, in light of the coming winter, suicidal.

sion in Tahiti, where crew members were allowed to wander freely on the island and mix with the native inhabitants, partaking of a smorgasbord of carnal and culinary delights. When it was time to move on, the crew balked at the prospect of leaving their newfound paradise, so they made their feelings clear in no uncertain terms— namely, mutiny.

Captain Bligh was set adrift in a rowboat on the high seas, but somehow he managed to make it back to land and later was promoted to admiral. Some of the mutineers were eventually caught and

Above: *The Arrest of Bligh*, a propaganda cartoon from 1808, Sydney, Australia, designed to show Capt. Bligh as a coward.
Left: Portrait of Vice-Admiral William Bligh (1754–1817), painted by Alexander Huey in 1814.

Paul McCartney Faked His Death

The possibility that the most popular band in the history of recorded music would be subject to its share of rumors and widely spread myths, and one of the biggest rumors surrounding the Beatles' seven-year career was that, after the completion of *Abbey Road* in 1969, Paul McCartney had died. The rumor, started by Detroit disc jockey Russ Gibb, quickly became a worldwide "truth" based on "clues" left behind in many of the Beatles albums, including *Abbey Road*. Gibb claimed that he had received an anonymous phone call informing him that McCartney was dead. It was said that Paul just died in a car accident, proof of which existed in the songs "A Day in the Life" and "I Am the Walrus." At the end of the song "Strawberry Fields," it was suggested that John

The Beatles greeting their fans in 1964. From left to right: John Lennon, Paul McCartney, George Harrison, and Ringo Starr.

Lennon could be heard chanting "I buried Paul." People believed that an actor had been hired to portray McCartney in album photographs, even undergoing plastic surgery to maintain a likeness to Paul. The album cover of *Abbey Road* depicted Paul barefoot and out of step with his bandmates, supposedly signifying his death because corpses are buried sans footwear in England.

The mass hysteria lasted for a week, until a team of *Life* magazine employees trekked through Scotland in search of McCartney's country vacation spot to photograph him. Of course, this is where McCartney had been all along, simply enjoying a holiday with his family, trying to avoid the relentless media hoopla that had accompanied the band's latest record release.

Daniel Boone Wore a Coonskin Hat

Fess Parker, the actor who played Daniel Boone on TV in the 1960s, wore a coonskin hat—and this prompted kids everywhere to do the same. But Boone himself did not. In fact, he thought the hat looked uncivilized. What the real Boone wore was a wide-brimmed, Pennsylvania-style, beaver-felt hunter's hat somewhat like the one on a box of Quaker Oats cereal. The wide brim helped keep the sun out of his eyes and the rain off his face. So whence the coonskin connection? The furry chapeau was traced to an actor in a minstrel show who became associated with Boone while depicting "The Hunters of Kentucky." The actor couldn't find a wide-brimmed beaver-felt hat, so he wore one made of coonskin instead. Go figure.

Lizzie Borden Axed Her Parents to Death

Lizzie Borden took an axe/ Gave her mother forty whacks/ When she saw what she had done/ She gave her father forty-one!

Or did she? No one knows for sure. But the jury deliberated for less than an hour before acquitting her. (By the way, the axed "mother" was actually her stepmother.) Also, the only other person in the house at the time of the murders was the maid, Bridget Sullivan. They didn't have a butler, so no one could say the butler did it, but some maintain it was the maid.

The townspeople of Fall River, Massachusetts, never accepted the verdict, however, and shunned Lizzie to her dying day in 1927. The fact is, Lizzie (shown at left) was a charitable person all her life and, before the murder, a respected member of the community. She even bequeathed the town a sizable amount for the upkeep of the family grave.

Catherine the Great Died While Having Sex with a Horse

How, you might ask, would such a bizarre notion come to be? For decades, college students have been springing this juicy historical "fact" on their unsuspecting peers, invoking expressions of drop-jawed astonishment. As the story goes, Catherine, empress of Russia, was so overcome with lust that she tried to have sex with a horse and was crushed while the horse was lowered via ropes and pulleys onto her naked body. Is there any truth to this?

To the great disappointment of sophomores everywhere, Catherine the Great died of a stroke while sitting on the toilet. That she had an enormous, if not insatiable, appetite for sex, however, may have some basis in fact. Her lovers were said to be legion, although some historians claim there were "only" a dozen or so.

In at least one instance, a former paramour pimped for her, so to speak, providing fresh bedmates from the ranks of soldiers and minor government officials. Her tastes were not indiscriminate, however, as she had her parlor maids give each prospective companion a trial run to be sure he "measured up."

Although Catherine was highly regarded as a monarch, such indiscretions didn't do much for her personal reputation, either in Russia or in Europe at large. No one knows for sure how the rumor of an equine demise got started, but Catherine had plenty of enemies to contend with, any one of whom could have gotten the ball rolling.

Cleopatra Was a Beautiful Egyptian Seductress Whom Roman Emperors Found Irresistible

Theda Bara, Claudette Colbert, and Elizabeth Taylor played her on the silver screen. She was rumored to be so alluring that men were willing to die for the chance to spend a night with her, right? Not exactly. Roman coins depict Cleopatra's face as hook-nosed and jowly. It's fair to say that her dalliances with the likes of Julius Caesar and Marc Antony were inspired more by her wit and charm (and the need to connect politically) than by her dubious pulchritude.

It's doubtful, in fact, whether Cleopatra was even Egyptian. In the middle of the third century BCE, Egypt was ruled by Macedonian Greeks, the heirs to Alexander the Great. The capital of Egypt was moved from Memphis to Alexandria and the Greeks, as was their practice throughout the lands they conquered, encouraged intermarriage between themselves and their new subjects. But the ruling class nearly always was Macedonian Greek—usually adopting the dress and lifestyle of the vanquished people.

Cleopatra was born in 69 BCE, the daughter of Pharaoh Ptolemy XII. She was crowned Cleopatra VII—meaning there were six Cleopatras before her. This Cleopatra, however, was different in that she laid claim to the throne, probably amid the confusion that ensued after the Roman conquest of the Greeks.

Speaking of confusion, there were reports that Cleopatra was indeed beautiful—but it happened to be the wrong Cleopatra. The pretty one was Cleopatra III, a distant relation to the more celebrated queen.

So how did the myth of Cleopatra VII's great beauty get started? It was probably the play by William Shakespeare, *Antony and Cleopatra*, that started it all. The play is based on the relationship between Cleopatra and Marc Antony from the time of the Parthian War to Cleopatra's suicide. In Shakespeare's view, Cleopatra was conceited, self-indulgent, and melodramatic, albeit quite beguiling.

In the early 1900s, George Bernard Shaw tried to correct history in a play entitled *Caesar and Cleopatra*. Shaw emphasized the political ramifications of a Roman Emperor marrying the Egyptian queen but then threw in some lurid subplots involving eunuchs and assassins. (The film version of the play starred Vivien Leigh as a sultry Cleopatra and Claude Rains as a somewhat hapless Caesar.)

Over the years, Cleopatra continued to be portrayed as a beautiful woman in literature, theater, and film. The most celebrated portrayal was Elizabeth Taylor's in the 1963 epic directed by Joseph L. Mankiewicz. What the film lacked in cinematic artistry was made up for in real-life melodrama: after the film, Taylor divorced her husband, Eddie Fisher, and married her costar, Richard Burton.

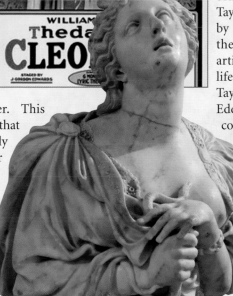

Film poster for the 1917 film *Cleopatra,* starring Theda Bara; and *Cleopatra VII Committing Suicide,* sculpture by Claude Bertin in the Louvre, Paris, France.

Carlos Castaneda Was Taught by Don Juan

World famous for his cryptic series of books that blend anthropology, shamanism, and psychedelia, Carlos Castaneda is a figure shrouded in self-cultivated mystery. His first three best-sellers—*The Teachings of Don Juan: A Yaqui Way of Knowledge*, *A Separate Reality*, and *Journey to Ixtlan*—were written while he was studying anthropology at UCLA. They were presented as factual accounts of his prolonged apprenticeship with a Yaqui Indian shaman named don Juan Matus.

Castaneda and his books (published from the 1960s to the 1990s) have attracted legions of adherents and legions of skeptics. His detractors question whether the "research" ever took place and whether a real shaman named don Juan ever existed. For example, only Castaneda and a few compatriots ever had personal contact with the shaman. No photographs of don Juan or other documentation have been offered up for scrutiny. And when the mentor departed, there was no record of a dead body.

Furthermore, Yaqui Indian experts note that the accounts do not have the ring of authenticity. For example, the descriptions of native shamanism don't jibe with other anthropological data, and the plants, animals, and landscapes Castaneda depicts are not consistent with what is known about Yaqui territory. Also, Castaneda had claimed his research was backed up with "voluminous" field notes, but no such notes have ever been found.

Other critics suggest that the accounts sound more like fiction than fact, and some aspects of the stories seem suspiciously familiar enough to have been lifted from other sources. A recluse who refused to comment on any of these accusations, Carlos Castaneda, who died in 1998, took the truth to his grave.

Clarence Darrow Was a Distinguished Law School Graduate

Famous in the 1920s for his role in the Scopes "monkey" trial, which tested the teaching of evolution in schools, and for his role in the trial of teenage murderers Leopold and Loeb, Clarence Darrow was regarded as the archetypal American defense lawyer. Although Darrow studied law for a year at the University of Michigan, he never graduated from law school. You could take the bar exam then without ever attending law school, and if you passed, you would be admitted to the bar and could practice law.

Davy Crockett Died Fighting at the Alamo

Davy Crockett died swinging his empty rifle ("Ole Betsy") at charging Mexican soldiers during their onslaught of the Alamo—or so the scene has been depicted in historical accounts and on the silver screen. But according to more recent research based on eyewitness accounts, Crockett was captured and brought before General Santa Anna to bargain for his life. Santa Anna, whose instructions to his men had been to take no prisoners, ordered that Crockett and other American captives be summarily executed—and that's exactly what happened.

Walt Disney Had His Head Frozen After He Died, and He Created Mickey Mouse

As the rumor goes, Walt Disney (1901–1966) had been fascinated with the promise of life extension via cryonics and had arranged for his head, or his entire body, to be placed in cryonic suspension—that is, frozen—right after his death. The hope of cryonics is that people who are frozen may someday be brought back to life when medical technology has advanced enough to make such a thing possible.

How this peculiar Hollywood rumor got started is the subject of much speculation based on a few loosely related suppositions—namely, that Disney loved new technology, he had an interest in cryonics, he had never made any funeral arrangements, the circumstances of his illness and death were enveloped in secrecy, there was no public observance of his funeral, and the family would not comment on his death.

So what are the facts? Simply that Disney died of lung cancer after months of rapidly declining health. He was cremated two days after his death, and his ashes were placed in a vault in Forest Lawn Cemetery in Glendale, California. The vault is identified only by an inconspicuous plaque on the wall containing the names of Disney, his wife, and his daughter.

As for Mickey, Disney may have inspired the character of Mickey Mouse (originally named Mortimer, incidentally), but the image itself, along with that of Mickey's predecessor, Oswald the Rabbit, was designed and drawn by Ub Iwerks, Disney's early associate (and a man with a name that sounds made up—by someone like Disney).

The fact is that Disney was never much of an artist, though he was often pictured seemingly drawing his cartoon characters and was loath to give his animators on-screen credit. Disney did provide Mickey's famous falsetto voice for the cartoons that were made between 1928 and 1946. But thereafter, while Disney was busy building his mega-corporation, others were assigned the task of voicing the animated mouse.

A story is told that at a surprise party for Disney, a cartoon created by two Disney animators explicitly showing Mickey and Minnie in compromising situations was shown. Disney watched the film with everyone else, apparently as amused as were all assembled. He asked the group, smilingly, who was responsible. The two animators stepped forward and took credit, expecting Disney to thank them. Instead, Disney fired them on the spot and promptly left.

By all accounts, Uncle Walt was not the easiest man in the world to work for.

Walt Disney, seen here in 1954, was an American film producer, director, screenwriter, voice actor, animator, and philanthropist. In 1923 he co-founded the Walt Disney Company with his brother, Roy.

Einstein Was a Bad Student—and in Old Age, He was Senile

It's true that Einstein began to talk later than the average child. But when he got around to it, he spoke in complete sentences. (When he finally started to speak, he was asked why he had waited so long, and he is reported to have said, "Until now, everything has been satisfactory.")

In school he never wore a dunce cap, as has been rumored. In fact, he got top grades and was doing physics and calculus by his early teens. Einstein did happen to fail a college entrance exam, but at the time he was two years younger than the average applicant, and he scored brilliantly in science and mathematics. His failure to pass the exam was due to one subject: French. After brushing up on the humanities, Einstein passed and was admitted the following year.

In the early twentieth century, the relationship between physics and mathematics was not as intimate as it is today. But Einstein's phenomenal command of the lofty mathematical concepts that his path-breaking theories required was clear from the very beginning of his career. People who recounted their experience attending his lectures in Berlin report that his mastery of mathematics was even more impressive than his insights within the realm of physics.

Einstein spent a great portion of his later years trying to accomplish a very difficult task—one that

Albert Einstein (1879–1955). Below: Photograph taken at the home of friends in Santa Barbara, California, 1933. At right: Childhood photograph taken in 1884.

still occupies the best minds in physics today. A kind of Holy Grail for physicists everywhere, the goal is to achieve the unification of all the forces of nature in one theory, expressible in one set of equations. Tentatively dubbed Unified Field Theory, it is sometimes referred to sweepingly as the Theory of Everything ("TOE"). Einstein was working on this subject on the very day he died.

Epicurus Was a Shameless Hedonist

Quite the opposite, actually. People often make the mistake of confusing "epicurean" with "hedonistic," assuming that both refer to a wanton pursuit of pleasure.

For Epicurus, the ancient Greek philosopher who lived from about 342 to 247 BCE, who gave epicureanism its name, pleasure was high on the list of desirable experiences, but it did not embrace the

kinds of orgies and drunken pig-outs we associate with hedonism. Rather, the movement's founder was a sensible fellow who advocated modesty, kindness, prudence, and moderation in all things. The pleasures that Epicurus aspired to were actually rather genteel: intelligent conversation, appreciation of the arts, and inner serenity—combined (of course) with good (but healthy) food.

Sigmund Freud Wrote about the Subconscious Mind and Advocated Sexual Freedom

The word "subconscious" was never used by Freud—in fact, he deliberately avoided the word, which he considered incorrect and misleading. Freud had a different term for all the repressed stuff in our psyches—namely "the unconscious." In it are stored childhood traumas, hidden resentments, disguised desires and fears, etc., which we can't access with our conscious mind and which Freudian psychoanalysis was designed to bring to the surface. So what's the difference in meaning between "subconscious" and "unconscious"? It depends on whom you ask, but it's safe to say that "subconscious" is a more nebulous term associated with some

Sigmund Freud (1856–1939) was an Austrian neurologist. He is considered the founder of the psychoanalytic school of psychology.

forms of psychotherapy, with pop psychology, and with hypnotism, and it doesn't always mean the same thing.

Despite his legacy as a pioneer who enlightened the twentieth century about the negative influence of sexual repression on our lives, Freud himself was rather inhibited, if not prudish and prurient, like many middle-class Europeans (and Americans) raised during the Victorian age. Freud was also guarded, controlling, meticulous, obstinate, and obsessed with cleanliness—traits one doesn't associate with the kind of freedom from repression that his theories seem in some cases to espouse.

Howard Hughes Became a Recluse

Howard Hughes was an eccentric millionaire recluse who lived most of his life surrounded by scandal and gossip. But his life is also a cautionary tale for anyone who suddenly becomes wealthy without any preparation or guidance. (Lottery winners are among the biggest losers in this department.)

One of the most notorious stories surrounding Hughes's later life involved his apparent phobia for germs and disease. It was often speculated that his drug addiction and questionable sanity had something to do with his reclusive and germ-avoiding nature. But Hughes had demonstrated this peculiar behavior very early on in his life. His mother had the same anxiety when it came to germs, which apparently rubbed off on young Howard. It was only later in life that his hypochondria and general paranoia became publicly known—his habit of storing his own urine in jars and then taking it with him wherever he went was hard to miss.

Howard Hughes (1905–1976) standing in front of his Boeing Army Pursuit plane in Inglewood, California, circa 1940.

Hardly a macho boy, Hughes had been a delicate and reclusive child. He also harbored a lifelong ambivalence regarding his sexuality. Hughes had been seduced by an uncle as a child and later on he frequently had affairs with both men and women. In 1935, he began a long relationship with Katharine Hepburn. The male lover Hughes reputedly abandoned for the actress was none other than Cary Grant.

Lady Godiva Rode a Horse Naked

It was supposed to have happened in England a few years before the Norman Conquest of 1066. Lady Godiva was the wife of Leofric, a nobleman who was said to have grievously overtaxed the poor citizens of Coventry. So far so good.

Sympathizing with the poor folk, Godiva implored her husband to lower the tax burden. He agreed to do so only if she would ride through Coventry naked. He assumed, of course, that she wouldn't (perhaps he had not been married for very long). But she did, covered only by the streaming locks of her Rapunzel-like hair.

In one version of the story, the whole town watched. In another, the town was ordered to hide in their homes and close their shutters so they couldn't peek at the naked lady. A man named Tom (later known as Peeping Tom) disobeyed and was struck blind.

So how much of this really happened? Scholars agree that Godiva was real and so was Leofric, both of whom lived near Coventry. But the dispute about taxes and the naked ride are at best the stuff of legend and at worst pure poppycock.

Harry Houdini Escaped from an Icy River

An escape artist par excellence, Harry Houdini was famous for being thrown off bridges while handcuffed, or being locked in a trunk. He claimed that in one instance he was lowered into the frozen waters of the Detroit River through a hole that was cut into the ice. He explained that after escaping from his bindings, he tried to swim back up to the area where the hole was but was unable to find it. He said that he survived by breathing the air trapped between the surface of the water and the layer of ice until he found a hole in the ice that permitted a way out. However, newspaper accounts of the event do not mention any ice or a frozen river.

Probably because of the Tony Curtis film, many believe Houdini died while performing an escape from a water tank. In truth, he suffered a ruptured appendix when he was punched in the stomach; he had invited the puncher to hit him as hard as he could to demonstrate his physical condition. Houdini lingered for several weeks and died on Halloween, October 31, 1926.

Hitler Was a House Painter

Early in life, Adolph Hitler was an aspiring painter—a painter of pictures, not of houses. The house painter myth is just one of many misconceptions surrounding Hitler. Here are a few more (with parenthetical corrections and comments): Hitler was born in Germany (he was born in Austria). Hitler's real name was Shicklgruber (his real name was Hiedler). Hitler was a paperhanger (never). Hitler was gay (perhaps latently—jury still out). Hitler was sexless (not; he had affairs with numerous women and had a sadomasochistic streak, requesting women to beat, kick, and urinate on him). Hitler danced a "victory jig" after France surrendered (not so—the film that showed him dancing was a fake). Oddly enough, the notion that sounds the most mythlike of all—that Hitler sometimes fell to the floor and chewed the carpet is true. It is said that subordinates who witnessed this behavior nicknamed him (out of earshot, no doubt) *Teppichfresser* (the "carpet-eater").

Adolf Hitler (1889–1945). Top: *Mother Mary with the Holy Child Jesus Christ*, painted by Hitler in 1913.

Ernest Hemingway Served in Four Wars

No one can say that Ernest Hemingway didn't have guts, but he never served in the military. He tried to join the army during World War I but was rejected because of bad vision. He then joined the Red Cross as an ambulance driver and was sent overseas. In 1918, while delivering candy and cigarettes to Italian soldiers, Hemingway was seriously wounded by fragments from an Austrian mortar shell. After months spent in the hospital recovering from his wounds, he returned to his hometown of Oak Park, Illinois, where he was greeted as a war hero. There he stayed with his parents, wore his Red Cross uniform around town, and gave presentations about his war experiences to civic groups. Hemingway's other war experiences, spanning the next three decades of his life, were as a civilian correspondent during the Greco-Turkish War, the Spanish Civil War, and World War II. Hemingway's experiences abroad, especially his time in the hospital, inspired his novel *A Farewell to Arms*.

Ernest Hemingway (1889–1961) at his home in Illinois, 1919.

Captain Kidd Was a Notorious Pirate

It's not that simple. He spent more time as a pirate catcher than a pirate, and some sources (including Kidd himself) maintain he was never a pirate at all. Kidd began as a model citizen—a wealthy, churchgoing family man. His career at sea was, shall we say, checkered.

William "Captain" Kidd (1645–1701); eighteenth-century portrait, artist and date unknown.

He did commandeer a few ships (some say legally), and he did kill one of his crew members (who, it turned out, had been insubordinate) by throwing a bucket at his head (probably manslaughter, not murder). But doubt remains as to whether Kidd was really guilty of either piracy or murder. He was, of course, tried for both, pronounced guilty, and hung. Kidd's bad luck followed him to the gallows, where the hangman's rope broke, and he had to be strung up a second time.

Grant Was Lincoln's First Choice to Lead the Union

Early in the Civil War, President Lincoln wanted Robert E. Lee, of all people, to lead the Union Army. Lee considered the offer, but when his home state of Virginia joined the Confederacy, Lee felt obliged to take the other side. Lincoln later appointed Grant as commander.

Ironically, General Grant defeated Lee at Appomattox, Virginia, ending the Civil War.

Lincoln Wrote the Gettysburg Address on the Back of an Envelope While Riding on a Train

If a president who had been asked to give a speech honoring fallen soldiers after an important battle had waited until the last minute to scribble his speech on a used envelope while riding on the train to the battleground, wouldn't it seem a bit disrespectful? On the other hand, school kids (especially those who have found writing of any kind to be painful) have long marveled at Lincoln's ability to come up with a brilliant piece of rhetoric in so short a time. But did he?

Lincoln did take the train to Gettysburg, but the rest is myth. Several months earlier, Lincoln had delivered an extemporaneous speech at Antietam right after the battle and was sorely criticized for what some viewed as desecrating sacred ground. So he began writing the Gettysburg speech weeks before in Washington and put the finishing touches on it in Gettysburg the evening before the speech was delivered. A copy was given to the newspapers before it was delivered so it could be printed. Five drafts of the speech, written on White House stationery, survive to this day.

Oddly enough, Lincoln's own supporters may be responsible for the perpetuation of this myth. The reaction to the speech was not one of universal praise. Lincoln haters (of which there were many) ridiculed it and called it just another example of Lincoln's disrespectful attitude toward the dead. Some Lincoln defenders who must have bought the myth excused the president by saying he had only enough time to jot down a brief speech on the train. In any case, what was missing from newspaper and other second-hand accounts were Lincoln's delivery and the solemn and poignant context of the speech.

The Nicolay copy of the Gettysburg Address (November 1863). From the Abraham Lincoln papers in the Library of Congress; the Lincoln bust from the memorial at Gettysburg, Pennsylvania.

77

Marylin Monroe Was Murdered Because She "Knew Too Much"

Marilyn Monroe—movie star, sex symbol, and magnet for scandal—is, of course, one of the most identifiable celebrities of the twentieth century. But everything about her has always been charged with ambiguity—including, most notably, her untimely death at the youthful age of thirty-six. Monroe's lifeless body was found in her bedroom on August 4, 1962. There was an empty bottle of sleeping pills next to her bed, which led some to the conclusion that she had committed suicide (from an overdose). Various theories have sprung up surrounding her death. Some conjecture that she took her own life after being told that president John F. Kennedy wanted to end their affair. Others say she was murdered because "she knew too much."

The more likely story is that her psychotherapist, Ralph Greenson, mistakenly overmedicated her. He was injecting the star with drugs and administering barbiturates to her on a daily basis. It is possible that Greenson tried to cover up his "error," thus creating fertile ground for all the other theories that attempted to explain the star's mysterious death.

Marilyn Monroe (1926–1962) entertaining troops at the Bulldozer Bowl, July 24, 1954.

Melville Died Rich and Famous

A titan of American literature, Herman Melville (1819–1891) was well known to the reading public early in his career. The stories he wrote based on his experiences as a seaman—*Typee*, for instance—found a wide readership. When *Moby Dick* (now considered his masterpiece) was published, however, the novel was greeted without much enthusiasm, and Melville's career took a downward turn. Things didn't improve much after that, and the great American novelist died poor and forgotten. Things got better for Melville starting in the 1920s, but by then he wasn't around to take notice.

Magellan Was the First to Sail around the Globe

As a Portuguese seaman sailing on behalf of Spain in the early 1500s, Ferdinand Magellan (right) did intend to sail around the world. Trouble is, he was killed by natives in the Philippines after sailing just past the halfway point. Of the five ships and two hundred fifty or so crew members that began the voyage, only one ship and eighteen sailors made it back to Seville, Spain, the starting point.

One can say, then, that Magellan's goal of circumnavigation was achieved, but Magellan himself got lost along the way. Francis Drake was the first to actually circumnavigate the globe—in the flesh.

Nixon Was an Ultraconservative

Lots of people hated Nixon for lots of reasons: Watergate, the Vietnam War, law-and-order politics, and even the fact that he sweated from his upper lip (which some say indicated he was lying). But ironically, Nixon was also hated by the truly ultraconservative John Birch Society. Why? He was too liberal!

So how was Nixon liberal? Let us count the ways. He built upon the liberal policies of the Johnson administration. He established the Environmental Protection Agency (EPA), the Occupational Safety and Health Administration (OSHA), and the National Oceanic and Atmospheric Administration (NOAA). He initiated the Strategic Arms Limitation Talks (SALT) to limit the spread of ballistic missiles. He encouraged detente with the

Soviet Union and, using Henry Kissinger as a go-between, normalized relations with Communist China.

Nixon also supported the Equal Rights Amendment and affirmative action, beefed up the food-stamp program, and even tried to replace welfare with a guaranteed annual income. In stark contrast to some other recent presidents, he doubled the funding for the National Endowment for the Arts and the National Endowment for the Humanities. So how liberal was Nixon? Looks like he was right up there with FDR, Johnson, Carter, and Clinton—and he got more things done. So what inspired him? Nixon's upbringing under impoverished circumstances left him with a profound regard for the downtrodden and the working class.

Napoleon Was a Shrimp

Napoleon Bonaparte (right) was not tall by today's standards, but he was taller than the average Frenchman of his day. At five feet six and a half inches, he was well within the range of modern-day men who are considered a bit short but by no means shrimps.

By comparison, Napoleon was half an inch taller than Dustin Hoffman and half an inch shorter than Tom Cruise.

So how did the myth get started? During his autopsy the coroner used a measuring system that was not properly converted to the one used today; hence the height recorded was off by a few inches. Also, the emperor may have looked small to onlookers because he was always guarded by soldiers who were all more than six feet tall. Napoleon did not avail himself of certain items of clothing—or style of dress—that would have made him appear taller, leading some biographers to believe that he saw his diminutive stature as a source of distinction.

Thoreau Lived as a Recluse on Walden Pond

The myth that many people harbor is that Henry David Thoreau was a misanthrope who spent his life as a recluse in a cabin deep in the woods near Walden Pond, during which time he avoided people and rarely saw another soul.

The reality is that, although eccentric, Thoreau was neither a recluse nor a misanthrope. He regularly had dinner with family and friends, and welcomed visitors to his cabin. The cabin was not located deep in the wilderness but on the edge of town, on property owned by his friend Ralph Waldo Emerson, just a mile or so from his family home.

This period of Thoreau's life followed his trip to New York, when he tried to break into the world of publishing, and he was, by all accounts, an ambitious, driven (and to many, obnoxious) young man—the nineteenth century version of a yuppie.

Richard Pryor Accidentally Set Himself on Fire While Freebasing

That's the way his agent explained it to the press. But the 1980 fire that severely burned the comedian was not an accident. It's true he had been freebasing—for several days. But the fire was caused when he poured high-proof rum on his body and lit it with a match in a drug-hazed suicide attempt. He later joked about the experience, but his close friends and family kept an eye on him for the rest of his life.

Picasso Became a Cubist Because He Was a Terrible Draftsman

According to his mother, Pablo Picasso could draw before he could talk. When he was just fourteen, he took the exams for the advanced program at the Barcelona School of Fine Arts. Told that he had one month to complete the exam, Picasso surprised everyone by bringing it back the next day, exhibiting more talent and expertise than students several years older than he.

His visual memory and gift for drawing were astonishing. He could draw complete figures with a single, unbroken line. During his Cubist period, he used real images as a point of departure before crossing into new visual territory.

Picasso produced more than 15,000 works of art during his ninety years, painting at least three canvases a day. He would fill a French country house with paintings, and when there was no more room, he would simply shut the door and set up shop in a new house. To call him prolific would be an understatement.

Truman Was a Nobody Before He Became FDR's Vice President, and His Middle Initial Stood for Nothing

Elected to the Senate in 1934, Harry Truman was nationally known by 1941, when he headed the Special Committee to Investigate the National Defense Program. An efficient administrator, he was also admired for being fair, decent, companionable, and extraordinarily competent. He saved taxpayers billions of dollars by uncovering waste and fraud in the Pentagon, and he saved the lives of countless servicemen by exposing defective weapons. Repeatedly called one of the most useful members of the Senate, he was also described as fearless and forthright. When asked to run for the vice presidency under FDR, Truman refused at first, but he relented after persistent arm-twisting.

Truman liked to keep a low profile. Groucho Marx was widely believed to have commented, "This country would be all right if Truman were alive"—*during* Truman's presidency. Marx denied saying it, but the quip stuck.

The notion that President Harry S. Truman's middle initial stood for nothing is not exactly false, but it's not 100 percent true, either. Truman himself

spoke of the initial as a compromise representing the *S* in both Anderson Shipp Truman and Solomon Young, the names of his grandfathers. Nor was the nameless initial unique: in Truman's home state of Missouri, as well as other states in the South, it was not uncommon for people to use initials rather than names. Some have claimed that the *S* should not have a period after it, but lots of historical documents, including those that bear Truman's signature, clearly do show a period after the *S*.

Harry S. Truman (1884–1972) was the thirty-third president of the United States. At left, he is at the piano, circa 1940.

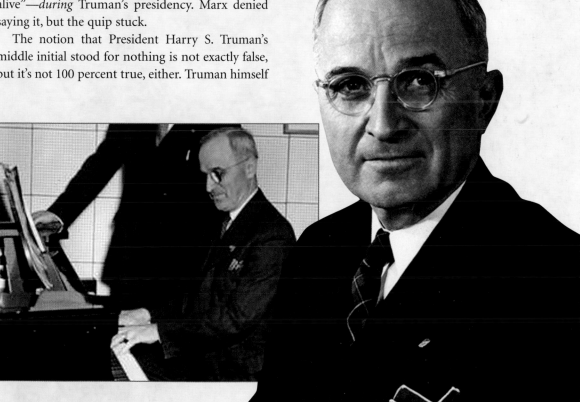

King Tut Was a Great Pharaoh

The discovery of Tutankhamen's tomb in 1922 made the "boy king" an instant celebrity the world over. But as pharaohs go, he was not much to write home about—or write history about. Tut was a minor king about whom not much is known—except that his reign took place more than 3,000 years ago and lasted through most of his teens (he died at 18). His claim to fame rests primarily in the fact that his tomb and all its magnificent contents (artifacts, furniture, jewelry, the stunning golden death mask, and thousands of other treasures) survived intact and untouched, unlike the tombs of other pharaohs that were looted and ransacked before archaeologists could get at them. The discovery of Tut's tomb took Egyptology a quantum leap forward and vastly expanded our understanding of ancient times.

Mask of Tutankhamen's mummy, from the Egyptian Museum in Cairo, Egypt. English Egyptologist Howard Carter didn't discover the tomb until 1922.

George Washington Had Wooden Teeth

President Washington began losing his teeth during his twenties, after a childhood plagued by poor dental health. To compensate for the loss of his missing molars (and their twenty-eight companions), he arranged for John Greenwood, the nation's leading dentist, to fashion several sets of dentures. The first set, worn during Washington's inauguration in 1789, were crafted from a base of hippopotamus ivory carved to fit the gums. The upper denture had ivory teeth, and the lower plate consisted of eight human teeth fastened by gold pivots that screwed into the base. The set was secured in his mouth by spiral springs.

In 1791 and 1795, Greenwood made a second and third set of dentures. In 1796, James Gardette made a large and very clumsy set. Apparently Washington was not pleased with these dentures and reportedly ordered another set from Greenwood in 1797. His final set was made in 1798, the year before he died.

The fact is, none of Washington's false teeth were made of wood, so the only splinters he would have

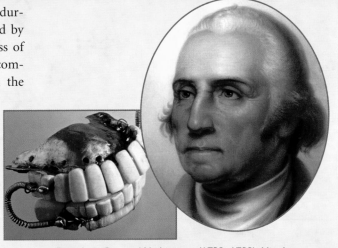

President George Washington (1732–1799). His dentures were made of ivory and/or human teeth, not wood. The teeth were taken out when not needed for chewing.

experienced (if any) were the ones he received chopping down the cherry tree (yet another myth). If you are curious enough to ogle our first president's dentures for yourself, and I'm not sure why you would be, they are on display at Baltimore's Dr. Samuel D. Harris National Museum of Dentistry.

Queen Victoria Was a Stuffy Prude

Her image is one of a stuffy, prudish, unsmiling killjoy who was the justifiable prototype of everything "Victorian." Not so. Victoria had no aversion to sex (she had nine children), she loved to drink (and was not unkind to drunks, even in the royal court), and she loved to laugh.

After she was widowed, Victoria hung out with a few hunks (such as her "personal servants" John Brown and Abdul Karim) and was even the subject of much whispering among royalty-watching Nosy Parkers and assorted busybodies.

Regardless, the queen is probably the last historical figure one would ordinarily associate with a brand of risque lingerie, but she did have her secrets, and she is, in fact, the same Victoria who lent her name to Victoria's Secret.

Science and Technology

Arabic Numerals Were Invented by Arabs

Arabs didn't invent them, and, for the most part, Arabs don't even use them. So why are they called Arabic numerals? These days the familiar figures are more properly called Hindu-Arabic numerals. Invented by Hindus in ancient India a few centuries BCE, the numbers from one to nine were later introduced by Arabs to Europe between the eighth and tenth centuries and so were mistakenly thought to have been invented by them.

Arabic numerals soon replaced the awkward and unwieldy Roman numerals. Today, Arabs themselves use their own unique set of numerals, and they refer to our Arabic numerals as "Indian numerals."

Earth's Atmosphere Forms a Thick Blanket of Air Around It

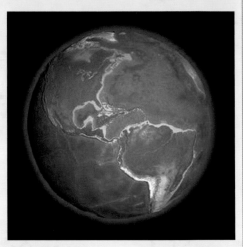

The earth's atmosphere is made up of four layers: troposphere, stratosphere, mesosphere, and thermosphere. It consists of 78% nitrogen, 21% oxygen, trace amounts of other gases, and water vapor.

One might think that between the solid ground beneath our feet and the edge of space, a distance of merely sixty miles, a voluminous blanket of air envelops the earth. How voluminous? It seems reasonable to assume, for example, that if the earth were the size of a baseball, the earth plus the surrounding atmosphere would be similar in size to a softball, right? Not so. Relatively speaking, the atmosphere just isn't that thick. If the earth were the size of a baseball, the atmosphere would be thinner than the baseball's leather skin.

Bicycles Are Stable because of the Gyroscopic Effect of the Wheels

Sounds plausible—how else would a cycle-challenged klutz be able to stay on a bike? But careful analysis shows that there is not enough torque—the force that produces the gyroscopic stability of a spinning wheel—to keep the bicycle and the rider upright. The fact is, if the bicycle is designed right, it will roll a long way without tipping over even when no one is riding it. Exactly why is one of the enduring (and pesky) mysteries of classical physics. And the answer is not in the wheels.

Remarkably, this problem (which seems to be of about the same vintage as the bicycle pictured at right), is still being pondered, but from a more human perspective. It now seems that additional bodily balancing mechanisms—over and above the balancing tools of the inner ear—are triggered and activated in people by motion. If you've ever tried to walk a narrow plank, you may have noticed that it's easier to maintain your balance if you walk it quickly.

It's Cheaper to Let a Lightbulb Burn All Night Than to Turn It On in the Morning

This myth has been propagated by tightwads and environmentalists alike, but it isn't true. For both incandescent and fluorescent bulbs, the energy-saving choice is to turn off a light whenever it's not needed.

It's true that fluorescent bulbs have a set number of starts in their ballasts (the apparatus in the bulb that converts electricity into light) and one is used each time the bulb is lit. It is theoretically possible to use them up, thereby necessitating the bulb's replacement; however, for that to ever happen, you'd pretty much have to devote your life to the pursuit of turning it on and off.

It's also true that when any light is turned on, it creates a slight electrical surge. The key word here, though, is "slight." The charge is equivalent to about one-tenth of a second's worth of normal burning. So if you're planning on leaving the room longer than that(!), the responsible choice is to turn it off. Mother Earth will be better off, and so will your wallet.

Boiling Water Gets Hotter When It Comes to a Full Boil

In order for water to boil, it has to reach 212 degrees Fahrenheit. As everyone knows, the process begins calmly enough with just a few little bubbles. From there it gradually develops into a noisier and more agitated state, called a full boil. An observer may assume that the more advanced the boil, the hotter the water. Not so. A boil is a boil, and from start to finish it stays at 212 degrees. Adding salt, however, raises the temperature of the water so that it reaches the full boil more quickly. Therefore, salting can help speed up the overall cooking process a bit.

Copernicus Was First to Say the Earth Orbits the Sun

A Renaissance man who grew up in Poland in the late 1400s, Copernicus excelled in a number of pursuits. He was so busy with other things, in fact, that he regarded astronomy as a mere hobby. In any case, Copernicus was not the first to suggest the notion of a sun-centered ("heliocentric") solar system, in which the earth orbits the sun rather than vice versa. The concept was an ancient one, appearing in Sanskrit texts dating from the seventh century BCE. The notion was also tossed around by the Greeks in the third and fourth centuries BCE and by an Arab astronomer in the 1300s, a century before Copernicus was born.

So why was Copernicus credited with this theory (which repudiated mankind's notion that the earth was the center of the universe, discombobulated the clergy, and knocked down the collective human ego a few hundred notches)? It's simple. He didn't just propose the theory: he proved it mathematically. Fortunately for Copernicus, he avoided the vengeful wrath of the ignorant (who might easily have burned him at the stake) by giving up the ghost many years before his revolutionary theory took hold.

An Unprotected Body Would Explode in Space

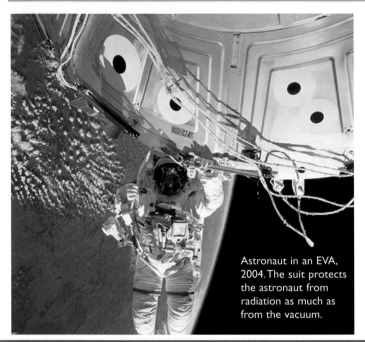

Astronaut in an EVA, 2004. The suit protects the astronaut from radiation as much as from the vacuum.

So what would happen if you went out the door of the space station but forgot to put on your space suit (like the astronaut in the film *2001: A Space Odyssey*)? Opinions on this differ, but all sources agree on at least one thing: you would not explode. Your flesh would swell up, your eardrums would probably burst, the air might be sucked out of your lungs, gas might be sucked out of your lower intestinal tract, and your blood and other bodily fluids might boil or vaporize. On the brighter side, you would have up to fifteen seconds of consciousness to get to safety, and if you passed out you would have up to two minutes to be rescued before the vacuum did you in.

Science Says Bumblebees Can't Fly

According to this long-standing myth, "the flight of the bumblebee" should be relegated to the musical world of Rimsky-Korsakov. Why? Because, supposedly, certain men of science have said that a bumblebee that flies also flies in the face of the laws of aerodynamics. Its wings are too small, its body too big, and its muscles too weak.

This notion, which some say began with aerodynamicists in the 1930s, was based on a presumption that bumblebee wings are "static airfoils" without the required lift to get the insect's mass off the ground. But the fact is, bumblebee wings are mobile, creating lift by moving through the air in many different directions. The wings beat, or some say "oscillate," about two hundred times per second. In its manner of flight, the bumblebee, like the dragonfly and other insects, can be roughly compared to a hel-

icopter, which has the ability to hover in one place or move up, down, backward, and sideways.

Naturalists have also noticed that the wings of bats are not blessed with the airfoil shape that keeps birds aloft and which is mimicked by man-made airplanes. Bats, like bumblebees, achieve flight only through the circular flapping motion of their non-aerodynamic wings.

All Crop Circles Are Hoaxes

These spectacular formations baffled everyone for years—until the 1990s, that is, when two elderly British gents named Doug Bower and Dave Chorley confessed to producing the complex designs with a handful of simple tools. After their widely publicized confession, much of the world leapt to the conclusion that all crop circles were hoaxes, if not produced by Doug and Dave then by legions of imitators. So are they all fakes? And how can we tell the difference between man-made crop circles and the real thing?

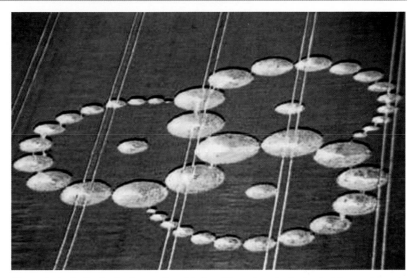

Crop circle design in the form of a triskelion (three interlocked spirals) superimposed over a series of parallel tractor tracks. In the past, a few circles have been made by hoaxers, but that's no reason to dismiss all of them as fakes.

First, some basics: Crop circles have appeared not only in England and the U.S. but in dozens of other countries, and some experts claim they have been around for not just a few decades but hundreds of years. The mysterious designs have been seen in fields of grain, in grass and reeds, in rice paddies, even in expanses of snow, ice, and sand.

So are true crop circles different from the man-made hoaxes, and if so how? There is a long list of characteristics that make it unlikely if not impossible for the "natural" crop circles to have been fabricated by humans:

- The leaves and stems of the plants manipulated in genuine crop circles are woven together in a fashion so intricate as to be impossible for pranksters to duplicate.
- Nodes on the plant stems are elongated, or stretched, in peculiar ways that no human could have managed.
- The soil beneath natural crop circles often remains dry, even after heavy downpours.

- The stalks of plants, some as brittle as celery, are bent at angles of up to ninety degrees. If handled by humans they would snap apart at a mere forty-five degrees.
- Farmers have reported increased crop yields from areas where the circles have formed.
- Microscopic changes have been observed, such as enlarged cell walls, in wheat plants found in crop circles.
- Some crop circles have been found in restricted areas, including military installations, which are securely fenced off from public access.
- Of the legions of crop circles scattered all over the world, many are far too complex in design to have been fabricated by pranksters.

As you can see, there's a convincing list of features distinguishing artificial crop circles from the genuine articles. So where do we go from here? Is there yet any reasonable explanation for this fascinating worldwide phenomenon? Nope. When it comes to answers, we're back to square one.

Diamonds Are Indestructible and Rare

Diamonds are harder than other gems—in fact, they are the hardest natural substance—but they aren't indestructible. Like most other substances, they can be destroyed by extremely high temperatures. Time is another natural enemy. Since diamonds are made of carbon, it's possible that they could eventually degrade into garden-variety graphite. Not that we'll ever know one way or the other—the process would take billions of years.

Another misconception about diamonds is that they are the rarest gem. They are not; rubies are rarer and more expensive—carat for carat, they're roughly four times pricier than diamonds. Large natural rubies, as opposed to man-made ones, are rarely seen outside of museums.

An octahedral diamond crystal from the United States Geological Survey.

Electrons Orbit the Nucleus of an Atom

In science classes of the not-too-distant past, an atom used to be pictured as a nucleus surrounded by orbiting electrons, the way the sun is surrounded by orbiting planets. If the nucleus were the size of, say, a tennis ball, we imagined its electrons to be like little ball bearings, spinning in an orbit a few feet or a few yards from the nucleus.

More recently, the way quantum physics envisions an atom has changed dramatically vis-à-vis relative size and distance. For example, suppose you have an atom whose nucleus is the size of a pea. The size of the atom itself, then, taking into account the amount of space occupied by its orbiting electrons, would be the size of the Notre Dame cathedral.

And rather than little balls whizzing around the nucleus, electron "orbitals" are now described as "shells" or "clouds," fuzzy zones that exhibit the properties of both waves and particles.

But can we be more specific? Unfortunately, no. When it comes to the question of what atoms, electrons, and other subatomic particles (or waves) really "look like up close," no one knows for sure. And it may not be possible to know—ever.

Ben Franklin's Kite Was Struck by Lightning

And that's how he proved that lightning is electricity, right? Not exactly. If a bolt of lightning had actually hit his kite, Franklin would not have made history in the usual sense—in fact, he would have *been* history, as in dead, departed, kaput, or (more to the point) "toast." In other words, if lightning had struck the kite or the ground under the kite, anyone standing nearby would have been killed or seriously injured from the ferocious blast of electric current. (Elsewhere, we point out that you don't have to be struck by lightning directly to be seriously harmed by it.)

Not to say that Franklin's experiment wasn't a success. He set out to show that lightning is a form of electricity, and he managed to prove his point. Electrical charges in a storm leak downward toward the ground. Franklin demonstrated that the kite and the key attached to the kite string became positively charged. Strands of twine on the kite string stood on end, like hair on a person's head after an electrical shock, and Franklin induced tiny sparks to jump from the key to his hand. These harmless little sparks were the closest thing to lightning that ever occurred during the experiment, and they substantiated Franklin's hypothesis.

So Franklin's adventure with the kite didn't happen quite as reported in grammar school science books. Furthermore, after thoroughly examining Franklin's notes from the period, a few skeptical historians have suggested it may never have happened at all.

Given how colorful a character Franklin was, it's surprising that more myths and misinformation haven't collected around him. One thing is certain: Franklin did not generally take his own well-articulated advice. In spite of coining "A penny saved is a penny earned," Franklin was not all that frugal. His friends would chastise him constantly about his spendthrift ways, and he would reply with an aphorism that you won't find in *Poor Richard's Almanac*: "An egg today is better than a hen tomorrow."

Franklin also did not subscribe to the adage "Time is money."

After he retired from the printing business, he spent most of his time doing … virtually nothing. When his friends would get on his case for being idle, he would simply reply that since the soul has all of eternity before it, what need is there for us to be in any hurry?

Beyond performing many solemn roles—as statesman, diplomat, scientist, entrepreneur, writer—Franklin obviously had a whimsical streak and well-honed wit.

Glass Is a Liquid

Scientists classify glass as an amorphous solid, not a liquid. Some characteristics of glass are liquid-like, but not enough to qualify glass as a liquid. Repeaters of the urban legend have claimed that, given enough time, glass will actually "flow," but there is no empirical evidence that this is the case.

There Is Zero Gravity in Space

When you see astronauts floating through the air inside the space shuttle, it's not because there is no gravity there. In fact, there is almost as much gravity as there is on the ground. If the shuttle suddenly stopped cold, the floating astronauts would fall to the floor.

The reason the astronauts float is because they are in "free fall," as if they were skydiving or practicing weightlessness in a diving airplane. So how can they be in free fall if they always remain at the same altitude while orbiting the earth? In other words, how can they be in free fall if they are not really "falling"? Because the force of gravity is balanced by, or virtually canceled out by, the orbital velocity of the shuttle. The same principle applies to satellites and even to the moon.

At an altitude of sixty miles, the orbital velocity of the shuttle has to be 17,500 mph. If it were less, the shuttle would be pulled down toward the earth. If it were more, the shuttle would fly off into space. When they say those big engines are needed for the shuttle to "escape the earth's atmosphere," we tend to picture the shuttle being launched straight up until it is outside the earth's atmosphere and outside the pull of gravity, at which time it just plops into orbit and is then hurtled around the earth. Not so. For one thing, the launch path is not straight up. It starts that way but then turns horizontally until it is almost parallel to the earth. The big engines are needed not to "escape the earth's atmosphere" but to propel the shuttle to orbital velocity once it gets into space.

A One-Way Mirror Lets You *See* Them, but They Can't *See* You

One-way mirrors aren't exactly what movies and detective shows make them out to be. Mirrors are simply polished surfaces that reflect rays of light. What is passed off as an exclusively "one-way" mirror simply has a thinner coating of metal (a "half-silvered" mirror). The metal coating must be thin enough to both reflect light and let some light pass through. When a room on one side of the mirror is darker than the other, light passes only from the light side to the dark side. This allows those in the darkened room to clearly see what is going on in the lighted room, but not vice versa.

Icebergs Are Made of Frozen Salt Water

Icebergs are big hunks of ice found floating in oceans and seas, so they must be made of frozen salt water, right? Wrong. Icebergs are not born of oceans and seas, but of freshwater sources on the land—namely, ice sheets or glaciers in areas where the climate is frigid. When glaciers ooze down to the edge of a body of water, big chunks

of ice break off, or "calve" (like a cow giving birth), and fall into the water to become icebergs. Incidentally, suppose you are on a boat in the ocean and run out of drinking water. As in Samuel Taylor Coleridge's *The Rime of the Ancient Mariner*, you are surrounded by "Water, water everywhere, nor any drop to drink." All is not lost if you happen to be near an iceberg, because you can chip off a chunk of ice, melt it, and drink fresh water.

A Magnet Never Wears Out

They certainly *seem* durable. Magnetic catches on kitchen cabinets, for example, work for many decades without showing any sign of getting weaker. But in fact magnets do wear out, though under ordinary circumstances the process takes a long time—perhaps hundreds of years. Magnets work the way they do because their atoms are aligned, creating a net electrical current loop that gives rise to the magnetic force. If the magnet is dropped, struck, or heated, the atom alignment can be disturbed and the magnetic force will lessen or disappear. Even ambient heat will wear away at the alignment and lessen the power of the magnet—not soon, but eventually.

The Dark Side of the Moon Is Always Dark

It's dark only when the sun isn't shining on it. "Dark side" is more metaphorical than factual. It would be more accurate to say "far" side of the moon or "hidden" side of the moon, in that we can never see it from the earth. Unlike the earth, the moon doesn't rotate (spin around its axis), so only about half of its surface is ever visible from the earth.

You could compare the situation to a boy (the earth) spinning around in circles while holding onto a taut string (gravitational force) at the other end of which is a ball (the moon) which does not spin because the pull of the string always keeps one side visible and the other side not. If you were standing on the moon, of course, you would be able to see the earth from all angles due to its constant rotation.

The Meteorites We Call Shooting Stars Are Very Large

If we can see them burning up from way down here as they enter the earth's atmosphere, they must be pretty big, right? Wrong. Most shooting stars are tinier than a grain of sand. But they slam into the earth's atmosphere at such an enormous speed that the heat caused by friction makes them burn up within a split second, producing a light bright enough to be seen from the ground. Rarely, a meteorite may be as large as a golf ball, making for a spectacular light show. Much more rarely, a meteorite is large enough to make it to the ground (you can see them displayed in natural history museums), but the chances of this happening are extremely remote.

The "old woman" meteorite (left) is the second largest in the United States. At right is a standard meteorite.

Objects outside the Milky Way Galaxy Are Not Visible to the Naked Eye

A recent misconception about the night sky is that nothing from beyond the Milky Way (our home galaxy) can be seen with the unaided eye. It's true that the circumstances for viewing the heavens are becoming less and less ideal because of both "light pollution" (interference from earthbound sources of light) and smog. But on a clear night—a really clear night—the Andromeda galaxy, our galactic neighbor about 2.2 million light-years (some 13 billion miles) away is visible with the naked eye. And some claim to have seen (and correctly located) the M33 galaxy in Triangulum, which is 3.3 million light-years away. Even so, sky-watchers in very remote areas know that light pollution can interfere with the view, even when the light is coming from several hundred miles away, because adverse atmospheric conditions can diffuse the light over a wide area. As this kind of interference continues to increase, we may be inching our way toward a time when such faraway observations will only be possible from space-based telescopes, or perhaps from telescopes situated on the dark side of the moon.

Pluto Marks the Outer Edge of the Solar System

Pluto is the farthest planet (relabeled a non-planet or a "dwarf planet" in 2006) from the sun, but the solar system itself keeps on going—and going and going and going. Suppose we could board a spaceship and travel to Pluto and then travel to the end of the solar system. How long would it take?

cloud (after Jan Oort, a Dutch astronomer). Assuming our ship continues at the same speed, how long would it take us to reach the inner fringes of the comet-laden Oort cloud? About 10,000 years.

And how thick, or deep, is the Oort cloud? Let's put it this way: the inner boundary of the cloud is

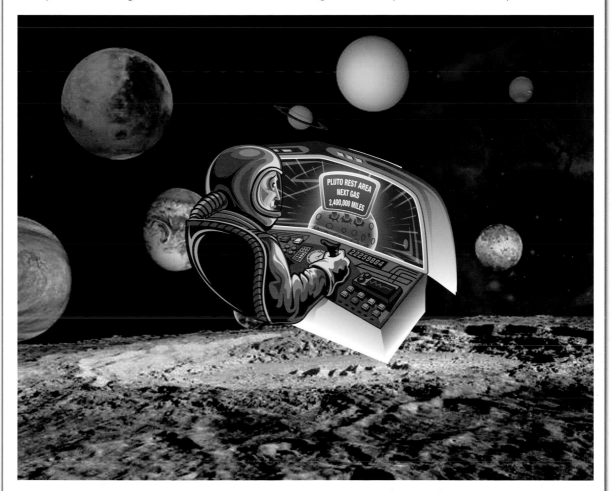

If the ship were going at the modest speed of 35,000 miles per hour—about the same speed as *Voyager* and other unmanned NASA spacecraft—it would require twelve years to reach the orbit of Pluto. Way beyond Pluto is a vast array of comets that also orbit the sun. They are collectively called the Oort

about one light-year from the sun. The outer boundary is about three light-years from the sun. That makes the solar system at the very least about six light-years in diameter—about 50,000 times the diameter of Pluto's orbit—which is very, very, very big.

Light Always Travels at 186,000 Miles per Second

Not always. Light travels at that speed only in a vacuum. It travels slightly more slowly through air and much more slowly through glass. And electromagnetic impulses, made of the same stuff as light, travel much more slowly than light speed through coaxial cable. In other words, the speed of all electromagnetic waves depends on the medium through which they are traveling. Recent experiments using super-dense media have been able to slow light down to a virtual crawl.

The Planets Move, but the Sun Doesn't

The sun doesn't stand still. Just as the moon orbits the earth and the earth and the other planets orbit the sun, the sun orbits the center of the galaxy at a speed of nearly 500,000 miles per hour. Instead of a sun at the center of our galaxy, there is a so-called super-massive black hole (SMBH). The time it takes the sun and its planets to orbit the SMBH is more than 200 million years, and it has completed about 20 orbits since the "dawn" of the solar system. Our galaxy itself is not standing still, either. The Milky Way is part of a cluster of galaxies (including Andromeda) that are moving toward the Virgo Cluster, our nearest neighbor among galactic clusters. At the risk of overheating your brain, keep in mind that in our galaxy alone there are billions of stars, and beyond our galaxy there are billions of other galaxies.

Other Planets in the Solar System Have No Effect on Earth

Astrological suppositions aside, the other planets in our solar system—particularly Venus and Jupiter, and to a lesser extent Mars (because it's so small)—have had and will continue to have a significant effect on the earth.

Other planets influence the earth's motion around the sun in three important ways: (1) the eccentricity of the earth's orbit (how far the orbit diverges from a perfect circle); (2) the inclination of the earth's axis (the tilt of the earth relative to its orbital plane around the sun); and (3) the precession of the axis (how the axis wobbles slightly as the earth spins). These effects, all caused by the gravitational pull of other planets, produce what are known as the Milankovitch cycles—named after a Serbian engineer and mathematician. These phenomena, which occur over tens of thousands of years, lead to large-scale changes on Earth. It is believed that the Sahara Desert was once lush with vegetation and became an arid expanse as a result of the Milankovitch cycles. These cycles have also been correlated with the ice ages that have come and gone throughout Earth's history.

Ecologically Speaking, Paper Is Better than Plastic

When the cashier at the grocery store offers you the choice of "paper or plastic," do you choose paper because you believe it's better for the environment? Or, at the risk of frowns from the Green Squad, do you choose plastic because the handles make the bag easier to carry? If you opt for the latter, you can assuage your guilty conscience with the fact that, when all the various environmental issues are taken into account, plastic emerges as the lesser of two evils.

Why? Some fifteen million trees are cut down each year to supply paper bags for American shoppers. Making paper bags takes four times more energy than making plastic bags. The paper bag manufacturing process produces greenhouse gases, acid rain, and water pollutants on a far greater scale than the plastic bag manufacturing process. Recycling paper bags takes ten times the energy needed to recycle plastic bags. In a landfill, paper bags take up much more space than plastic ones. And although one would expect paper to degrade much faster than plastic, without heat, light, and oxygen, paper buried in landfills takes decades to decompose.

Plastic bags definitely have their downside. They are ugly, especially when flapping in the wind from fences and tree branches. They clog drains and sewers, and some environmentalists say they are a threat to wildlife. However, the evidence that plastic bags end up in the throats of birds, raccoons, and seals is purely anecdotal.

So which is the better choice: paper or plastic? Clearly, when you consider all the environmental pros and cons, plastic comes out on top. The best choice of all, however, is neither. If you want to protect the environment, do your shopping with a reusable canvas bag you bring from home.

A Mushroom Cloud Is a Sure Sign of a Nuclear Explosion

In a major explosion—like that of a nuclear bomb—hot, low-density gas is produced. It is then forced upward, and more air rushes in to fill the void. That air then rises, along with smoke, soot, and other particles, to form a "stem." When the stem reaches the cool air in the upper atmosphere, its density decreases and the particles dissipate, forming a "cap" and creating a mushroom-like shape.

The disturbing images of World War II and the subsequent fears of the Cold War combined to inextricably establish mushroom clouds as a symbol of the horrors of nuclear war in the American psyche. But the truth is that any big aboveground explosion that happens in relatively calm weather—including those produced by volcanoes—can create a mushroom cloud, and there's nothing nuclear about it.

Mushroom clouds form during volcanic eruption of Mount Redoubt, Alaska.

Seasons Are Caused by the Earth's Distance from the Sun

Actually, the earth is closest to the sun in January and farthest from the sun in July. What causes the seasons is not how far we are from the sun but how long and at what angle the sun shines each day. In summer, not only are the days longer, allowing more heat to accumulate, but the sun's rays strike the earth at a steeper angle, which makes things even hotter. In winter, it's just the opposite, because the days are shorter and the angle at which the sun's rays hit the earth is more slanted.

So what causes all these changes in the length of days and the angle of the sun's rays over the course of a year? It's the tilt of the earth's axis. Despite the rotation of the earth, its axis remains at the same fixed angle as it revolves around the sun. To show yourself how this works, light a candle in a dark room and try moving a globe around it in a circle. Keep the axis of the globe in exactly the same position vis-à-vis the candle and watch how the light is distributed when you rotate the globe at different points around the circle. One consequence of the earth's tilted axis, of course, is that the seasons in the northern and southern hemispheres are reversed—summer in Canada means winter in Argentina.

The Speed of Sound Is Always the Same

The speed of sound is far from constant. It depends entirely on the medium sound is traveling through—and the density of that medium. At sea level, sound travels through air at about 760 mph. But up in the sky where the air is thinner, it travels more slowly. Sound travels much faster in liquids and solids—e.g., 3,300 mph in water and 13,000 mph in glass. In a vacuum, of course, there is no sound at all.

We Have Five Senses

Children are taught that there are five senses: sight, sound, smell, taste, and touch. But in the last century or so, biologists, neurologists, and other experts have added to the list considerably—and that's not even counting the so-called sixth sense, which didn't make the cut. Anyway, the extended list includes the following: heat, cold, pressure, pain, hunger, thirst, balance, and body awareness.

The Pressure Difference between the Inside and the Outside of an Airplane Can Suck You out an Airplane Window

It is a fact that action movies tend to stretch and embellish the laws of physics. Often, in a particularly high-paced sequence, a bad guy might get sucked out of a depressurized passenger compartment when a stray bullet cracks a window in the fuselage, à la the James Bond classic *Goldfinger*. It is a common misconception that this could actually happen in real life.

In actuality, airplanes are not entirely airtight. Continually pumped-in air keeps cabins pressurized because air is constantly being leaked out small cracks throughout the aircraft. Incidents have occurred that involved doors and pieces of fuselage flying off planes in mid-flight. For the most part, no major injuries occurred during these accidents, but the planes were forced to descend to a lower altitude just to allow people to breathe without masks.

In an incident involving a blown-off roof, one standing flight attendant was swept out of the plane, but the rest of the passengers remained in their seats—even the ones not strapped in.

Saturn Is the Only Planet Surrounded by Rings

Generations of wall charts and textbooks depicting planets could easily convince you that this was so—and they certainly are a spectacular sight. But Saturn's are not the only planetary rings in our solar system. Jupiter, Neptune, and Uranus have them too, but none are as brilliantly lit as Saturn's. The rings of Uranus were discovered in 1977 when they passed in front of a star that kept fading in and out of view as it passed the planet in the sky. Further investigation revealed a system of eleven rings around Uranus. Jupiter was found to have three rings by *Voyager 1* in 1979, and Neptune was found to have four rings by *Voyager 2* in 1989.

Long ago it was thought that Saturn's rings were solid discs, but that was shown to be impossible in 1859 by James Clerk Maxwell, who showed that

showed in 1979 that Saturn's rings included a remarkable system of "shepherd moons"—small moonlets that maintain the structure of the rings and prevent them from hurtling into space. This explained why the rings of Saturn are so stable, but it only deepened the mystery of their origin. The best guess today is that the rings are the remains of a comet that brushed by the planet and was pulverized by its gravitational field.

solid rings would have been torn apart long ago by Saturn's gravitation. At one point, it was conjectured that the rings were the remains of a moon that had gotten too close to the planet and was torn apart by tidal forces, but that theory has not stood up—for one thing, the icy structure of the rings is not what one would expect from such an astronomical catastrophe. The *Pioneer 11* probe further

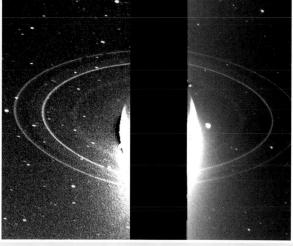

Top: Saturn. Left: Uranus (artist rendering). Above: Rings of Neptune, image taken by the *Voyager 2* camera in 1989.

The Stars We See Are All Real

This probably strikes you as a pretty odd item, doesn't it? But the fact is, many of the stars we see in the night sky now are long gone. It takes so long for light to travel across vast distances in space to us that all we see today is the light that has reached us long after the stars themselves are defunct.

For example, the light from the closest star, Proxima Centauri, takes more than four light-years to reach us, so if its light went out today we wouldn't know for more than four years. Some stars we "see" now died out twenty years ago, some before the Civil War, some before Columbus sailed to America, etc.

The most distant stars visible to the naked eye belong to the Triangulum Galaxy, which is 2.6 million light-years away. Some of its stars whose light we still see today may have died out a few hundred millennia before man showed his puzzled, stubbly face on terra firma. The fact that we receive light from sources so far away is one of the surest indications that the universe is very, very old.

Electrons Travel inside Wires at the Speed of Light

In science class, you may have been taught that electricity consists of electrons traveling through wires at or near the speed of light. Not so. Electrons are a bit more sluggish than that. In direct current (DC), electrons flow more slowly than molasses, at a rate of an inch or two per minute. In alternating current (AC), the electrons don't flow at all. They stay in one place and vibrate.

So why do electrical appliances work as soon as you switch them on? Because the electrical energy itself, not the electrons, skips from electron to electron at nearly the speed of light.

Here's an analogy from the world of sound: when a bell rings, it is not the molecules of air that move from the bell to your ears at the speed of sound. It is the energy itself, expressed in sound waves, that is transmitted at the speed of sound from one vibrating molecule to another.

If Mental Telepathy Were Possible, It Would Have Evolved Already

Maybe; maybe not. The question of the possibility of mental telepathy and extrasensory perception finds an apt parallel in a question that the great atomic physicist Enrico Fermi posed (and was thereafter known as "Fermi's Paradox"). When he was asked what he thought about the possibility of alien beings visiting Earth, Fermi asked, "Then, where *are* they?" If alien visitation were at all possible, he reasoned, then it should have happened already and should be a common occurrence. That it hasn't indicates, according to this point of view, that it's just not possible to begin with.

Science fiction writer Isaac Asimov applied this reasoning to mental telepathy: if it were at all possible, it would have evolved already because such an ability would give the creature (human or otherwise) an enormous advantage in the battle for survival. That it hasn't proves that it's not possible in the first place (this approach became known as "Asimov's Paradox").

The problem with this kind of reasoning is that telepathy may well have evolved already—but we just haven't seen it. And who knows, there may even be telepathic aliens who disappear when they sense us coming.

Wormholes Are Nothing but Science Fiction

On TV's *Star Trek*, space travelers seem to rely on wormholes almost as routinely as city dwellers rely on the local subway system. They use them as shortcuts to get from one place to the other in the vast expanse of "spacetime." Also, in the sci-fi film *Contact* (based on the Carl Sagan novel of the same name), an astronaut travels through a wormhole to distant stars and galaxies in a matter of seconds.

The name "wormhole" comes from a metaphor about a worm and an apple: if the worm wants to take the shortest route to the other side of the apple, it would burrow through the center rather than crawl around the outside. (This is neither here nor there, but given the arduous task of burrowing, wouldn't the worm save more time by taking the long way? I guess we're not supposed to take the metaphor too literally.)

Back to the question at hand: are wormholes real? According to theoretical physics, they may be perfectly real, but no one has seen one or been through one lately. In other words, these mysterious tunnels

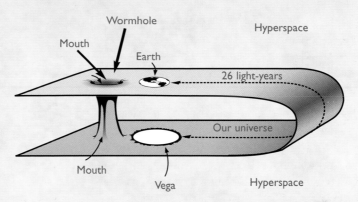

A theoretical construct of a wormhole. If such a thing exists, the passage connecting earth with a star like Vega 26 light-years away would be only one kilometer long. The challenge would be to keep the wormhole open long enough to get through it—the "tunnel" would last only fractions of a second—and not to be torn apart by the gut-wrenching forces that a traveler would experience inside.

through the folds of time and space are still, well, hypothetical—and possibly a key to the elusive Unified Field Theory that Einstein was searching for.

But consider this: another concept that started out as purely hypothetical—the existence of black holes—is today considered virtually certain … and may have already been observed.

Nature

"The Antelope Play" in the American West

Strictly speaking, if you were given a home on the range "where the deer and the antelope play," it wouldn't be in the American West. According to zoologists, no true antelope live in North America. The ringer here is the pronghorn, an unrelated species. The closest thing to an antelope in these parts, oddly enough, is the Rocky Mountain goat. To take this tiresome nitpicking one step further, the song should really go, "Give me a home, where the bison roam, and the deer and the pronghorn play."

The pronghorn, by the way, is a species unique to North America, and it is endangered. Uncontrolled hunting in the eighteenth and nineteenth centuries, as well as the disappearance of the animals' natural habitat, contributed to their near extinction. Then, thanks to conservation efforts in the seventies, their ranks swelled somewhat. The bison has fared even worse than the pronghorn. Though it once roamed not just the American West but the entire country—from ocean to ocean, down into Mexico and up to northern Canada—it now is on the verge of extinction. Odd how the same culture that so romanti-

cized the bison as a symbol of the Old West had no qualms about first displacing them and then hunting them almost to the point of annihilation.

The Arctic Is the Coldest Place on Earth

In the first place, the Arctic region is slightly warmer than Antarctica because it is, for the most part, at sea level, while Antarctica is an elevated plateau, and higher areas generally experience colder temperatures. Moreover, beneath the ice of the Arctic region is a sea that is warmer than land would be under comparable conditions. On average, the North Pole registers temperatures ten to fifteen degrees Fahrenheit colder than the region around the South Pole. But colder still are several areas on the globe that, although located at some distance from the poles, are subject to climatic conditions that create extreme cold. In Siberia, for example, temperatures reaching ninety degrees below zero have been recorded, and similar cold spells have occurred in Tierra del Fuego, an island off the coast of South America.

Baby Birds Handled by Humans Are Rejected by Their Parents

This is one of the most common misconceptions about birds—and about wildlife in general. For one thing, a bird's sense of smell is not very good, so the scent of a human would probably not be picked up at all. Furthermore, birds wouldn't be bothered by the scent even if they could smell it.

So what should you do if you find a baby bird on the ground? It depends on whether the bird is a nestling or a fledgling, so you should be aware of the difference. A nestling is fuzzy or featherless and belongs in the nest. If you can locate the nest, try to gently place it back there. Fledglings, on the other hand, have feathers and are learning to fly. They may look helpless and lost to a would-be Good Samaritan, but fledglings should be left alone. As a normal part of their development, they spend several days on the ground until they get the knack of using their wings for flight. During that time their parents watch over them and bring them food. So it's best to curb your adoptive impulses. Besides, baby birds taken home by humans have a very low rate of survival. One exception to this scenario: if you spot a fledgling that seems to be threatened by cats, dogs, or humans, place the bird behind some shrubbery, on a tree limb, or otherwise out of harm's way.

What about other baby animals? Are they ever rejected by their parents after being handled by humans? For the most part, no. But the broader question is, can humans help baby animals in distress? The answers are varied and depend on the circumstances. For a guiding light that will explain what to do when you find a baby animal, be sure to visit this helpful site: www.paws.org/wildlife/injured/rescue.

Audubon Protected Birds and Other Wildlife

Founded in 1905, the National Audubon Society has long been revered for its efforts at wildlife conservation and the protection of birds. Oddly enough, the esteemed organization was named for a man who shot more birds in an average week than a zealous duck hunter did in an entire season. John James Audubon, of course, produced a whole slew of bird paintings, many of them considered masterpieces. Like most birds, his models would not sit still for a portrait—unless they happened to be dead, of course. Hence the artist packed a rifle along with his palette and brushes. Audubon was said to have shot as many as a hundred birds a day. Taking the long view, one could say it was all worthwhile. The birds did, after all, achieve a kind of pictorial immortality after they were gunned down.

Covered Bridges Were Covered to Protect Travelers from Bad Weather

The roofs of these quaint relics from the American past served a practical purpose, and it was not to keep the wind, rain, and snow off travelers. Rather, it was to protect the bridge itself, the supporting structures of which were subject to rot and to damage from harsh weather. Keeping the bridge's roof in repair was much cheaper and less dangerous than rebuilding the whole bridge.

Dogs Don't "Get" Television

Most people believe that the optical structures of dogs (and cats, for that matter) are so finely tuned (like their hearing and sense of smell) that they are not able to make visual sense of television—they don't "connect the dots" the way we do in making those pixilated images that blur across the screen into coherent images of people who dance, sing, cook, or report the news. But James (the "Amazing") Randi has tested this with a particular dog that seemed to be watching TV and following images across the screen. Was Fido (actually a poodle named Terr) merely responding to the spectacle of color and shapes (at one end of the spectrum), or did the dog have an interest in knowing if Miranda would ever recover from her amnesia or what Jack Bauer (of *24*) does on his day off? Randi carefully observed Terr's reactions to the appearance of another dog on screen and to cats as they appeared. Terr perked up when a dog appeared, followed it across the screen until it left—as he did with other four-legged creatures—and went positively berserk at the appearance of a cat. Can it be long before the Nielsen people create an Office of Mammalian Monitoring? On second thought, naah…

Only People Are Either Right-Handed or Left-Handed; All Animals Are Ambidextrous

Since we're not exactly sure what causes some people to be right-handed and others left-handed, or why the majority of humans—in all epochs and in all societies—are right-handed, by at least eight to one, and usually nine to one, it would be difficult to say what the case is with animals. We do know that elephants are usually "right-tusked"—which means they favor the right tusk in performing tasks, as evidenced by the degree of wear and tear on that tusk. But this elephantine tendency is not nearly as marked as it is for humans—more like three to two. A similar ratio holds for chimpanzees, our closest relative on the genetic tree: chimps tend toward right-handedness, but, again, by no more than three to one.

With many animals, it is difficult to determine handedness at all. But meticulous studies conducted in the last few years have shown that even more primitive mammals, such as mice, show a clear tendency toward right-handedness—and, again, by only a slight margin. So what causes handedness in the first place, and why are humans so predominantly right-handed? These questions are still being pondered. But at least we now know that the tendency is there and that it pervades (to one degree or another) the entire animal kingdom.

A Compass Needle Points to the North Pole

The earth's "magnetic north pole" is not located at the true North Pole, which is determined by the axis of rotation of the earth. The question is, why not? Well, the earth's magnetic pole is the result of two opposing forces that constantly struggle for supremacy in determining the earth's magnetic field. On the one hand, there is the earth's molten-iron outer core, extending some eighteen hundred miles beneath the surface of the earth. This sea of magma flows contrary to the spin of the earth, rising and descending in response to internal geological forces, all of which causes variations in the earth's magnetic field.

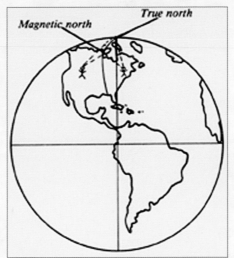

Magnetic north   True north

Working in opposition to this is the relatively stable magnetic field created by the solid inner core of the earth. As a result of the perennial battle between these two titanic forces, the magnetic north pole "wanders" over the North American landscape, sometimes at the remarkably fast pace (geologically speaking) of twenty-five miles per year. Right now, the ever-shifting magnetic north pole is about six hundred miles from the North Pole.

Eventually, the balance of those two opposing forces will become so skewed that the earth's north and south magnetic poles will reverse. This has, in fact, happened some twenty times over the last five million years and is believed to be in the process of happening again.

Geological evidence indicates that the earth's magnetic field has been growing steadily weaker over the past two thousand years, which is what generally precedes a magnetic pole reversal. It is theorized that, at some point several thousand years hence, the earth's magnetic field will virtually vanish.

The ecological consequences of that event can not yet be determined. But it is known, for example, that the earth's magnetic field deflects a small portion of harmful radiation from space. Also, many ecological patterns that depend on migratory behavior are thought to be sensitive to the earth's magnetic field, and they may well be disrupted.

Dew Falls from the Sky

Unlike rain, snow, or hail, dew does not fall from the sky. It is formed when water vapor in the air condenses on the surface of a cool object (such as a blade of grass). The temperature of the object has to be lower than the dew point for dew to form. Not a precise temperature per se, the dew point is associated with relative humidity. A high relative humidity means that the dew point is closer to the current air temperature than it would be with a low relative humidity. If the relative humidity is 100 percent, the dew point will be equal to the current temperature. In any case all that wet grass you see on a cool morning is not the result of dew falling, but of dew forming.

Fish or Birds That All Turn at Once Are Following a Command from Their Leader

If you've ever gone snorkeling, you may have seen this astonishing sight: an entire school of fish suddenly changes direction en masse, as one unit. The same goes for flocks of birds that climb, turn, and swoop all at once, as if they were a single entity. So are they all following the commands of a leader, like the members of an aerobics class aping the movements of their instructor?

Researchers have determined that there is no leader or controlling force. Rather, the individual fish (or bird) is reacting almost instantly to the movements of its neighbors in the school (or flock). Any individual can initiate a movement, such as a change in direction, and this sends out a "maneuver wave," which spreads through the group at an astounding speed. Because individuals can see, or sense, the wave coming toward them, they are ready to react more quickly than they would without such advance notice. What appears to us as simultaneous is actually a kind of "follow your neighbor" behavior moving faster than the eye can see.

The Century Plant Blooms Every Hundred Years

The long-lived succulent known as the "century plant" belongs to the genus *Agave*, the most familiar being *Agave americana*. Although the plant does bloom infrequently, it does not take anywhere near one hundred years to do so. Plants belonging to the *Agave* family may bloom in one year or fifty, depending on the species. Also, the common belief that the century plant dies after it blooms is false; while the leaves of the plant die, the roots remain alive underneath and continue to produce new growth.

Agave americana is originally from Mexico but is now cultivated worldwide.

Leaves Change Color in the Fall

They appear to change color, but the yellow and orange pigments (carotenoids) we see in autumn foliage were already there, hidden under the green pigment (chlorophyll). As the chlorophyll breaks down, it disappears, lifting the veil from the yellows and oranges. The same kind of "unveiling" does not hold true with the bright reds and purples that appear on some leaves in the fall (such as those of the spectacular sugar maples). Unlike the yellows and oranges, these colors are produced by sunlight striking residual glucose stored in the leaves, turning them red or purple. Thus, in the latter instance, the leaves actually do change color.

Lemmings Commit Mass Suicide

You've heard about these Norwegian rodents rushing en masse to the edge of a cliff, then hurling their mouselike bodies into the sea due to some horrifying and inexplicable urge to end it all, right?

This particular myth began as folklore and was dramatically etched into the public consciousness in 1958, with the release of *Wild Wilderness*, a film by Disney. Footage of the lemming "suicide" was also shown repeatedly on the Disney TV show, and it was further depicted in a popular Disney comic book.

So what's really going on with those seemingly desperate and impulsive creatures? Well, lemmings do in fact fall off cliffs, but it's not a deliberately self-destructive act on their part. It's entirely accidental. Every few years, a species of lemming that inhabits Scandinavia undergoes a population explosion of such magnitude that they set out frantically in search of something to eat. Some manage to swim across lakes and streams to reach food on the other side. The less fortunate ones, pushed forward by the hordes behind them, fall off cliffs into the sea and drown.

Exactly what role did the Disney film play in all this? Since wild animals tend not to cooperate when a director shouts "action," the filmmakers facilitated the mass migration by putting the lemmings on a spinning turntable covered with snow (so future viewers wouldn't be able to see the turntable). The lemmings were then herded over a cliff so their "suicidal" plunge into the sea could be recorded on film.

The fact is, when lemmings have to compete for food, territory, or mates with any degree of desperation, they are more likely to fight to the death with each other than to bid the cruel world adieu by jumping off a cliff.

Man Is the Only Animal That Wages War

Clockwise from left: man, chimps, ants, and hyena. These four species exhibit territorial battle behavior.

This idea seems to stem from the notion that creatures in nature are not as nasty and bellicose as we humans—and that, except to hunt for food and to survive, animals live in peace and tranquility, inhabiting a kind of warless Eden. This may be generally the case, but not always. Ants go to war en masse. Groups of hyenas do battle with each other, as do groups of chimpanzees.

Whenever animals that live in groups (or packs or colonies) need to compete with other groups for food or territory, the condition for collective conflict is set, and wars can happen.

Humans Are Descended from Apes

This notion seems to suggest that a few hundred thousand generations back, the mother of all humans looked like Coco the gorilla. But that makes no more sense than to say that all lions are descended from tigers, or all Caucasians are descended from Asians. In each of these cases, the theory is that the two groups share a common ancestor from which the separate groups descended.

Apes and humans share a common ancestor that lived in the distant past and no longer exists. But some apes, to borrow a phrase from George Orwell, are "more equal [to humans] than others." We are more closely related to gorillas and chimpanzees, for example, than to monkeys. In evolutionary terms, this means that the common ancestor we share with gorillas and chimps is a more recent one than the common ancestor we share with monkeys.

There Are More People Alive Today Than Have Ever Lived Before

This "fact" might have the beneficial effect of drawing our attention to the problem of overpopulation, but it isn't accurate. There are a lot of people on the planet right now—6.5 billion as of 2006—but that doesn't come close to the number that lived and died before us.

Of course, the number of people that lived before us is not easy to calculate. Only in recent times do we have reliable population figures, as accurate demographics and census information do not exist for ages past. Also, there is no agreement on exactly when our primate ancestors officially became human. In spite of the lack of hard data, experts have come up with a figure of between sixty and a hundred billion— far more than the earth could ever support at one time.

It should be noted, however, that the number of people living now is greater than at any other time in history—and it's still climbing.

Quicksand Sucks You Down

In the movies, it's usually a villain or a dispensable character who ends up in the quicksand, because once they're in it, they don't come out. They get sucked down irreversibly to an awful, gloppy grave. So what would happen if you were to get mired in real-life quicksand? If you struggle, your feet may create suction that can work your body deeper into the quicksand, so it can be hazardous. If you don't struggle, however, you won't go any deeper than you would in water—that is, up to your chest or shoulders. Instead of pulling you down, quicksand is so dense that it actually tends to buoy you up, just as the Great Salt Lake does to swimmers. The best way to get out of quicksand is to swim in slow motion or lie on top of it and roll off. Flaying your arms in panic, as we see people do in movies, is not advisable.

Steam Is Visible

The white cloudy stuff you see shooting out of a geyser, a teakettle, or an old locomotive is not

steam. It is the mist composed of (visible) water droplets formed when the emerging steam begins to cool off. Steam itself is an invisible gas.

Sea Cucumbers Are Plants

Couch potatoes are not the only animals that have been compared to plants. The sea cucumber may look like the vegetable you slice

up for a salad, but it's an echinoderm, a marine scavenger that lives on plankton and other organic material. Asians eat them and also use them for medicines, creams, and cosmetics.

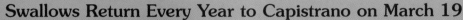

Swallows Return Every Year to Capistrano on March 19

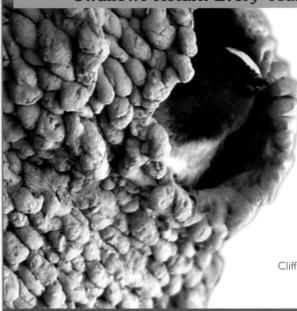

To the mission at San Juan Capistrano, that is. Anyway, the birds celebrated in the famous song spend the winter six thousand miles away in Argentina and supposedly arrive back in one great flock every year on March 19. The fact is that they don't return in one flock, they nest at many other locations in southern California, and they may arrive any time between late February and late March. In any case, the tourists who flock to the mission to see them every March 19 are very punctual.

Cliff swallow in its nest, Bird Point, Alaska.

Heat Lightning Has No Thunder

Often observed on hot evenings, "heat lightning" is soundless, faint, and far away. The reason it is soundless, as you may have suspected, is that its thunder is too far away to hear. Also, due to variations in air density and land formations, the sound of thunder may be refracted in such a way that it reaches some places and not others.

In any case, lightning is always accompanied by thunder, whether you hear it or not. The "heat" in heat lightning is not descriptive but simply coincidental, in that thunderstorms occur more often in warm weather.

Trees Leak Sap onto the Hood of Your Car

So what is that sticky stuff that falls from trees onto your car—and is almost impossible to get off? You probably assume that it's some sort of tree sap, but it's more likely to be bug sap.

Euphemistically called "honeydew," the stuff consists of undigested waste products excreted by the aphids and scale insects that feed on leaves. Ick …

California Redwoods Are the World's Tallest Trees

They're tall, but as a rule, the tallest trees are the eucalyptus trees of Australia. The Australian giant eucalypt (or peppermint) tree grows to heights of 450 to 480 feet, while the sequoia of California rarely gets taller than 350 feet. The redwoods do have the distinction of having the largest girth, often growing to diameters of more than thirty-five feet, while the Australian eucalyptuses generally have diameters of ten to fifteen feet.

It Can Get Too Cold to Snow

People often say this, but in order for the air to become so drained of moisture that snow cannot form, the temperature has to reach forty to fifty degrees below zero Fahrenheit. In the Arctic region, it routinely snows when the temperatures are twenty to thirty degrees below zero. It is true that extremely cold air is often stagnant or slow moving, and that is not conducive to the kind of atmospheric volatility needed—on the part of fronts, clouds, and air masses—to produce snow.

The Full Moon Makes People Act Weird

If the moon is powerful enough to pull oceans back and forth, as shown by the changing tides, it's got to affect our behavior, right? Especially since our bodies are about two-thirds water (salt water at that, like the ocean). The notion seems fairly logical, but countless scientific studies comparing lunar cycles with human behavior (such as the incidence of violent crime, suicide attempts, road rage, fistfights, lovers' quarrels, emergency room visits, etc.) have come up with nothing that is statistically significant—in other words, zip, zilch, and zero.

Some theorize that the notion got started because untoward events that happen during a full moon are more likely to be noticed—especially by those predisposed to see a link. In spite of the lack of evidence, New York City police dispatchers keep insisting there is a correlation.

The Chernobyl Accident Left the Area Uninhabitable

The 1986 nuclear disaster at Chernobyl in the Ukraine included a series of explosions and a reactor meltdown, resulting in a major increase in local radiation. Even so, the Chernobyl area is far from uninhabitable today. People still live and work there, some twenty years later.

According to a 2000 United Nations report, there has been no scientific evidence of an increase in birth defects, congenital malformations, stillbirths, or premature births that could be linked to radiation. Even though there were approximately 1,800 cases of child thyroid cancer reported at the time, "there is no evidence of a major public health impact attributable to radiation exposure." Apparently the increased radiation levels were not significant enough to cause inheritable genetic damage.

The explosion immediately affected the environment in the area surrounding the reactor (see the image at right), especially since much of the land around Chernobyl had been used for agricultural purposes. But as early as three years after the accident, the trees had begun to grow back and had even regained their lost reproductive functions. And as proof of the area's habitability, the largest density and diversity of animals in the area can be found in the exclusion zone.

The Dinosaurs, like All Reptiles, Were Cold-Blooded

First of all, reptiles aren't all cold-blooded. The leatherback turtle, for example, is one of the largest living reptiles at 1,600 pounds. It travels in both cold and tropical waters. Scientists claim that the large size of this turtle contributes to its apparent "warm-bloodedness." The same was probably true for the larger dinosaurs. Polar dinosaurs were found in Australia and Antarctica, suggesting that they must have been able to somehow regulate their body temperature internally (unlike most reptiles). Because of their size, large dinosaurs would have lost heat to the surrounding air relatively slowly.

This characteristic adds considerable weight to the argument that they were "homeotherms"—animals that are warmer than their environments purely because of their size rather than because of special adaptations like feathers or fur.

It is probable that not all dinosaurs were reptiles—at least as we know them today. But there seem to be exceptions to just about any rule, and since the existence of the leatherback turtle changes the definition of the reptile, dinosaurs might just fall into a classification all to themselves.

A Bee (or Wasp) Can't Sting You If You Hold Your Breath

Stinging insects are associated with a number of folk beliefs—holding one's breath, making a fist, grabbing one's wrist with the other hand—but none of them will help you avoid being stung. It is true that keeping still lessens the chance that you will be stung,

and staying calm will help too (since bees are sensitive to body odor). But the idea that holding one's breath, say, somehow closes the pores and makes the skin impenetrable to the stinger of a bee or wasp is nothing more than wishful thinking.

Pandas and Koalas Are Not Bears

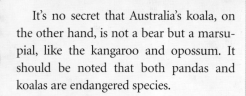

You already knew that, right? So what exactly are pandas, anyway? Stay tuned, you may be surprised. The giant panda, which lives in central China, looks a lot like a black-and-white version of a North American bear. For a long time zoologists had claimed the panda was in a family by itself, its anatomy seeming more like a raccoon than a true bear. After a century of debate, recently obtained DNA data confirm—and experts now agree—that yes, the giant panda is in the bear family.

It's no secret that Australia's koala, on the other hand, is not a bear but a marsupial, like the kangaroo and opossum. It should be noted that both pandas and koalas are endangered species.

To be a bear or not to be a bear? Above: Koalas are not bears but are classified as marsupials. Picture taken in July 2004 at Cape Otway National Park, Victoria, Australia.
Left: Pandas are genetically related to North American bears. Giant panda in the National Zoo, Washington, D.C.

Lightning Travels from the Sky to the Ground

Lightning begins when a negative charge, called a "stepped leader," moves from a cloud toward the ground, but this stage is invisible. What we see as lightning is a positive charge from the ground moving upward to meet the invisible negative charge that is on its way down from the cloud—but it moves too fast for us to determine that it is moving up and not down. The branches of lightning that appear to be moving from the sky to the ground are actually other stepped leaders that never reached the ground. They are illuminated by the upward-traveling bolt of lightning that was activated by the stepped leader that did reach the ground.

Porpoises Never Sleep

This idea is based on the very real observation that these frolicking members of the whale family really don't seem to sleep—ever. Remember that porpoises are air-breathing mammals. Therefore, if they ever did go to sleep, they would risk drowning by inhaling water. So do they sleep, or not?

Well, it turns out that porpoises have developed the remarkable ability to sleep a half a brain at a time! First one hemisphere of their brain sleeps while the other maintains a wakeful state that keeps them afloat and breathing—and then the other half sleeps while the first one minds the store. It's a remarkable adaptation and makes one wonder whether there's any way we can learn this neat trick.

Northern Lights Make Noise

Reports of noises heard during the aurora borealis, or northern lights, date back to the 1800s. Despite the many accounts of "swishing" or "crackling" sounds during the astronomical display, no such sounds have ever been recorded. These anecdotal reports of a "sound and light show" seem hard to verify. For one thing, there is insufficient air between the aurora and the ground to transmit audible sound waves. Also, the sounds would have to travel from an approximate altitude of fifty miles all the way to the ground, creating a considerable gap in time between the light and the sound. Since viewers have reported the light and the "accompanying" sound to be in synch, the sound must either be coming from somewhere else or be the stuff of the viewer's imagination.

The Phases of the Moon Affect Farming

This notion is as ancient as our ancestors who worshiped heavenly bodies, and many people still believe it today. *Old Farmer's Almanac* still publishes detailed information about the moon's phases because some farmers believe the moon affects their crops. The idea is, for example, that the moon affects ground water just as it does the tides, and the brighter light from the full moon may affect the growth of plants.

The difference in moisture and light caused by the moon's phases is extremely small, however, and not nearly enough to make a difference in plant growth. Besides, even if the moon did have an effect, it would not be nearly as great as that of modern technology, which allows crops to be irrigated, fertilized, chemically treated, and exposed to artificial sunlight. (See also "The Full Moon Makes People Act Weird.")

Whales Commit Suicide When They Beach Themselves

Whales often die after they are beached because of dehydration, suffocation, or drowning at high tide. Scientists cannot agree on any one cause of whales to be beached. However, suicide is a human action that cannot be attributed to any animal (see entry "Lemmings Commit Mass Suicide"). Whales probably do not know what they are doing when they are beached, which is a likely reason for ending up in such a predicament in the first place. Some theories suggest that intense underwater noises from anti-submarine sonar or oil drills cause the whales to become disoriented and surface too rapidly, resulting in hemorrhaging and decompression sickness (otherwise known as "the bends"). Others claim that radical changes in the earth's magnetic field prior to earthquakes interfere with the animals' ability to navigate. The latter theory is used to explain whale or dolphin beachings that occur en masse.

Regardless of the true cause (or causes), most scientists agree that whales are beached as a result of confusion and disorientation, not because of any desire to end their lives.

Beached whale painting by Kazumasa Ogawa, 1896, printed in *Dobutsu Shashin Sho* (*Album of Annual Photography*).

Animals

Beaver Are Nocturnal Creatures by Nature

By nature, beaver are (or were) predominantly diurnal (active during the day). They became creatures of the night as the result of human encroachment—that is, the extensive trapping that took place during the two centuries of the North American fur trade. In its heyday, the eighteenth and nineteenth centuries, beaver hats were very popular in Europe, and they made rich men

Beaver do not use their tails to tamp down the mud in their dams. Instead, their teeth and claws perform both of those functions. The beaver does, however, use its tail as a prop that, together with its hind legs, forms a tripod that allows it to stand upright. The tail is also used as a rudder for swimming and as a warning device when slapped on the water's surface.

of John Jacob Astor and his ilk. At that time, beavers were easy targets, because they were active during the day and trappers could find them easily. After years of exploitative trapping, the beaver adapted by hiding under the cover of darkness, and the adaptive trait remains to this day.

Several other misconceptions are associated with beaver. For example, their teeth are not white or yellow but orange—a fact that certain toothpaste advertisers who use the beaver's teeth as a symbol of whiteness would not be happy to hear. A beaver's teeth are constantly growing, so that it has to gnaw at trees just to keep its teeth from getting too big.

Because of the sophisticated dams they build, beaver are thought to be extraordinarily intelligent. But a careful analysis of the dams shows that the structures are no more complex than the types of underground tunnels burrowed by other rodents. Also, the fact that beaver are often killed by falling trees they have just gnawed to the tipping point does not reflect well on their intelligence.

Finally, a number of folk remedies and aphrodisiacs have been attributed to the tails and testicles of beaver (Ojibwa Indians, for instance, were said to treat cuts with extract of beaver testicle). To date, such claims have not been verified.

The Blue Whale Is the Largest Creature That Ever Lived

Until recently, the largest creature that ever lived (including all the known dinosaurs) was believed to be the blue whale, which can reach up to one hundred feet in length and weigh up to one hundred seventy-five tons. Its heart is the size of a compact car, and its largest artery is wide enough for a human to swim through. Blue whales are also the loudest creatures on earth—perhaps the loudest ever. Their calls (used for intraspecies communication) rack up more decibels than a jet engine and can be heard for hundreds of miles.

But let's get back to the subject at hand—the largest creature that ever lived. Although the blue whale dwarfs most known dinosaurs, new evidence suggests that a group of plant eaters called sauropods must now take first place in the size department. Recently discovered fossils indicate that some sauropods were more than one hundred sixty feet long and sixty feet tall. If alive today, one of these gargantuan lizards, while standing with their feet on the ground, would be able to nibble the greenery on the patio of a seventh-floor penthouse.

Sapporo Snow Festival featuring dinosaurs.

Bats Are Blind

The expression "blind as a bat" is heard so often that it might conceivably lead some folks to believe that bats are sightless. In fact, however, all species of bats can see to one degree or another. Fruit bats, for example, have conspicuous eyes that can see quite well.

Most bats are nocturnal and spend much of their lives in dark caves. Therefore, whether they can see or not, they must rely on a system of sonar, or "echolocation," to hunt and navigate. But even the cave dwellers can see and will rely on their sight as long as there is enough light with which to hunt and fly.

Birds Sing Because They Love to Make Music

Granted, birds sing because in order to survive they must attract mates and defend their territory. But do they also sing because they enjoy it? Recent studies are leaning in that direction. Regardless of a bird's aesthetic tastes, the notion that they derive pleasure from singing makes sense from a Darwinian perspective, in that most activities related to survival—such as eating, sleeping, and sex—happen to feel good.

One point to bear in mind is the avian need for economy of size and weight: birds have to be designed very precisely if they are to achieve flight and evade other airborne predators, so as little weight as possible needs to be devoted to noisemaking. Therefore, bird sounds must be generated by air (whistles, chirps, warbles) rather than by the sounds of resonating bulk (growls, roars, barks, chest-beating, foot-stomping, etc.).

One thing that some claim to have noticed about bird songs: when studied scientifically and analyzed in a sound lab, they don't sound as beautiful as they do coming from the branch of a tree at sunset or on a dewy morning.

Boa Constrictors Crush Their Prey to Death

These muscular snakes don't crush their prey, as is commonly believed. They suffocate their victims by squeezing them so hard they can't take in any more air. As an encircled victim exhales, the lung cavity gets smaller, and that's when the boa tightens its grip. Soon, the victim has no room

to expand its chest to inhale. If you should ever find yourself in the "embrace" of a boa (which probably indicates you are having a very bad day), the strategy is to get an arm between the boa and you and apply pressure. Unless the boa is particularly stubborn or just plain mean, the snake will give up as soon as it realizes its usual tactic isn't working.

If asphyxiation doesn't do the job, the hapless prey will probably die of heart failure. You may think of suffocation as slightly more "civilized" than crushing victims to death. But be reminded that constrictors do not have the most elegant table manners. They do, after all, swallow their victims whole.

The Color Red Makes Bulls Angry

This would be a very neat trick, considering that bulls are color-blind. Fact is, it's not the color of the matador's cape (his muleta) that the bulls react to; something else is irritating them. Could it be the fact that the matador is lunging at the bull with cape and sword; or the dozen or so darts that have been stuck into the bull by riders on horses, who also taunt the bull and bump it around the arena, around which thousands are screaming for the bull to be killed; or could it be the beating the bull gets in its stall before it ever gets into the arena? Like most animals, bulls are territorial, and one can cause a great deal of damage inadvertently by tossing its horns around. But whatever provokes a bull's rage, it won't be the color of your clothes that causes it to (metaphorically) "see red."

Chickens Can't Fly

Yes they can, but not like eagles, robins, or even wild turkeys. Chickens fly in short spurts. They can flap their way to a fence post, a low tree branch, or the top of an idle tractor wheel in order to stay out of danger or even roost for the night. A spirited bantam or free-range bird is more likely to get off the ground than a cumbersome laying hen, but even the most agile of chickens has its limits.

Horseshoe Crabs Are Crabs

The horseshoe crab resembles an old-time combat helmet with legs and a tail. So primitive-looking is this creature that it seems like one of the Creator's more rudimentary efforts at animal-making. And maybe it was, since the horseshoe crab's origins go back more than five hundred million years. Despite the superficial resemblance, horseshoe crabs are not crabs; they are arthropods—that is, they are more closely related to spiders and scorpions than to "true" crabs, which are crustaceans.

Camels Store Water in Their Humps

Bactrian camels (camels with two humps) are native to Asian deserts.

Even in the heat of summer, these remarkable creatures of the desert can go for eight days without drinking water. In winter they can go for up to eight weeks! During each refill they can drink up to twenty-five gallons in ten minutes. So where do they put all that water? Are their humps just big water tanks, as many have believed?

Actually, the only thing they store in those humps is fat, and when the fat is used up, the humps shrink and flop to the side. The water, it turns out, is stored throughout the camel's body, mainly in the bloodstream. Yet the humps do turn out to be an indirect source of water in that for every pound of fat metabolized (by reacting with oxygen from the air), a pint of water is produced as a by-product. The camel's water lasts a long time because the animals don't sweat until their body temperature reaches about 105 degrees Fahrenheit.

Also, they don't urinate very often. In one of nature's more remarkable examples of adaptation, camels concentrate their urine and sometimes recycle it within their bodies rather than excrete it from their bodies.

Killer Bees Are Deadly

They make for alarming news stories and scary movies, but killer bees (also known as Africanized honeybees) don't present nearly the threat to humans that we've been led to believe. The bees were brought from Africa to South America to be studied by entomologists. Some escaped and began to thrive in the Brazilian forest. There is some truth to the myth that they are dangerous, in that killer bees do have a greater tendency to swarm. Also, they defend their hives more aggressively and at greater distances from the hive than New World bees. But the image of swarms of angry bees going on a murderous rampage—stinging everything in sight—is the stuff of fiction.

More problematic is the fact that Africanized bees produce less honey than their New World cousins. As the two bee populations intermingle, a stasis will be reached somewhere in the middle on the scale of both aggressiveness and honey production.

Cats Always Land on Their Feet; Their Eyes Shine in the Dark; and They Purr as a Sign of Contentment

They certainly seem to be endowed with the uncanny ability to right themselves while falling, and they do happen to land on all fours. What is perhaps equally remarkable is the aplomb with which they perform this feat. That's because it is a reflex action that cats perform involuntarily. However, even the most nimble cat requires some time to right itself. A cat falling a short distance from an upside-down position will not make the turn in time—but then the fall will not be injurious because it has fallen only a foot or two. In 1880, news stories circulated widely that a cat fell from the top of the Washington Monument and survived the one-hundred-sixty-foot fall. However, something about the various versions of the story and the description of the cat led many people to conclude that the incident never occurred.

Cats (and certain other nocturnal animals) have an extra membrane in their eyes called the *tapetum lucidum*. This layer is a bright metallic blue or green and reflects light a second time through the retina, allowing the cat to see in very low light. (But not even a cat can see in total darkness.) It is the reflection from the *tapetum lucidum* that makes a cat's eyes seem to shine—especially in low light.

Do cats purr out of contentment? We're not exactly sure, and for a long time, it wasn't at all clear how they do it. It used to be thought that cats were able to vibrate blood vessels that surrounded their voice box, but it now appears that what is vibrating is not blood vessels but muscles connected to the voice box. Cats allow air to pass through their throat in a very controlled way, and the vibration radiates through the cat's body. It has a soothing, even a healing effect on bones, muscles, and ligaments, which are easily strained or torn in the course of a day of mouse hunting. Purring, then, seems to be an accommodation by the domesticated cat to the behavioral leftovers of its feral (wild) past.

Physicians find that similar vibrations stimulate the healing of damaged bones in humans. It is unlikely that cats express contentment by purring—any more than rubbing against a human leg is a cat's way of showing affection. It's part of the territorial instinct of felines to mark their domain, in this case using legs instead of plants or tree trunks. One might be tempted to speculate that cats are the way they are because they were domesticated later than, say, dogs or cattle. But maybe not—after all, cats have been chasing mice away from our food supplies since time immemorial.

A Centipede Has a Hundred Legs

It's no secret that the name of this nasty, venomous arthropod means "one hundred legs." But some centipedes have as few as thirty legs and others have more than two hundred. If you factor in all of the thousand or so species of centipede, the average number of legs is about thirty-five. But no matter what the actual count, they certainly *look* like they have a hundred legs.

The Bald Eagle, Our National Emblem, Is a Noble Bird

With its formidable beak, determined glare, and white-feathered crown, no bird appears bolder and more dignified than the bald eagle. No wonder, then, that the bird was chosen to become the symbol of the United States of America. Appearance is one thing, however, and behavior quite another.

As revered a figure as Benjamin Franklin was not at all happy about the choice. He complained, "For my own part I wish the bald eagle had not been chosen the representative of our country. He is a bird of bad moral character. He does not get his living honestly. You may have seen him perched on some dead tree near the river, where, too lazy to fish for himself, he watches the labor of the fishing hawk [osprey]; and when that diligent bird has at length taken a fish, and is bearing it to his nest for the support of his mate and young ones, the bald eagle pursues him and takes it from him."

Franklin insisted the bird is not only a thief but also a coward, because the bald eagle is easily driven away by the much smaller, sparrow-sized king bird when protecting its territory. Finally, Franklin regarded the eagle as a symbol of European royalty, and, indeed, it appears on the coat of arms of the Hapsburgs and other royal families. The symbol of the new democracy—the United States of America—should not, Franklin reasoned, also be the mascot of the aristocracy.

A better choice, for Franklin, would have been another familiar American bird: "The turkey is in comparison a much more respectable bird," wrote Franklin, "and withal a true original native of America. He is besides, though a little vain and silly, a bird of courage, and would not hesitate to attack a Grenadier of the British Guards who should presume to invade his farm yard with a red coat on." He of course meant the wild turkey, not the obese, farm-bred specimens we serve to our families on Thanksgiving.

So does Franklin have a point? It depends on your perspective. If we judge the bald eagle on how well it measures up to human moral standards, the bird is a thief, a coward, a scavenger, and a bully. If we judge it from a more biological perspective, based on its ability to survive, then it gets the gold medal. The bald eagle is an opportunistic predator that takes advantage of every chance to obtain food, regardless of the source, and does so with a clean conscience. Perhaps, then, it is not such an inappropriate symbol for America after all.

Now being removed from the endangered species list, the bald eagle was once on the brink of extinction. Inset: The symbol of the bald eagle on a United States quarter.

Elephants Are Afraid of Mice

Reports have been issued time and again documenting the fact that elephants are not the least bit afraid of mice or any other small animal. Elephants are sometimes bothered by barking dogs, snakes, and human beings, but they're not really afraid of anything. Even the big cats don't frighten adult elephants, and instances where elephants do get agitated at the smell or presence of a lion, say, are due to concern for the calves. Even a pride of lions is no match for one reasonably healthy elephant.

So how did this story get started? One possibility is that someone noticed that elephants often rest their trunks on the ground and then wondered about the possible consequences. Since elephants' eyesight is very bad, for example, they will make no attempt to avoid mice scurrying around their feet because the elephants, in all likelihood, can't see them. To carry the conjecture a bit further, someone must have wondered: what would happen if one of those mice scurried up an elephant's trunk? Out of that came the myth that rodents could make their way into the elephant's brain—hence elephants were supposedly fearful of the deadly consequences. Not surprisingly, this is all nonsense. A rodent couldn't get a fraction of the way up an elephant's trunk, which is lined with sensitive tissue and powerful muscles that expand and contract, inhibiting anything foreign from entering the elephant's inner sanctum. So do elephants have anything to fear from mice or any other rodents? No way.

Giraffes Have More Neck Bones Than We Do and Have Little Horns on Their Heads

Even with necks that are six feet long, giraffes (like most mammals) have the same number of neck bones we do—seven—and their necks are structurally similar to ours. However, each of their neck vertebrae can be up to ten inches long, and the neck itself can weigh six hundred pounds.

As far as the horns are concerned, they aren't really horns but bony knobs covered with skin. They appear to be horns because they are located just where two horns would ordinarily be.

The biggest misconception regarding giraffes, however, is the notion that they are docile, humble creatures.

(This idea is fostered by the fact that giraffes are very quiet. They either can't make noise, choose not to make noise or, as some zoologists believe, communicate ultrasonically.) In any case, giraffes are hardly wimps. Experts at self-defense, they have virtually no natural enemies. A single well-placed kick from a giraffe, in fact, will kill a lion.

Top left: Giraffe in South Africa at Landolozzi, 2003. Giraffes are the tallest of all land-living animals, with males reaching heights of sixteen to eighteen feet.

Electric Eels Are Eels

They may look the part, but electric eels are different from "true" eels (as marine biologists like to call them). *Electrophorus electricus* is a South American knifefish. Measuring up to nine feet in length and weighing fifty pounds, it can deliver a formidable electric shock of more than six hundred volts. A supercharged nervous system enables it to navigate, defend itself, and kill prey. As you may have guessed, electric eels don't make good pets. "True" eels,

although not electrified, grow even larger: some are more than nine feet long and weigh up to one hundred forty pounds.

Gorillas Are Bellicose Brutes

Although gorillas are often portrayed as fierce monsters and although they are equipped with scarier canine teeth than a Doberman and enough strength to snap your arm like a toothpick, gorillas are by nature slow, lethargic, and gentle. They are also vegetarians.

There are cases on record where people have acted subservient toward gorillas, and the creatures responded by petting, hugging, and even grooming them in what might be called a parental manner. The most famous example of gorilla-human rapport was that of field researcher Dian Fossey, who lived with gorillas in Rwanda. Fossey went to great lengths to protect the gorillas. Unfortunately, she made enemies of Rwandan poachers, who eventually killed her.

On rare occasions, gorillas will display aggression symbolically by beating their chests—generally this is done to ward off intruders or to show dominance within the "troop" (the name for a group of gorillas). But since gorillas avoid people whenever possible, this behavior has been observed only rarely.

Incidentally, a surprising number of people confuse "gorilla," the primate, and "guerrilla," the style of warfare. The latter, of course, has nothing to do with the animal; it derives from *guerra*, Spanish for "war."

Cheese Is the Favorite Food of Mice

Omnivores, mice will eat anything. But when it comes to favorites, cheese is not at the top of their list. They'd rather feast on peanut butter, pretzels, oats, fruit, vegetables, flower bulbs, beans, cookies, nuts, pasta, chocolate, worms, spiders, and insects.

Moths Eat Woolen Clothes

In your closet you may be alarmed to see a moth fly up from an old woolen sweater, but adult moths don't eat clothes. It's their larvae that do the eating. And they don't limit their menu to wool. The larvae also dine on fur, feathers, leather, bristles, silk, and felt.

The "Grey" in Greyhound Refers to the Dog's Color

A few greyhounds happen to look grey (or gray), but the origin of the name has nothing to do with the dog's color. In fact, most greyhounds come in colors other than grey. "Greyhound" derives from the Old English term

grighund. The *hund* part is obvious, but no one is exactly sure what *grig* means, or meant.

The etymological theories vary widely, including such oddly diverse possibilities as "shine," "twinkle," "piglet," "dawn," "great," "Greek," "badger," and "bitch."

Moose and Deer Are Different Species

To some people, moose and deer seem like blood relatives, but most people think they're two different species. Moose are actually big deer. They are the largest members of the deer family (Cervidae) and belong to the same subfamily (Capreolinae) as mule deer, white-tailed deer, and reindeer.

Grizzly Bears Are So Named Because They Are Scary

The behavior of grizzly bears is often gruesome, grim, and gory—one could even say "grisly." But the name of the bear is "grizzly," not "grisly." The two words are pronounced the same,

but "grizzly" refers to the color of the bear, which is grayish or grizzled. The confusion is easy to understand, as the coincidence is apt.

Grizzly bears are huge, ferocious-looking animals, it's true, but they are generally docile and non-confrontational. Most of a grizzly's diet is vegetarian, with less than 20 percent made up of fish and, very occasionally, other meat.

An exception to their polite behavior occurs when a female grizzly believes her cubs are threatened, and that can happen even when an animal (and that includes, of course, the human animal) innocently passes between a mother grizzly and her young. In the wild, this is considered predatory behavior and a hunting tactic. When this happens, a grizzly *will* attack, bearing down on its adversary faster (over short distances) than a racehorse and with great ferocity. Grizzlies have been known to rip off car doors to kill an attacker.

The Lion Is King of the Jungle

Lions don't even live in the jungle, so they are hardly kings of that domain. They live on the African plains, where they can chase down hoofed prey such as gnus, zebras, and antelope. And it's not the majestically maned males (the would-be kings) who do most of the hunting. It's the females, for the most part, who stalk, capture, kill, and bring home the bacon. Also (I say at the risk of an audible groan), lions may not be royalty, but they do have their pride.

Raccoons Wash Their Food

When you see them with their paws in a stream, these masked forest-dwellers may appear to be cleaning their edibles in the flowing water, but the truth is that they aren't nearly that fastidious. Raccoons are really searching the stream bed for food in the form of crustaceans (crayfish and other small animals) underneath the rocks and sand. Some theorize that raccoons also wet their food because they have no salivary glands and the moisture makes their meal easier to swallow.

All Mammals Bear Their Young Live

They say "a camel is a horse built by a committee." But the platypus (with its duck bill, webbed feet, hairy body, and habit of laying eggs) takes that eclectic hodgepodge of characteristics one step further—so much so that scientists at first believed the animal to be a hoax. Along with five species of spiny anteaters, the platypus belongs to the order Monotremata, which, believe it or not, taxonomists classify as mammals. Unlike other mammals, they don't bear live young. But they do demonstrate other mammalian characteristics, such as a single bone in their lower jaw, three middle ear bones, high metabolic rates, and hair.

Ostriches Bury Their Heads in the Sand to Escape Danger

They may not be Einsteins, but no ostrich is going to believe for a moment that sticking its head into the sand is going to save it from a predator because it believes that if the bird can't see the predator, the predator can't see the bird. First of all, there's little need for an ostrich to resort to such a tactic. Ostriches are very swift, able to reach speeds of thirty-five miles per hour; they are very high jumpers, able to clear twelve-foot obstacles with ease; and they have amazingly acute senses—ostriches are able to hear or see danger long before other animals in the vicinity.

Even if an ostrich were cornered, the predator would have more to worry about than the bird. An adult has a kick powerful enough to kill a horse. Handlers of ostriches know this and are extremely careful with them; they may appear to be docile, near-domesticated animals, but there's no telling what will happen when one is suddenly frightened—a broken bone, perhaps, or worse.

So how did the ridiculous head-in-the-sand story get started? Below are three explanations—a natural one, a historical one, and a literary one.

The natural explanation: Ostriches habitually poke their heads into any hole or crevice in search of food (and an ostrich can and will eat virtually anything). An observer may think that the only chance a predator has of felling an ostrich (assuming the predator could get close enough) is to catch it with its head in the ground, supposedly placed there to evade the predator.

The historical explanation: The earliest reports of this behavior are in Roman natural histories citing Arab merchants who claimed to have observed ostriches doing this. Now, a tried-and-true sales technique practiced in bazaars and souks all over Asia is for the merchant to tell the shopper a harmless but outrageous story to see if it is believed. If it is, the merchant knows he has a "live one"—a gullible mark. One can easily imagine this story about ostriches being told by merchants to amazed customers as part of the selling strategy.

The literary explanation: There is something so instructive, so poignant, and so applicable about this supposed ostrich behavior as it applies to human behavior that it's deemed worthy of repeating and perpetuating, if only not to lose it as a pedagogical tool.

All Mosquitoes Bite

We use the word "bite," but most everyone knows that what mosquitoes do is sting. And only half of them do—namely, the females. The males live on plant juices and don't even have the proboscis needed to penetrate the skin and suck up blood. The females suck animal blood (and that includes human blood) because it contains proteins needed to produce eggs. In other words, mosquitoes bite you in order to make more mosquitoes to bite you later on. Lovely.

Piranhas Are Ferocious and Deadly

Hollywood legend suggests that anyone who swims with piranhas is quickly reduced to a skeleton. And that natives herding cattle across piranha-infested rivers must sacrifice one animal so the rest can pass safely while a throng of demonic fish picks the poor cow to the bone.

It's true that these South American fish have razor-sharp teeth, sometimes feed in large numbers, and can smell blood like sharks. But they are more of a threat to each other than they are to humans or large animals. They usually feed on fish, frogs, or other aquatic animals that are their size or smaller. Natives who live along the Amazon regularly swim among them without incident.

How did piranhas get such a bad rep? For one thing, their ferocious appearance hasn't helped. Also, a popular book by Teddy Roosevelt, *Through the Brazilian Wilderness* (1914), about his trek through the rain forest recounts how one member of the expedition lost part of his foot while crossing a stream. Roosevelt only guessed the culprit was a piranha—but for most people, that was enough.

In case you're planning to take a swim in the Amazon in the near future, however, here's some advice from the locals: don't swim during drought season (when the fish are most hungry and aggressive) and stay out of the water if you have any open cuts or sores.

Notwithstanding all this, you'll probably find it reassuring to know that zookeepers in New Orleans moved the piranhas in the aquarium to another city as Hurricane Katrina was approaching for fear the fish would somehow get loose and start spawning in the Mississippi. Good thinking.

Piranhas at the Bell Isle Aquarium, Detroit, Michigan, 2005.

Opossums Play Dead to Elude Predators

The phrase "play dead" (or "play possum") implies that opossums instinctively and voluntarily *pretend* to be dead as a tactic to deter predators, but this is not the case. When threatened, they *involuntarily* fall into a catatonic or comatose state that mimics death—and it's *very* convincing. The eyes glaze over, the lips pull back, baring the teeth, saliva foams around the edges of the mouth, the tongue falls to the side, and a foul-smelling juice is secreted from the anus. Even more impressive, the body stiffens and becomes insensitive to touch—including lifting, poking, shaking, and whisker-pulling. After a period of minutes or hours, the opossum awakens from its trance and trots away. At times this defense backfires: well-meaning humans who believe the creature is dead may take it upon themselves to bury it—alive.

Pigeons Are Different from Doves

They are ornithologically the same, but the larger ones tend to be called pigeons and the smaller ones tend to be called doves—especially those that offer olive branches in a gesture of peace. (No doubt the opponents of war would rather be called doves than pigeons.) The original name of the common city pigeon was "rock dove." They built their nests in the crevices of rocky cliffs. That's why they gather in cities—because the facades of man-made buildings look like cliffs and there are plenty of crevices to nest in.

Salmon Die after Spawning

There are many different kinds of salmon scattered all over the world—from Canada to Australia and from Siberia to Scandinavia. But only one kind—namely, the Pacific salmon, located along the west coast of North America—dies after spawning.

In contrast, other species, such as Atlantic salmon, for example, may live to make the arduous journey to the sea and back to spawn again and again.

Pit Bulls Are Vicious by Nature

This breed has gotten a lot of bad press over the last three decades. Stories of attacks, mauling, and even lethal encounters with pit bulls have made for banner headlines. And their reputation has not benefited from the fact that they were bred to be fighters of other dogs (in the "pit," often for gambling purposes) and fighters of other animals (such as bears and bulls). Under such combative circumstances, they are justly regarded as fierce and tenacious.

Another strike against the breed has come from the havoc perpetrated by irresponsible owners and breeders. That includes people attracted to pit bulls because of their fierce reputation—owners who want to come across as macho men not to be messed with, who themselves may be violent by nature, hence likely to abuse the dogs and use the dogs to abuse or frighten other people. Some reports have described pit bulls as "ticking time bombs," and because of this some owners have been intimidated into dispensing with their otherwise ideal pets.

Now for the good news: when bred and cared for responsibly, pit bulls are among the most affectionate of canine companions. Really. Although they were bred to fight other dogs, they were also selectively bred *not* to attack *people*. For the most part, pit bulls that attacked people were not allowed to reproduce. Dog experts say that, ironically, pit bulls have a friendlier disposition than most other breeds. In a recent study of breed temperaments, pit bulls were rated very favorably—on a par with beagles and golden retrievers.

St. Bernard Dogs Carry Brandy to Lost Travelers

Monks at the hospice and monastery known as St. Bernard's, located in the Swiss Alps, began keeping dogs in the 1600s. Over the years, the breed they developed there assumed the name of the hospice. The St. Bernard dogs, descended from mastiffs, were used to locate and rescue travelers lost in the treacherous mountain terrain.

So did they carry kegs of brandy? Never. The myth stemmed from a painting in 1820 that showed a mastiff with a barrel around its neck beside an exhausted traveler. Brandy can make the body *feel* warmer. But it or any other alcohol would fail as first aid, since it dehydrates the body and speeds heat loss. Also, a bag around the dog's neck would slow the dog down, get in the way of the dog's ability to sniff for a scent, and give off a scent of its own, which would further confuse the dog.

The monks do keep a few little kegs around the hospice and occasionally place them on the dogs, but only for the tourists who expect to photograph the dogs wearing them.

Wasps Die When They Sting

Wasps and hornets can sting you repeatedly without losing a beat, let alone their lives. For honey bees, however, it's quite another story. Stinging a person (or any other mammal, for that matter) amounts to a kamikaze mission, because their stingers are barbed and can't be pulled out without eviscerating the insect. This may seem a glaring error on the part of natural selection, but the fact is that honeybees can sting other insects repeatedly (when defending the hive, for example) without suffering any suicidal consequences. Incidentally, honeybees (unlike wasps and hornets) are very reluctant to sting humans unless stepped on, say, or otherwise provoked.

"Thoroughbred" Means "Pedigreed"

It's true that Thoroughbred horses are purebred and pedigreed, but that's not what "Thoroughbred" means. Thoroughbred is the name for a breed of horse, as is Morgan, Clydesdale, pinto, mustang, or Arabian.

All Thoroughbred horses racing today are descended from three Middle Eastern stallions—two Arabians and one Turk—that were brought to England in the 1600s to be mated with British mares. For more than three centuries now, Thoroughbreds have been bred selectively as racers par excellence.

Wolves and Sharks Are Vicious Predators with a Special Taste (and Hatred) for People

Two animals that get bad press on a regular basis are wolves and sharks. Now, that doesn't mean anyone would want to get up close and personal with either animal—but neither would anyone want to do that with any number of creatures with far more benign reputations.

The fact is that wolves are very docile animals, with a highly developed family system and a warm,

mutually supportive and, in many ways, incredibly sophisticated social structure. Wolves are loyal to one another and especially faithful to their spouse. That's right: wolves mate for life and are devoted to their offspring—male wolves no less than females—caring for them well into adulthood. The use of the term to describe a lecherous, promiscuous man couldn't be less apt—wolves are monogamous to a fault. When a mate dies, the survivor goes into a prolonged, depressed celibacy, rarely connecting with another wolf.

As hunters, wolves subsist mainly on fish, mice, and carrion, only rarely hunting deer and caribou, and then only culling old and injured animals from the herd. Occasionally, wolves will hunt in packs, but that's generally when the herd does not have any stragglers. And wolves do not howl at the moon; they howl often as a means of socializing, communicating, and courting other wolves.

Wolves have been portrayed as evil creatures that have a particular appetite for people. From "Little Red Riding Hood" to the carnage depicted in Willa Cather's *My Antonia* (in which wolf packs hunt down six sleighs that are part of a wedding party and devour fifteen people and fifty horses), the popular myth is that wolves and humans are natu-

ral enemies. The fact is—investigated and corroborated by such respected naturalists as Vilhjalmur Stefansson, Barry Lopez, and Farley Mowat—that wolves do not hunt or attack people, not singly or in packs. The number of cases of a healthy wolf attacking a human is minuscule—more people die from bee attacks every year than from wolf attacks in an entire decade.

The same goes for sharks, although a shark is likely to occasionally mistake a swimming human for a seal, its favorite food. Sharks will very rarely attack divers underwater, unless they perceive an encroachment into their territory. There are literally hundreds of different species of sharks, and only a few are large and predatory enough to pose any threat to people. Shark populations have been decimated around the world, fueled partly by good old-fashioned greed, and by even older-fashioned fear, promulgated by such depictions as the great white shark in *Jaws*. But, as one naturalist put it, sharks have a great deal more to fear from us than we do from them.

Food and Drink

The Baby Ruth Candy Bar Was Named after Babe Ruth

The final answer on this is hazy. Since the candy bar and the slugger appeared on the scene at the same time, it's natural to assume the bar was named for the ballplayer. But the candy bar's manufacturer, the Curtiss Candy Company, always claimed the bar was named for President Grover Cleveland's baby daughter, Ruth. Since baby Ruth died some fourteen years before Baby Ruth appeared, however, one wonders about the timing. Curtiss had never signed a permission deal with the Sultan of Swat, so it's possible the Ruth Cleveland explanation may have served as a convenient insurance policy in case the company had to fend off any untoward litigation from the Babe or his estate.

Banana Oil Comes from Bananas

It smells like bananas, but that's as close as it gets to the popular fruit. Banana oil is a synthetic compound (usually amyl acetate and nitrocellulose) that happens to have a banana scent. The substance is used as a solvent and as a food flavoring. Bananas themselves produce no oil that is marketed commercially.

Chocolate Gives You Acne

According to scientific studies, chocolate does not cause acne. One dermatological study, for example, showed no difference in the amount of acne in subjects who ate real chocolate bars for a month and those who ate fake-chocolate "control" bars for the same amount of time.

Acne results from overactive sebaceous glands, which are found all over the body. The glands produce an oily secretion called sebum, which is a complex mixture of fats. Acne is a mixture of sebum, keratin, and pieces of dead cells that plug up the mouth of the gland, which then swells up. Because both chocolate and sebum are rich in fats, some have tended to assume a cause-and-effect relationship between chocolate and acne. Others have thought that if you eat a lot of chocolate your body tries to get rid of the excess fat by squirting it through your sebaceous glands, which would then be blocked and cause acne.

Studies using radiation to track the fats in chocolate have shown that almost none of the tracked fats appeared in the sebum, proving that there is no chemical or physiological link between chocolate and acne.

Beer Won't Make You Blotto

Although there is less alcohol in one ounce of beer than in one ounce of hard liquor, beer is no less intoxicating than any other alcohol. There is just as much alcohol in a twelve-ounce can of beer as there is in a five-ounce glass of wine or a one-and-a-half ounce shot of eighty-proof liquor. Because beer is consumed in much larger quantities, the amount of absolute alcohol actually taken in is about the same—as are the effects.

Cashews Are Nuts

Cashews are not true nuts but the seeds of a tropical and semitropical fruit called the cashew apple, which grows on trees. About the size of regular apples, cashew apples are edible, pear-shaped, and sour. Hanging from the fruit itself are several comma-shaped, nutlike pods, which contain the seeds, or the "cashew nuts."

Cashews are not sold in their natural form because the seedpods have a double-layered, leathery covering that contains an irritating and caustic oil called cardol. Because of the danger cardol presents to human skin, the outer covering of the cashew is risky to remove by hand, so machinery is required. Once the covering has been removed, the cashews are roasted to remove all traces of the oil, making them safe for consumption.

Bottled Water Is Better than Tap Water

Not always. For one thing, the EPA and FDA don't regulate bottled water as tightly as tap water, meaning bottled water could contain unsafe levels of bacteria and metals (as in the 1990 finding that a popular brand of bottled water contained unsafe levels of benzene). And bottled water doesn't have fluoride; adding it is a public health measure that has gone a long way toward preventing tooth decay and gum disease, which can lead to other serious medical problems.

Besides, bottled water isn't all that special. Often, it's nothing more than filtered tap water (this is the case whenever it says "purified" or "filtered" rather than "spring"). And taste tests show again and again that most people can't tell the difference between bottled and tap anyway, so you might as well save your money (or buy your own water filter).

Breakfast Is the Most Important Meal of the Day

This popular misconception developed in the 1940s and 1950s at the time of what became known as the "Iowa Breakfast Studies," a series of experiments conducted by nutritionists. The studies were later deemed flawed, and current studies show that there is no substantive evidence to support the belief that breakfast is any more nutritionally important than meals eaten later in the day.

However, for young people who wake up hungry in the morning and aren't getting enough total daily nutrients from other meals, not eating breakfast can cause extra stress that could affect concentration and cognitive skills—and that translates into poor school performance.

Betty Crocker Was Real, but Aunt Jemima and Sara Lee Weren't

Aunt Jemima wasn't her real name, and the pancake formula wasn't hers either, but the person herself was very real. Born a slave in 1834, the future Aunt Jemima was named Nancy Green. She grew up to be a wonderful cook, and her personal warmth, as depicted in her famous image, was genuine. Discovered at age fifty-nine by the pancake people, who gave her the name Aunt Jemima, she and her supply of pancakes attracted huge crowds at the historic Chicago World's Fair of 1893. After that, pancake sales took off, and her image was on packaging, magazine ads, and billboards worldwide. More recently, in response to complaints that the famous face sent a message that was stereotypical, Aunt Jemima's image has undergone a makeover.

Sara Lee was a real person too. She is the daughter of bakery entrepreneur Charlie Lubin, who decided to put her name on his cheesecakes when Sara Lee was eight years old. Lubin sold his business to Consolidated Foods in 1956 and continued there as an executive for many years. The outfit changed its name to the Sara Lee Corporation in 1985. The flesh-and-blood Sara Lee never held a management position in the company, but she appeared in a few ads and promotions. Today, she is a philanthropist who spends most of her time supporting the education and advancement of women and girls in science.

1936 1955 1965

1972 1980 1986

Betty Crocker, the spokespersona for General Mills since the 1920s, is quite fictitious. Betty was pieced together from various sources. The name Crocker belonged to a company executive; her famous signature was that of a company secretary; and her various radio voices over the years belonged to a number of different actresses. In the 1930s, Betty acquired a face. It was an artist's composite of several women who worked at General Mills. The image has morphed many times since then, presumably to reflect changes in the culture at large. Viewed as a group, however, the bevy of Bettys could all be sisters. For some segments of the population, at least, Betty was more fact than fiction, since opinion polls consistently rated her among the most famous women in America.

Betty Crocker first got her face in 1936. Artist Neysa McMein created an image from the faces of all the women in the company's home service department. The portrait was then widely circulated and reinforced the popular belief that Betty Crocker was a real woman. Her face changed seven times over the next sixty years—she was made to look younger in 1955; more "professional" in 1980; and in 1996 she was given an "ethnic" look with a slightly darker skin tone.

1969

1996

Coffee Comes from Latin America

The coffee plant is believed to have originated in Africa, more specifically in Kaffa (or Kava), a southwest province of Ethiopia (etymologists connect the word "coffee" to Kaffa). Coffee's origin is one thing, but its cultivation is another. Arab traders brought the seed home from Africa and grew their own plants, called *Coffea arabica*. Later, Jesuit missionaries introduced the plant to Colombia and the rest of Latin America, where it flourishes today.

Bananas Are Picked Green to Allow Time for Shipping

Unlike many other fruits, bananas are not at their best when ripened on the vine. In fact, they taste awful. Bananas are picked green because they ripen in a more palatable fashion after being separated from the plant. The picked bananas are refrigerated and shipped to their destination. Then they are ripened in airtight "ripening rooms," which are filled with ethylene gas to enhance ripening. Bananas that arrive at the market green are unlikely to ripen well enough to taste good.

Russian Dressing Came from Russia

Russian dressing is about as Russian as hot dogs and ketchup. Invented in America, the dressing was so named because earlier versions of the recipe contained a relish of caviar, which was associated with Russia in the popular mind.

Buttermilk Has Butter in It

Butter is made by churning cream until it reaches a much creamier, semisolid state called—guess what—butter. The watery liquid left behind is buttermilk. Although a residue of butter-making, buttermilk itself does not contain butter. It does, however, contain bacteria that are added to create a fermented milk product. The bacteria turn the natural lactose in the milk into lactic acid, resulting in the tart and thick liquid that some of us love to hate.

The Caesar Salad Was Named after Julius Caesar

Nope, it's not that old. The salad got its name from a chef named Caesar Cardini, who invented the dish at his Tijuana (Tijuana!) restaurant in 1924. Although the salad is char-acterized of late by its optional anchovies, the salty fish played no role in the original recipe, which included romaine lettuce, garlic, crou-tons, Parmesan cheese, coddled eggs (boiled in the shell for one minute—not raw, as is some-times the case), olive oil, and Worcestershire sauce (and try adding cranberries—yum!).

Chop Suey and Fortune Cookies Came from China

The exact origin of chop suey and fortune cookies is not 100 percent certain, but everyone seems to agree that both first appeared in America, not China. Chop suey arrived on the scene in the late 1900s. Some say it was invented by Chinese immigrants in San Francisco or by Chinese laborers working on the transcontinental railroad. Others claim it originated in 1896 in New York, where the Chinese ambassador's chefs prepared a version of "Chinese" food that they thought would be acceptable to American guests.

Most agree that fortune cookies were invented in San Francisco. Some say they were devised by the Chinese founder of the Hong Kong Noodle Company in 1918. The more likely story is that they were the creation, some ten years earlier, of Makoto Hagiwara, the Japanese immigrant who designed Golden Gate Park's famous Japanese Tea Garden. He served the cookies to his guests with tea and placed a thank-you note inside each one. Chinese restaura-teurs copied the recipe and put fortunes inside.

Brown Eggs Are Richer than White Eggs

For years, people believed that brown eggs were more nutri-tious than white eggs—the belief stemming from the notion that nutrients of the yolk "overflowed" and were responsible for the coloration of the shell. On the other hand, in certain parts of the Midwest, people believed that white eggs were fresher than brown eggs, the brown of the shell impressing people as a sign of staleness.

Neither of these beliefs has any basis in fact: brown and white eggs are indistinguishable inside and the coloration of the shell has no effect on either the nutritive value or the freshness of the egg. (So shouldn't they cost the same?)

A Disgruntled Customer Has Been Giving Away a Company's Secret Cookie Recipe on the Web

This urban legend is actually older than the Internet. In the original story, the cookie brand was Mrs. Fields. In the story going around the Internet these days, the brand is Neiman Marcus. Here's how it goes:

In the restaurant at a Neiman Marcus store, a shopper was served an incredibly delicious chocolate chip cookie. She asked for the recipe. The waiter said, "I'm sorry, madam, but it's a secret." She wheedled and cajoled, and finally the waiter summoned the manager. "I'll give you the recipe," the manager whispered, "but you must keep it quiet—and it will cost you two-fifty." Surprised at the price, she eagerly accepted. Later, she found the recipe written on her receipt along with the words "Cookie Recipe, $250." She protested that she'd been hornswoggled, but the manager insisted that she did get the recipe she ordered—and it was, after all, a secret one at that. Now, to get even, she proceeded to send the recipe free to everyone in the world. "Please forward it to at least ten of your friends," says the e-mail, "and tell them to do the same!"

It's true that Neiman Marcus sells a delicious chocolate chip cookie. But the recipe isn't secret. In fact, the company publishes it on its own Web site, along with a note inviting everyone to "Copy it, print it out, and pass it along to friends and family. It's a terrific recipe. And it's absolutely free."

Neiman Marcus Chocolate Chip Cookie Recipe

Ingredients

1/2 cup unsalted butter, softened

1 cup brown sugar

3 tablespoons granulated sugar

1 egg

2 teaspoons vanilla extract

1/2 teaspoon baking soda

1/2 teaspoon baking powder

1/2 teaspoon salt

1-3/4 cups flour

1-1/2 teaspoons instant espresso powder, slightly crushed

8 ounces semisweet chocolate chips

Directions

Cream the butter with the sugars until fluffy.

Beat in the egg and the vanilla extract.

Combine the dry ingredients and beat into the butter mixture. Stir in the chocolate chips.

Drop by large spoonfuls onto a greased cookie sheet. Bake at 375 degrees for 8 to 10 minutes, or 10 to 12 minutes for a crispier cookie. Makes 12 to 15 large cookies.

Danish Pastry Originated in Denmark

For heaven's sake, where else would Danish pastry come from? These sweet and flaky breakfast treats can be traced not to Danish bakers but to Viennese bakers who worked in Denmark. How the Austrian bakers got to Denmark is open to debate, but their recipes were decidedly Viennese. Nor do the Danes claim to have invented the Danish pastry. In Copenhagen, what we would call a Danish is referred to as *Vienerbrod*, which means "Viennese bread." Go figure.

The Special Formula for Coca-Cola Is a Closely Guarded Secret

Coca-Cola has always had a flair for style that makes up for whatever it happens to lack in substance. The inordinate media hype over Coke's "secret formula" has really set it apart from its many rivals—giving Coke more of an edge than its supposedly unique taste ever could. In other words, it's all about advertising, and over the years a series of Coke's savvy ad copywriters have succeeded in making Coca-Cola an American institution.

It's true that, historically, Coke's elusive recipe has been known only to a privileged few—according to rumor, only two—and that they were supposedly sworn to secrecy. And Coca-Cola has never applied for a patent that would protect the formula, because patents are matters of public record

(anyone can look it up), and patents eventually run out—and are no longer protected.

But let's get real—these days it would be awfully hard to keep such a secret from competitors. A routine chemical analysis can (and has) revealed exactly what is in Coke and in what proportions (by the way, these ingredients have changed many times over the years). Among the hush-hush ingredients are vanilla, lime juice, extract of coca, cinnamon, coriander, nutmeg, citrus oils, and caramel. So other than the famed use of a tiny amount of cocaine, which was removed from the formula in 1906, everything in Coca-Cola is relatively common, inexpensive, and unexotic—albeit very tasty when mixed together. In 1985, the company launched "New Coke," with a different formula. The effort tanked, and the classic formula was reinstated.

English Muffins and English Breakfast Tea Were Invented in England

English muffins were first given that name in New York City around 1880 by Samuel Bath Thomas, a baker who had emigrated from England. Even today, the name Thomas' (oddly pronounced "Thomas-ezz," even with the single apostrophe) is virtually synonymous with English muffins. Speaking of British immigrants who named things, a popular tea owes its name to an Englishman who also settled in New York City. Richard Davies concocted the blend from a mix of congou, pekoe, and pouchong and dubbed it "English Breakfast." In most parts of England, ask for English breakfast tea and you're likely to get a blank stare (before they serve you whatever they have on hand).

Marco Polo Brought Ice Cream and Pasta to Italy from China

After visiting China, Marco Polo is said to have returned to Italy in 1279 with recipes for ice cream and pasta, or at least that's what your second-grade teacher told you. But first of all, no one knows for sure whether Marco Polo ever made it to China. Moreover, pasta had been consumed in Italy for hundreds of years before Marco Polo ever sailed to ... wherever it is he sailed to.

As for ice cream, it may have been invented in China, or it may have been invented in the Middle East, or it may have just "evolved" by taking many different forms in many different places. The closest thing to a sub-

Ice cream and pasta—or their precursors—were well known in Europe well before Marco Polo traveled to the Far East.

stantiation of the lore about Marco Polo vis-à-vis pasta and ice cream is that the explorer *may* have brought back recipes for a different *kind* of pasta (made with rice rather than wheat) and for a sorbet-like flavored ice (but he didn't have to go all the way to China for iced confectioneries— they were common in much of the Middle East by the Middle Ages).

A precursor of ice cream called *kulfi* was popular in India and all of Central Asia by the sixteenth century. But the closest thing to ice cream as we know it today seems to have been developed in France in the seventeenth century.

Prohibition Made It Illegal to Drink Alcohol

Prohibition began in 1919, when the Eighteenth Amendment was passed, ushering in an era of illegal booze and speakeasies that turned into a field day for organized crime.

So, one might ask, didn't the amendment make drinking illegal? The answer is no. It was not illegal to drink or possess alcohol—only to make it, sell it, or transport it. So if you had been a customer at a speakeasy and the police raided the joint, you couldn't have been arrested (except maybe for public drunkenness). But the people who ran the place could be hauled off to the slammer.

"Mama" Cass Elliot Died from Choking on a Ham Sandwich

Cass Elliot—the overweight singer dubbed "Mama," from the 1960s rock and roll band The Mamas & the Papas—died in London on July 29, 1974. Initial press reports said that her doctor had guessed she "probably choked to

death on a sandwich." Sadly, she did die, but it was from a heart attack and not from food. Coroners found no trace of food (or drugs) in her system after an autopsy. However, the "sandwich" story stuck and was soon embellished with the word "ham."

Cocoa Is the Same as Chocolate

Others might say the popular misconception is that cocoa and chocolate are different. In fact, they are the same—and they are not the same. Cocoa and chocolate are both derived from the seeds of the tropical tree *Theobroma cacao*. The seeds (or beans) are roasted, shelled, and ground and then allowed to cool in pans. The result is at first a paste and then solid bars. The bars consist partly of a fat called cocoa butter, and the combination of cocoa butter and cocoa is what we know as "chocolate." But if the paste is put into pressurized containers, the fat separates from the mixture and the result is cocoa. Hence cocoa is chocolate with all or most of the cocoa butter removed.

Cocoa became popular when it was noticed that it dissolved in liquid (particularly hot liquid) better than the fatty chocolate. Visually, when people speak of "hot chocolate," they mean "hot cocoa," though the two terms have come to be used interchangeably.

French Fries Come from France

Many Americans believe that french-fried potatoes originated in either France or America. In fact, "french fries" were invented in neither of those countries but in Belgium. Since the nineteenth century, they have been made and served there by street vendors, traditionally in waxed paper cones. The popular snack food traveled quickly to France and then to England, where they are referred to as "chips."

Corn Is Used to Make Corned Beef

Before the days of refrigeration, some beef was treated by rubbing thick pellets of salt, some the size of corn kernels (the salty equivalent of peppercorns), into the meat to facilitate preservation. Coarse salt is still used to pickle beef, so the *corn* in corned beef refers not to kernels of corn but to the kernels or "grains" of salt used in the preparation process.

You Should Only Eat Oysters in the *R* Months

The notion that oysters should only be eaten in the *R* months (September through March) may have begun in the days before refrigeration, when oysters were shipped at temperatures that could cause them to spoil. These days the old adage can, for the most part, be ignored. However, at certain places in the South, some people still avoid eating oysters harvested locally in the summer (in the non-*R* months). The reason is that in some southern climes the oysters grow in places where they are covered by water only during high tide but not at low tide. This exposes them to the sun, making the bacteria count (and the possibility for illness) greater in warm weather.

Very Rare Steaks Are Filled with Blood

The bright red juice that one sees dripping out of uncooked meat and steaks cooked very rare is not blood—although it's a close relative. The explanation for this requires that the reader endure a quick lesson in high-school biology.

Oxygen is conveyed through the body by the bloodstream in a chemical called hemoglobin, an iron-based compound that is responsible for blood being red. Many animals, however, need that oxygen in their muscles much faster than the circulatory system can deliver it, so they store another iron-based compound called myoglobin in their muscles. When a very fast reaction is needed by muscle tissue—say, when running away from a predator—the muscles utilize the myoglobin while the "real stuff," the hemoglobin, is en route.

It is this myoglobin that oozes out of the meat we eat and not blood (which was disposed of in the slaughterhouse). There is actually almost no blood in a very rare steak. Also the less an animal requires a quick burst of energy, the less it needs myoglobin—and the lighter (in both color and weight) the meat.

Spinach Makes You Strong

Spinach isn't a high-energy food, and it doesn't have an exceptionally high concentration of iron. Although Popeye (being a cartoon character) could consume the vegetable and rapidly become stronger, it doesn't work in real life. In fact, the body doesn't even absorb most of the nutrients found in spinach.

If you were to rely on spinach alone for your daily requirement of

iron, you would have to consume twice your body weight of spinach each year—and simply ingesting large amounts of iron will not make you strong. Consuming too much spinach will also load you up with large amounts of oxalic acid, which could concentrate in the urine and cause kidney stones.

Wine in Screw-Cap Bottles Is Inferior

Unscrewing a metal cap may lack the seasoned éclat of popping a cork, but screw tops on wine bottles are almost certainly the wave of the future. True, screw caps in the past were associated with cheap, low-end wines—but now it is clear that the once-elegant corks have a deal-breaking downside. To an increasing degree, a mold that grows in corks has been contaminating wine with trichloroanisole (TCA), a compound that leaves up to ten percent of wines tasting musty and flat. The twist caps, called stelvin lids, leave the wine untainted, and their acceptance has gathered considerable momentum among producers, sellers, and connoisseurs alike.

Vodka Won't Give You a Hangover

The theory is that all spirits contain "congeners"—impurities such as esters, aldehydes, methanol, etc.—which are responsible for causing hangovers. Clear beverages such as vodka and gin contain fewer congeners than darker ones, and fewer congeners mean fewer (or less nasty) hangovers. There is some truth to all this, but congeners are not the only cause of hangovers. The main one is dehydration: alcohol is a diuretic that sucks the water out of your cells, resulting in headaches and general discomfort. Alcohol also irritates the gastrointestinal tract, which can bring on nausea or diarrhea.

White Wine Comes from White Grapes, and All Red Wines Improve with Age

Although many white wines come from white grapes (such as Chardonnay and Sauvignon Blanc), the pale color of white wine has nothing to do with the color of the grapes used to make it. When red grapes (such as Pinot Noir and Zinfandel) are used to make white wine, the skins are removed before fermenting, leaving only the colorless inside portion. Red wines get their color because the dark-colored skins are left in the mix throughout the fermentation process. Leaving the skins in for only part of the process yields wines that are pinkish in color, or "blush."

Many people think that red wine always gets better with age. However, most red wines produced today are not meant to be aged for many years and should be consumed within a year or two of bottling. Keep in mind that wine isn't static: the fermentation process is ongoing, so that the wine is always changing. A bottle of red wine today will taste different a year, a month, or even a day later.

In fact, a character in *Sideways*, the classic film about wine-tasting (among other things) in northern California, describes wine as nothing less than "a living thing." Real-life wine-lovers often utter the same phrase.

Yams Are the Same as Sweet Potatoes

Nope, they are two different plants from two different botanical families. Sweet potatoes are native to South America, and yams to Africa and Asia. But the vegetables we call yams—the ones we buy in this country—are not true yams. They are a variety of sweet potato that happens to have orange flesh.

So how did this name mix-up get started? Marketers trying to sell the orange variety of sweet potatoes in the U.S. wanted to distinguish them from regular white-fleshed sweet potatoes, so they intentionally mislabeled them "yams" (from the West African word *nyami*). Today, the government requires that they be labeled "sweet potato yams." So who eats the real yams? In tropical areas of Africa, Asia, and Latin America, they are a starchy staple about as common as regular potatoes are here. True yams can grow up to seven feet long and weigh up to 150 pounds.

Health and the Body

All the Cells in the Body Are Replaced Every Seven Years

Not quite. Some cells in the body are replaced fairly often, while others take much longer to be replaced—and there are some that are never replaced but last as long as you do. To be specific, some blood cells have lives measured in hours; the visceral cells of some internal organs are replaced every few days; and

not replaced, and that is the nerve cell—the neuron. The cells in your brain and nervous system are yours for a lifetime—you die with the cells you were born with. The question is why—what adaptation made it advantageous for these cells to not be replaced—especially when, as is the case with other cells, it would

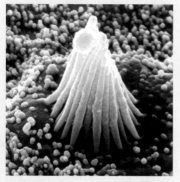 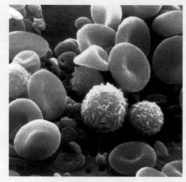 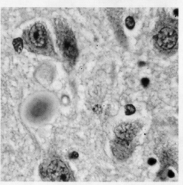

From left: hair cells (sensory receptors in the auditory and vestibular systems of all vertebrates); scanning electron microscope [SEM] image of human blood, showing red and white blood cells; brain cells (made up of neurons and glial cells).

red blood cells last about four months. The skin is completely replaced (cell by cell) roughly every month, and the cells of the skeleton are replaced every ten years. In a typical lifetime, therefore, you will "have" about a half-dozen or more skeletons and up to one thousand skins. But there is one type of cell that is

seem advantageous for them to be replaced. Since we locate sensations, memory, and consciousness in the neurons (in some as-yet imperfectly understood way), might there be some aspect of an enduring sense of identity that is enhanced by the fact that neurons are unreplaced? I suppose we'll find out eventually.

Bubonic Plague Is a Thing of the Past

Known as the Black Death, which killed millions throughout Europe in the Dark Ages, the bubonic plague (transmitted from rats to fleas to humans) has recently made a few curtain calls. A pandemic of the plague occurred, mainly in India, between the 1890s and the 1920s. And between 1900 and 1910, the disease was discovered in San Francisco, possibly transmitted from rats aboard a ship from Hong Kong. In the 1970s, an outbreak occurred in war-torn Vietnam, killing some 4,000 people a year.

Since the 1960s, more than 1,500 cases per year

have been reported internationally by the World Health Organization, mainly in developing countries in Africa and Asia. Even in the U.S., an average of about a dozen or so cases per year have been reported in recent decades.

Unlike the Dark Ages, the twenty-first century has the resources to treat the disease, so fatalities may be markedly reduced. Some contend, however, that unless we make renewed efforts—by developing new antibiotics and more effective pest control—another pandemic may be in the offing.

A Man Can't Get Pregnant

There is no recorded case of it happening outside of the magical world of movies, but according to David Bodanis, science writer and former lecturer at Oxford University, it is actually possible for a man to carry a fertilized egg to term.

Bodanis has written about the process that would be involved, including the necessity of a moist tissue to latch onto with suitable blood supply. His theory is based on cases where eggs have slipped out of fallopian tubes in women and wound up attached to the pelvic wall. In most cases, nine months later a healthy baby was delivered via cesarean section. Based on this, if supplied with the proper hormones, a fertilized egg should be able to survive and grow within a man in one of the following locations: the "greater omental fat pad," the bladder, the peritoneum, or the "kidney capsule."

Even though a man can't get pregnant in the traditional sense, he can, if given the right amount of hormones, carry a healthy baby to term and give birth through a cesarean section. The lingering question, however, is what man would ever want to do this, and why? Feminist wags have joked that if the human race ever had to depend on men to give birth (and it may now be possible), there'd soon be no human race.

Men Don't Have Any Estrogen

A common misconception widely held is that testosterone is the male hormone and estrogen the female hormone, and never the twain shall meet. But the fact is that all men and all women have both hormones in their bodies. An imbalance between the two can cause a number of problems, including a less-than-satisfying sex life. As men age, their testosterone levels decrease and their estrogen levels increase. In some cases, testosterone supplements may be appropriate, but the benefits should be carefully weighed against the risks.

The Cesarean Section Was Named after Julius Caesar

The word "cesarean" derives not from Julius Caesar (right) but from the Latin word *cadre*, to cut. It's easy to understand why the procedure was associated with the emperor, since "Caesar" and "cesarean" sound alike. More to the point, some historians say Julius Caesar himself was delivered that way. Others insist he was not. Go figure.

Birth Rates Go Up Nine Months after a Blackout

In spite of the many rumors that spread of a spike in the birth rate in the New York area nine months after the blackout of 1965, the actual birth rate dipped during that period. Snuggling in candlelight might seem romantic, but the fact is emergencies like storms and power outages increase anxiety, and that is not conducive to the process of baby-making.

Carrots Improve Your Night Vision

Carrots do provide beta-carotene, transformed by the body into vitamin A, which is needed for night vision. But lots of other foods provide vitamin A, so carrots aren't particularly helpful in that way. If you have normal night vision, more carrots or more vitamin A won't improve it. However, if you are deficient in vitamin A, carrots may help you to see at night, as will lots of other foods rich in vitamin A, including liver, cantaloupe, sweet potatoes, spinach, mangoes, egg yolks, and mozzarella cheese. Another source of the vitamin, of course, is a vitamin pill.

The association between carrots and night vision may be traced to World War II, when British pilots were supposedly given lots of carrots to help them see the enemy in the dark. Tests conducted at the time indicated that the body uses as much vitamin A as it can and disposes of the excess. So eating more carrots than the body can use won't help anyone's vision. British pilots and antiaircraft gunners shot down lots of Nazi planes during the war, but their success was due not to the carrots but to a new radar technology, which the Germans didn't have. Naturally, the British wanted to keep their secret from the enemy, so they used the carrot story as a smoke screen.

The Color-Blind Can't See Color

Not true. The phrase "color-blind" is misleading, because most people who are so labeled can see most colors. Typically, people with this genetic condition (more common in males than females) can't tell the difference between red and green, because certain color receptors in their eyes are missing. They can drive safely, however, because they can see which light is flashing, and on a stoplight red is at the top and green is on the bottom. Another form of color-blindness affects yellow-blue perception, but this is very rare. Rarest of all is achromatic vision, or the inability to see any color. For those with this condition, life is like a black-and-white movie.

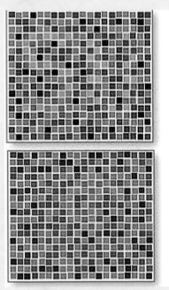

Ishihara color test plates. The numbers and letters (from top left: 58; 18; 17; E) should be visible to people with normal vision.

Coffee Sobers You Up after Drinking Alcohol

Drinking coffee won't get rid of the alcohol in your system. Only time and your liver can do that. Coffee will, however, make you more alert. So if you find yourself in a situation where falling asleep could harm you or someone else, drinking coffee may help you to stay on your toes. Also, since the passage of time is what really sobers you up, drinking coffee may help for the simple reason that it takes some time to drink.

If You Burp and Fart at the Same Time, You Will Die

This ridiculous notion, which falls into the category of kid lore, is usually conveyed with an air of authority, amazement, and grave admonition from one young boy to another (girls don't have much truck with this sort of thing). That the same "little-known fact" is sometimes passed along tongue-in-cheek from a prankish adult to a gullible child may provide a clue as to how the whole thing got started. In other words, it probably began as a mildly sadistic, intergenerational joke—a third cousin, perhaps, to Santa Claus and the Easter Bunny but more disgusting. The number of bodily functions that need to happen at the same time in order for you to die varies with the version you happen to hear. The simplest includes only a burp and a fart. More elaborate renditions include a burp, fart, sneeze, cough, and hiccup.

You Can Catch a Cold from Cold Weather

All the scientific studies say cold itself does not give you a cold. You have to be exposed to a rhinovirus, of which there are hundreds. Okay, but won't being cold compromise your immune system so that you're more likely to become susceptible to a virus? Studies say not, but personal experience may lead you to believe otherwise. So why do more people catch colds in the winter? The usual answer is that people spend more time indoors, hence they are more exposed to each other's viruses. The more complete answer is that the air indoors is much less humid in the winter, drying out noses and throats, so fewer viruses are intercepted by the protective mucous membranes. Also, many cold viruses thrive better in drier air, and in winter this creates more opportunities for exposure.

The rhinovirus is responsible for 50% of all cases of the common cold.

We Dream in Black and White

We all can dream in color, but some people may have an occasional dream in black and white. Psychologists have suggested that the notion of black-and-white dreams got started in the mid-twentieth century, when black-and-white photos, films, and TV dominated the media.

Those who claim they dream only in black and white may be basing their assumption on the *memory* of their dreams. Less vivid than the real thing, the memory of a dream may consist of vague, shadowy images in hazy gray tones—tones that do not reflect the colors that appeared in the original dream. Colors that one specifically notices while dreaming—a bright red scarf, an iridescent lizard—are more likely to be remembered when one wakes up.

Some People Don't Dream

It's true that some people don't *remember* their dreams, but tests show conclusively that every person dreams—and does so at least four to six times a night. Dreaming, known in sleep labs as REM (rapid eye movement) sleep, is essential for processing experiences that have accumulated during one's waking hours; hence dreaming is unavoidable. Tests also show that people are more apt to remember a dream if they have it later in their period of sleep and closer to the time when they wake up. Also, the longer a dream is, the more of it the dreamer will remember. So how long *are* dreams? Longer than the few minutes we often think they are. Dreams can last from a few minutes to half an hour and, in rare instances, more than an hour.

A Nightcap before Bed Will Help You Sleep

Sure, having a drink or two before retiring will help you *fall* asleep. But you won't sleep very well. The sedating effect of alcohol is only temporary. After a couple of hours, other effects start kicking in that disrupt sleep. They include shallow sleep, tossing and turning, frequent awakenings during the night, sleep apnea, waking up too early in the morning, and feeling tired the following day. The more you drink before bedtime, the worse the consequences.

Dieting Shrinks Your Stomach

Dieting for several days in a row decreases your appetite, but it's not because your stomach gets smaller. Your stomach can't shrink, no matter how little you eat. It can get bigger if you stuff it with food, but once the food is gone it returns to its original size. Actually, frequent overeating can stretch a stomach by a small percent, and this will mean more food will have to be ingested to fill the stomach to the top, where the nerve receptors that tell the brain you're full are located. But this change in stomach size is not large enough to make a difference.

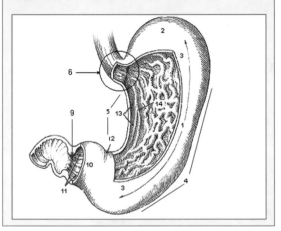

Everyone Is Born Either Male or Female

Not every baby is born male or female. One out of a hundred is born somewhere in between, with physical characteristics (especially genital organs) that belong to both sexes. And one or two out of a thousand have such pronounced sexual ambiguity that surgery may be considered as an option.

Sexually ambiguous people used to be called hermaphrodites (from a combination of the Greek god Hermes and the goddess Aphrodite), but these days the term has mostly been replaced by "intersexual" or "intersexed." (In contrast, the term "transsexual" refers to someone born male or female who surgically switches to the opposite sex. The term "transgender" is a much broader term that may or may not refer to intersexuals, depending on who is using it.)

In this country alone, there are hundreds of thousands of people who, to a greater or lesser extent, can be classified as intersexuals. So where are they? Why don't we hear more about them? For the most part, due to ignorance, intolerance, and abuse on the part of the general public—and the personal shame and fear that it prompts in people who are "different"—intersexuals tend to remain in the closet.

Hair and Nails Keep Growing after Death

It may look that way to someone who makes a point of periodically checking up on the grooming attributes of corpses, but it's not the case. It's an illusion caused by the shrinkage  of skin around the nails and hair. After death, dehydration makes tissues recede, exposing more of the nails and hair than was visible when the person was alive and kicking (and trimming).

Only Women Can Get Breast Cancer

Men get it too, though much more rarely. Why? All people, men and women, have breasts. The tissue does not normally develop in boys as it does in girls, but it's still there. Roughly 1,500 men develop the disease every year (compared with more than 200,000 women), and about a third of those men lose their lives. The average time between the first symptom and diagnosis is more than a year and a half for men—much longer than for women—partly because men are not ordinarily expected to get breast cancer.

Your IQ Is Fixed at Birth

An IQ (intelligence quotient) is simply a score obtained from taking a particular IQ test at a particular time under particular circumstances. Many people think of the score as absolute and fixed at birth—a characteristic as immutable as one's face or fingerprints. The truth is that IQ varies with age, health, thinking habits, and life experiences. It also depends on the test one takes. A score of 120 on one test may translate into 110 on another test and 130 on yet another. If one takes a test at age twelve and the same test at age eighteen or twenty-five, the scores may be quite different. If one takes a test this year and again next year after taking courses that have sharpened one's reasoning skills, the score may jump considerably.

Also, IQ tests tend to confine themselves to logical, verbal, and mathematical intelligence—a rather limited approach. Psychologists (Howard Gardner, among others) maintain there are many other kinds of intelligence that conventional IQ tests ignore (such as observational, organizational, philosophical, spatial, kinesthetic, musical, interpersonal, emotional and spiritual, and multiple subdivisions within each of these broad categories). So how seriously should we take IQ tests? Just remember that scores are never etched in stone, and the tests reflect a relatively narrow segment of a much broader spectrum of abilities.

Reading in Poor Light Will Hurt Your Eyes

Everyone has heard this from Mom, along with the advice never to go swimming right after lunch because you will get a cramp and drown. But for the most part, reading in low light will not hurt your eyes. It can strain them, leading to such temporary discomforts as soreness, headaches, or blurred vision, but these effects soon subside. On the other hand, it should be noted that some eye experts claim that habitually reading in dim light over the course of months or years can make you more nearsighted—especially if you are young or are somewhat nearsighted already.

You Can Get Leprosy from Touching a Leper

In books and movies, leprosy is a creepy, macabre, incurable disease that makes your flesh rot and causes your fingers and toes to fall off. It is supposedly so contagious that you can get it merely by shaking hands or rubbing elbows with a leper. As a public health precaution, those afflicted had to be confined to leper colonies, where they lived out their grim and hopeless lives until they finally succumbed to the disease.

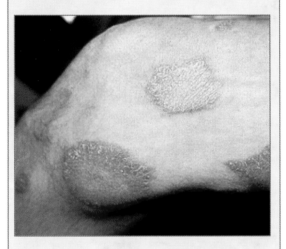

Well, all of the above is false. Leprosy, also known as Hansen's disease, is not very contagious. Caused by a slow-growing bacterium related to the one that causes tuberculosis, the disease affects the skin, nerves, and mucous membranes. It may cause skin lesions, numbness, and some disfiguration, but nothing like what is described above.

As of 1982, leprosy is considered curable through a treatment that uses a mix of several medications to defeat the disease-causing bacteria. For the milder form of the disease, a six-month course of tablets is sufficient. For the more severe form of leprosy, the medication must be taken for two years.

To Avoid Being Hit by Lightning, It's Best to Lie Flat on the Ground

Decades ago it was standard practice to lie flat on the ground during a lightning storm because it was assumed that the lower you got, the safer you'd be. Now we know better: when lightning strikes the earth, it can create lethal electric currents in the ground up to one hundred feet from the point where it hits, and lying on the ground would make you more vulnerable to those currents.

So what to do? Assume what is called the "Lightning Crouch"—that is, crouch down on the balls of your feet (minimizing your contact with the ground) and cover your ears. This position will reduce your chances of being struck, but it won't guarantee your safety. The best plan of action is to go indoors.

Most Food Is Digested in the Stomach

The stomach serves as a food processor and storage unit. Contrary to popular belief, most of the digestion process (especially the absorption of food) occurs farther along, in the small intestine. Much larger than the stomach, the coiled-up small intestine, if unraveled, would be about twenty-two feet in length.

Fact is, digestion begins the instant food enters the mouth and continues right through every inch of the alimentary canal, shown at right.

The Mind Goes as You Get Older

The word "senility" comes from *senex*, the Latin word for "old." At one time, and to some extent even today, physicians and everyone else assumed that people's minds—particularly their memories—gradually failed as a natural part of getting older. But lots of anecdotal evidence contradicts this. And it's a fact that, for example, although Einstein's "miraculous year" (1905) took place while he was still in his twenties, he published his seminal paper on the paradoxes of quantum theory—a set of observations that

still agitates the world of physics—when he was in his fifties. Artists like Michelangelo and Frank Lloyd Wright (above) did their most ground-breaking work when they were well past sixty-five. As Dr. Richard Restak says, in *Mozart's Brain and the Fighter Pilot*, a well-exercised brain can perform better as time goes on.

Adorning the Neck with Rings Makes the Neck Longer

Adding metal neck rings incrementally between childhood and adulthood is a practice peculiar to the women of a tribe known as the Padaung, who live in Burma (Myanmar) and Thailand. One traditional answer to the question "Why?" is that tigers won't be able to bite them in the neck when they are wearing all that metal. The more common explanation is that a long neck with lots of rings on it makes a woman, to the Padaung anyway, more beautiful. Meanwhile, back to the question of whether rings make the neck longer. Anatomically, the answer is no. When rings are added over the years, the effect is not to stretch the neck itself but to force the collar bone downward until it reaches such a dramatic angle that it seems to be part of the neck. A woman may be carrying up to twenty pounds of rings on a "neck" that is up to fifteen inches long. If the rings were removed—a punishment for adultery—the woman's atrophied neck muscles would not be able to hold her head up, so it would flop to the side. Not surprisingly, adultery is extremely uncommon among the Padaung.

Cutting the Jugular Vein Causes Instant Death

In the first place, as a vein, the jugular carries deoxygenated blood away from the brain back to the heart, where it can then be pumped to the lungs to be oxygenated. So cutting the jugular will not cause the brain to be deprived suddenly of oxygen and thus be instantly lethal. Only if air enters the jugular and an air bubble (an "embolism") enters the bloodstream, causing a heart attack, will a cut jugular prove fatal. Second, there are several veins in the neck called jugular veins and if any one of them is severed, it can be treated with pressure if the cut is not too severe.

Finally, there are two arteries, called the carotid arteries, that send blood to the brain, and at high pressure, so that cutting of these vessels can cause a very quick death. The familiar phrase "going for the jugular," which of course conveys ferocity, should more properly be worded "going for the carotid." How, then, did "jugular" earn its place in common parlance? Possibly because the word somehow got substituted for "jugulum"—the part of the body where the neck meets the shoulders. To "go for the jugulum" would then simply mean "go for the neck." Or it may have come from an association with animal predators that attack their prey by going for the neck. Since the jugular is closer to the surface of the neck than the carotid, it is more accessible to the fangs of predators. Hence "go for the jugular" would seem quite logical as an expression of ferocity.

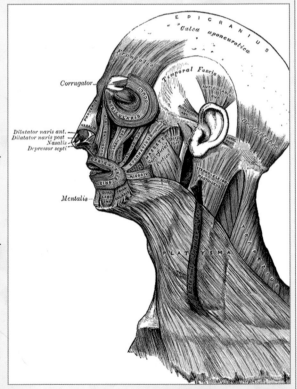

The jugular vein, highlighted. The carotid arteries are deeper in the neck and are protected in part by the neck muscles, making it more difficult to cut off blood flow to the brain.

Mummies Were Well Preserved Because the Egyptians Were Masters at Embalming

Egyptian embalming practices were elaborate, and not very affordable—unless you happened to be a rich man or a pharaoh. Hence not all that many dead Egyptians became mummies. Draining the body of fluids, removing waste matter from the intestines, and wrapping the body in absorbent sealant—all routine burial procedures today, were then practiced only on the wealthy. But the remarkably preserved mummies that have been unearthed in the last century owe more to the dry Egyptian climate and a lack of bacteria than to any lost art of embalming. In the sands of the desert, whole animals have been unearthed that were as well preserved as Egyptian mummies.

Egyptian embalmers may not have had many secrets, but they did develop techniques that we would recognize as scientifically valid.

Sharks Don't Get Cancer

Sharks have plenty to worry about from humans—from vengeful hunters who consider them evil, and from Japanese fisherman who slice off their fins for shark fin soup before dumping their carcasses back into the sea. Now we want their cartilage! The notion that sharks are naturally protected against cancer came from William Lane's 1992 book, *Sharks Don't Get Cancer,* which received what seemed like an endorsement from the TV program *60 Minutes.* The problem is that 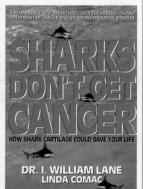 sharks *do* get cancer—they just don't get bone cancer because … they don't have bones. It's said that cartilage—the sinewy tissue that sharks have in lieu of bone—is less prone to cancer, but the evidence that sharks are resistant to cancer and other diseases is mostly anecdotal. There have been few, if any, scientific studies to confirm it.

Hair Can Go White Overnight

A normal adult's hair can go white in about a month, but nothing can turn a person's hair white overnight—not excessive worry or sudden fright—simply because hair that is already of a certain color remains that way until it is replaced by new hair, which may or may not be white.

Hair does sometimes seem to go white in a very short time, however. Genes play a huge role here, but stress might contribute as well. Recent studies have indicated that stress can accelerate the aging of the body's cells on a genetic level, and that includes hair cells.

Stress can also make hair fall out, so if you lose pigmented hair and are about to go gray anyway, the regrowth will reflect that. And there's actually some evidence that pigmented hair may be more likely to fall out than gray, meaning if you're so stressed your hair is falling out, your hair will not only be thinner, it will also be grayer.

Poison Ivy Spreads When You Scratch It

It may *seem* to spread when you scratch it, but it doesn't. Since some parts of the body have thicker skin than others, it takes longer for the plant's toxic oil to soak into the skin in those areas. The delay makes it appear that the rash has spread by scratching one area and then touching another. Furthermore, the liquid in poison ivy blisters does not contain any of the offending oil, so you can't spread it by breaking blisters and spreading the contents around. Remember also that poison ivy is not contagious, so you can't give it to a friend. Tip: after you touch the plant, the oil takes about fifteen minutes to soak below the surface of your skin, so if possible, wash it off quickly with soap and water. That way, you may avoid that awful itch that keeps on itching.

Suicides Are More Common at Christmas

Suicide is no more common during the winter holidays than at any other time. Studies reveal that the number of suicides during that period, supposedly brought on by loneliness and depression that spills over into self-destructive behavior, is average or below average. Hence it seems that this notorious bugaboo, which the media love to call attention to ad infinitum, is about as real as Ole Saint Nick.

In this quintessential holiday suicide movie, George Bailey(Jimmy Stewart) is about to throw himself into a river because of a series of adverse circumstances. But his guardian angel intervenes and reacquaints him with the meaning of life—and the will to live.

All Bacteria Are Bad for You continued opposite page

While humans are waging a war against the *harmful* bacteria of the world, they should actually be grateful for the majority of these microscopic cells. There are a multitude of bacterial species, most of which are helpful, or at least harmless. A bacterium measures about 0.5 to 1.5 microns, with one thousand microns in every millimeter. In the human body alone, the tiny bacterial cells outnumber human cells about ten to one. Outside the body, the skin is covered with bacteria, which help to keep out harmful bacteria—what we call germs. Inside the body, bacteria work with the body's chemicals in breaking down food, converting food into vitamins and minerals, and making sure intestinal walls can absorb nutrients for the blood-

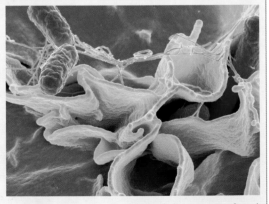

Bacteria are the most abundant of all organisms, found in soil, in water, and in virtually every living thing.

Testosterone Makes Men Compete, Get Mad, and Go to War

In the first place, the hormones produced by the body are very—and we should emphasize *very*—complicated, which makes a simplification like the one that follows virtually nonsensical. This much we can say:

We each have a set of hormones that interact with one another in ways that are not fully understood. Men and women both have—and need—testosterone and estrogen, the so-called female hormone.

Generally speaking, men have more testosterone in the bloodstream; women more estrogen. But that is only a generalization.

An imbalance in either direction—too much or too little of either hormone—can lead to behavioral shifts and changes. That means that too little testosterone can cause aggressive behavior, *as* can too much. The same is true of estrogen.

The brain converts testosterone into estrogen through the action of an enzyme called aromatase. In men, too much or too little estrogen produced from testosterone (just like too much or too little testosterone alone) can trigger aggressive behavior. Confused yet? As you can see, "complicated" is an understatement.

Gum Takes Seven Years to Digest

It is true that gum is not completely digestible by the human body, but, like other foods, it is expelled from the body. Sorbitol, sometimes used as a sweetener in gum, can even act as a laxative, which would actually help the movement of gum through the bowels.

The idea that chewing gum would sit and collect in the stomach because of its supposedly protracted digestion period probably comes from a widespread—but quite mistaken—notion about the size of the stomach. Ads depict the stomach as a rather large organ, taking up most of the midsection of a person's body, and much of what we call the stomach is actually small intestine.

In fact, the stomach is relatively small, thus unable to collect and store food that can't be digested relatively quickly. If the gum (or anything else) were to just sit there, it wouldn't take long for someone who chewed and swallowed a pack of gum a day to have nothing but gum in his stomach—and he would be unable to eat any other foods for the seven years it would take to digest all that gum.

• • • • • • •

stream to circulate. Without bacteria, we couldn't digest food. Also, exposure to harmful bacteria is necessary for the body to build up the resistance required to fight disease. When germs enter the body, they trigger the formation of antibodies to fight them. Some doctors believe that the current rise in the incidence of asthma and allergies in the U.S. is due to the oversterilized world children grow up in today. Their bodies aren't exposed to enough harmful germs to prompt the formation of disease-fighting antibodies. They are ill-prepared to deal with an invading dust or pollen particle, for example, because they have not developed the "T-helper-1" cells that make antibodies for allergens.

Bad bacteria, in the form of *E. coli*, salmonella, and cholera, affect the intestines. They also cause strep throat, pinkeye, and pneumonia. The bacteria that infect the inside of the body, such as *E. coli*, are killed only by properly cooking food and by treating water. Antibacterial soap and other disinfectants are helpful in killing other harmful bacteria, and the germs that cause pneumonia are easily killed with regular soap.

Ironically, antibacterial soap kills not only the bad bacteria (germs) on the skin but the helpful bacteria as well, and it prevents any new bacterial growth for at least one day. This may open the door for other harmful bacteria to invade the body, so care must be taken to guard against new infection.

Teeth Are Made of Bone

They may look and feel like bones, but teeth are made of other stuff—in fact, four different kinds of other stuff. Enamel, the white coating on the outside of the tooth, is the hardest substance in the body. Under the enamel is dentin, a yellowish, bonelike tissue that contains a few nerves. At the center of the tooth is the pulp (also called "the nerve"), which is made up of blood vessels and lots of nerves. Cementum, the fourth ingredient, is the substance under the gum that anchors the rest of the tooth to the jawbone.

You Can't Sneeze with Your Eyes Open

A bodily reflex makes most people close their eyes when sneezing, even when they try hard to keep them open. Some people, however, are wired differently and are able to keep their eyes open during a sneeze. No one knows exactly why, for the vast majority of people, sneezing makes the eyes close. But since the reflex involves the eyes, it may be related to the "photic sneeze reflex," which makes some people sneeze when their eyes are exposed to bright sunlight.

Tarantulas Are Poisonous

Because of their size and their horrifically hairy appearance, these giant spiders are more likely to scare you to death than harm you. It turns out that tarantulas are generally docile creatures that bite only when provoked, and their bite is no worse than a bee sting. In fact, some people even keep them as pets. So are tarantulas dangerous at all? In medieval Italy, it was believed that a tarantula bite affected the victim's nervous system, causing him to flail

wildly. Out of this belief came a lively folk dance—aptly called the *tarantella*. Strictly speaking, tarantula venom is not toxic. But like bee venom, it may (very rarely) cause an allergic reaction in some people. Harmless as they are, tarantulas continue to invoke the fear factor—big time. In film after film—*Dr. No, Raiders of the Lost Ark, Arachnophobia*—tarantulas are the quintessential scary spider. If they were a little smaller and not so hairy, the creatures would probably—in Hollywood anyway—be out of a job.

Normal Body Temperature Is 98.6°F

In fact, the body temperature of a healthy person will fluctuate during the day and will vary from day to day. Body temperature generally rises in the afternoon to about 99°F and will drop during sleep to 97°F. The body temperature of a woman will vary according to what part of her menstrual cycle she is in at the moment.

When "normal" body temperature was first defined, it was determined that the average temperature is somewhere between 98° and 99°F. Since thermometers were calibrated by fifths of degrees and not tenths, 98.6 was picked instead of 98.5.

Sex before Athletics Saps One's Ability to Compete

Many a coach has made "No sex before the game" a virtual commandment. And many a player over the years has made a habit of abstaining before a competition, believing that sex saps one's strength and determination. The supposed explanation, at least for male athletes, goes something like this: sex uses up testosterone, the hormone that makes a player aggressive; therefore abstinence will keep the stuff at a level that will allow him to play better.

Recent science has come up with another take on the matter—namely, that sex before a game actually *increases* the level of testosterone in the blood. So wouldn't that argue *for* playing around before playing?

The consensus these days—from sources claiming to be backed up by hard science—is that sex before the game does not make any difference one way or the other. But here's an afterthought based on what happens in nature: whenever male

animals in the wild (bucks, chimps, walruses, etc.) compete with each other—often waging ferocious battles, sometimes to the death—it's all about winning females, right? So suppose a buck had sex with a doe right before a big battle with another buck. Wouldn't it be reasonable for the buck to think, "I'm really not up for a fight right now—I already got lucky today, so I think I'll just chill and back off." Speaking of getting lucky, note that one of the more extraordinary NBA stars, Wilt Chamberlain (above), claimed to have had sex several times a day, *every* day, for years on end without it putting a dent in his performance on the court.

The Appendix Is Useless

The appendix, a slimy sac located between the small and large intestines, measures about a half-inch in diameter and is about three inches long. Although it isn't necessarily one of the body's most vital organs, it does still play a beneficial role.

Primates use their appendix to digest fiber and raw meat, suggesting that early humans used it for similar purposes. Although it is no longer required for this kind of specialized digestion, the appendix is far from useless.

The appendix makes endocrine cells in the fetus soon after conception. Endocrine cells secrete certain hormones that help with the development of the baby. After birth, the main purpose of the appendix is warding off disease as a lymphoid organ and producing white blood cells and antibodies. The organ is continually collecting and expelling food from the intestines; expos-

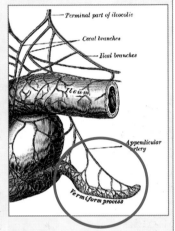

The appendix: an organ in search of a function. One indication that the appendix is a holdover from our evolutionary past is that only anthropoid apes have appendixes; other primates do not.

ing the white blood cells to bacteria, viruses, drugs, and bad food; helping the white blood cells to "learn" how to fight potentially fatal bacteria. Important as it is, this function of the appendix is dramatically reduced after a person reaches the age of thirty.

When food gets stuck in the appendix, it can cause an infection that can be fatal if not removed, especially if the organ bursts. While the body can function fine without an appendix, doctors have recently realized the organ's potential for reconstructive surgery, such as during bladder replacement. Appendix tissue can be used to re-create a sphincter, to replace a bladder, and to serve as a substitute ureter.

The Toilet Was Invented by Thomas Crapper

This one lends an amusing twist to the celebrated array of surname-career coincidences, standing alongside such fortuitous examples as a neurologist named Brain, a journalist named Pressman, a priest named Pope, etc. With a name like Crapper, he's perfectly matched for a career in toilets, right?

Thomas Crapper was a real person, an Englishman, and he was in the plumbing business, but the mechanism of the modern toilet was invented by Albert Giblin, an employee of Crapper's who allowed his boss to build and market the device under his name. Crapper's business flourished in the early half of the twentieth century, when cities were growing larger and, more important, sewer systems were being developed to transport waste to remote locations. After all, there is little point flushing anything down a toilet if it has nowhere to go.

The term "crapper" (for toilet) became popular in World War I, when American soldiers saw the name "T. Crapper—Chelsea" stenciled on British toilet tanks and didn't realize it was the manufacturer's actual name. The company was a thriving business well past World War II but shut its doors in the late 1970s. In any case, one can't deny that Thomas Crapper, in one way or another, lived up to his celebrated name.

Creative toilets on display at Seattle's Bumbershoot festival, 2005. Thomas would be proud.

Tetanus Starts with a Puncture Wound

Catching tetanus may be facilitated by a puncture wound (the result of stepping on a rusty nail, say), because the bacteria that cause this horrific disease thrive in places where there is little oxygen. However, the bacteria (which are found in the feces of sheep, cows, horses, dogs, cats, rats, and chickens) can contaminate not only puncture wounds but other kinds of wounds as well—such as cuts, abrasions, lesions, and lacerations. So avoid sharp surfaces the next time you visit a farm—and watch where you step.

Only Humans Have Belly Buttons

A belly button, or navel, is a scar where the placenta used to be attached via the umbilical cord. So any mammal nourished by a placenta before birth has one. This includes quite a lot of animals—rodents, sheep, cows, horses, dogs, cats, armadillos, whales, and bats, to name a few. And, of course, our fellow primates are all "placental" as well.

So why don't you see a belly button on your dog or cat? Because navels on most mammals are very faint scars, and they're often covered by fur. Sometimes, however, they take the form of a hairless line on the animal's underside.

Urine Is Unclean—and Thus Undrinkable

People generally look upon urine as a waste product, but this is not the case. Urine is sterile when it leaves the body and is safer to use to clean a wound than water from a polluted source. Urination is the body's way of regulating the concentration of electrolytes and key minerals in the blood.

Urine has long been used as a folk remedy for everything from athlete's foot to cancer, and imbibing one's own urine has been advocated by experts in both the East and the West. Some Western physicians believe urine contains substances (antigens) created by the body's own immune system that can, if ingested, help the body fight cancer and other diseases. Though this practice is highly controversial, a large body of anecdotal evidence suggests there is something to "urotherapy," which focuses on ingesting products derived from or contained in (one's own) urine.

In the East, Indian yogis have practiced the ritual of *amaroli* (drinking one's own urine) for centuries. They believe that urine contains elements that relax the body and promote meditation—and it actually does, in the form of the hormone melatonin. Also, some three million Chinese, convinced that the liquid contains important nutrients, drink a cup of their own urine every day to stay healthy.

Another more obvious benefit of the practice is avoiding dehydration. Someone caught in a desert or adrift at sea could survive longer by drinking his own urine—as the Kevin Costner character did in *Waterworld*. Incidentally, urine is not foul-smelling when it first leaves the body. The objectionable odor is caused by bacteria that enter the urine from the environment and break down its constituents.

Boys' Voices Change at Puberty, but Girls' Voices Don't

Androgens make the voice box grow larger in puberty, lowering the voice—and this is true of both sexes. The difference is more dramatic in boys, whose voices drop about an octave or so. Girls' voices also drop, but only about a quarter of an octave. The difference is magnified when they sing: men deliberately try to produce deep tones, while women aim for the higher end, in keeping with traditional sex roles vis-à-vis musical expression.

Arts, Sports, and Entertainment

The America's Cup Is Named for the United States of America

This most prestigious regatta is named not for a country or even a continent but for a boat. In 1851, a sailing vessel named *America* won the 100 Guinea Cup, awarded to the winner of a race around the Isle of Wight. The winners, members of the New York Yacht Club, donated the trophy to the Club, which was to hold it as a "challenge" trophy.

Oddly enough, although the Cup's name dates to a nineteenth-century seafaring vessel and the event took place in the British Isles, the United States does happen to dominate the event. Only three nations other than the United States have won what is often called the oldest trophy in international sport.

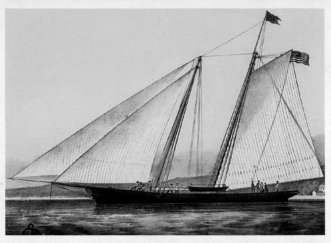

The America's Cup competition namesake, the yacht *America*, as painted in 1851 by Currier and Ives.

Ben-Hur Is a Biblical Figure—and a Stuntman Was Killed during the Filming of the 1959 Movie *Ben-Hur*

Charlton Heston may have enlivened the silver screen with his dynamic chariot-racing skills in the 1959 epic, but the man he portrayed never drew a breath. In the 1880 novel *Ben-Hur: A Tale of the Christ,* by Lew Wallace, Ben-Hur is a fictional Judean aristocrat who, during the reign of the Roman Emperor Tiberius, is enslaved after being betrayed by his Roman friend Messala. Embittered upon his emancipation, he is redeemed after encountering Jesus and witnessing his crucifixion.

Ben-Hur, the 1959 motion picture (other versions were made in 1907, 1925, and 2003), is no stranger to the misconception mill.

A rumor persists that a stuntman was killed during the filming of the chariot scene. While this story seems to have a life of its own, including the claim that director William Wyler left the death in the final cut, no one was killed or seriously injured during the filming of the chariot scene.

The only injury suffered was by Charlton Heston's stunt double, Joe Canutt, who incurred a gash on his chin when he was thrown out of a chariot during the race sequence. Canutt received four stitches and went back to work.

Cinderella Wore Glass Slippers

I've always wondered, where does anyone get glass slippers? In all versions of the folktale—a European tale with over five hundred variants and a version in virtually every culture—Cinderella wears glass slippers and drops one at the ball, but were they really supposed to be made of glass? Scholars have noticed that nearly all versions of the story in which the slippers are made of glass are derived from a French version in which the slippers are made from ermine—Old French for which is *vair*. Many believe a translator, Charles Perrault, who published the story in an anthology, *Tales of Mother Goose* (1697), probably mistook *vair* for *verre*, French for "glass"—with the same pronunciation.

But I suspect it's not that simple. There's something about the slippers being made of glass that has made that detail an endearing and enduring one. Glass is fragile, which means the prince has to take special pains to guard and protect it as he goes looking for the missing debutante.

Nineteenth-century engraving of Gustave Doré's *Cendrillon*.

Humphrey Bogart Tells the Pianist to "Play It Again, Sam" in the Film *Casablanca*

It may be one of the most famous and oft-quoted phrases from American cinema, but Humphrey Bogart never spoke the line. In this 1942 classic, Bogart's Rick crosses paths with his lost love, Ilsa (played by Ingrid Bergman). When Ilsa enters Rick's club she approaches the pianist, Sam: "Play it once, Sam, for old times' sake." Sam lies and replies that he does not know what piece she is referring to. She asks him again, and he reluctantly plays the song "As Times Goes By." Rick, not aware of Ilsa's presence, rep- rimands Sam for playing the song. Later, alone with Sam, he says, "You played it for her and you can play it for me. If she can stand it, I can! Play it!" And that's as close as he gets.

Woody Allen later wrote a play and then a 1972 movie entitled *Play It Again, Sam* in which a nebbishy divorced man receives dating advice from the ghost of Humphrey Bogart. Allen said he was fully aware that the line was never uttered by Bogie in the film but that he thought it funny to perpetuate the myth.

The Brooklyn Dodgers Were Named for Their Deftness on the Diamond

Because of the proliferation of trolley lines in old Brooklyn, which made it a challenge to get around on foot, residents of the borough were jokingly called "trolley dodgers." Despite whatever dodging may have occurred on the playing field, the team was named for the dodging that players and fans alike had to do on the way to the stadium.

Ebbets Field, Brooklyn, New York, circa 1913, the year the stadium opened. It was demolished in 1960, three years after the Dodgers moved to Los Angeles.

The *Encyclopaedia Britannica* Is British

Inspired by the Scottish Enlightenment, the *Encyclopaedia Britannica* was born in Edinburgh in 1768. But as of nearly a century ago, the revered reference has been owned, manufactured, and distributed by Americans. Between 1920 and 1943 it was the property of Sears & Roebuck of Chicago, which sold the encyclopedia through its famous mail-order catalog. Afterward, the *Britannica* was owned by a series of individuals and private corporations, but its home remained (and still remains) in Chicago.

Count Dracula Was a Fictional Character

He may not have slept in a coffin or sucked blood from the necks of his victims, but he was just as murderous and bloodthirsty as the Hollywood Dracula—perhaps even more so. Bram Stoker's Transylvanian castle-dweller was based on a real-life Transylvanian castle-dweller also called Dracula. His given name was Vlad IV, and he was a fifteenth-century nobleman assigned the honorific "Dracula," meaning "son of the dragon" or "son of the devil." (His father, Vlad III, prince of Walachia, a region in southern Transylvania, was known as Vlad Dracul, or "Vlad the Devil," so it seems Vlad IV was a chip off the old block.)

He was popularly known as Vlad the Impaler (depicted at right) because he had the corpses of his enemies—which included Turks, corrupt merchants, beggars, and whomever he regarded as criminals, traitors, or undesirables—mounted on sharp wooden stakes for all to behold.

On one occasion, in order to discourage an advancing army of Turks, he impaled more than twenty thousand Turkish prisoners and placed them in the path of the marching soldiers. At one point in his career Vlad was imprisoned for his horrific deeds. In his confinement, with no humans to impale, he was rumored to have impaled mice (some habits are hard to break, it would seem).

The Tombstone of W. C. Fields Reads, "On the Whole, I'd Rather Be in Philadelphia"

Everyone has heard one or another version of the famous curmudgeon's supposed epitaph, each of which implies that Fields had little love for his native City of Brotherly Love. The epitaph has appeared in a number of different forms, including "I'd rather be here than in Philadelphia," "On the whole, I'd rather be in Philadelphia," and "All things considered, I'd rather be in Philadelphia."

So what is actually inscribed on his grave at Forest Lawn Cemetery in Glendale, California? Simply this: "W. C. Fields, 1880–1946." Where, then, did all the "Philadelphia stories" come from? Actually, from the lips of Fields himself. As recorded in a 1925 *Vanity Fair* article, he appropriated a well-traveled quip of the day and proposed that his own epitaph read: "Here lies W. C. Fields. I would rather be living in Philadelphia."

During his final days in a hospital, Fields was seen reading the Bible. When asked why, he replied, "I'm checking for loopholes."

Chinese Checkers Came from China

Played with marbles on a star-shaped board, the game of Chinese checkers couldn't be less Chinese.

Depending on whom you ask, the game originated in Germany, England, or Greece. The German version was called Halma, which is Greek for "jump" (the players use marbles or pins to jump over other marbles or pins). When it reached the United States in the 1920s, the game may have been given its present name simply because "Chinese" sounded intriguingly foreign, making people curious enough to buy it.

That a seemingly Far Eastern origin has the effect of stimulating buyer curiosity was evidenced again in the unexpected popularity of the puzzle, Sudoku.

Grimm's Fairy Tales Were Created by the Brothers Grimm

The Grimm brothers, Wilhelm and Jacob, did not make up their famous fairy tales (among them "Cinderella," "Sleeping Beauty," "Little Red Riding Hood," "Hansel and Gretel," "Snow White," "Rapunzel," and "Rumpelstiltskin"—all well-known classics.)

The tales were passed down orally by German peasants from one generation to the next. The contribution of the Grimm brothers was to collect them, record them, edit them, and publish them for posterity. The Grimm brothers also included in their collections French folktales which would otherwise have been lost.

The Guitar Was Invented in Spain, the Banjo in the American South, and the Ukulele in Hawaii

Funny how a musical instrument can become so embraced by a place and its culture that it seems the instrument must have been invented there. (See the entry on bagpipes.) This is especially true when the instrument is relatively easy to construct. The guitar, many believe, originated in Spain, evolved into the banjo in the American South, and then morphed into the ukulele in Hawaii. The historical record says otherwise. First, let's agree that a guitar is not a harp with a hump. Harp-like (and lyre-like) instruments go back to antiquity and are depicted in wall drawings from ancient Egypt

and Mesopotamia. The innovations introduced by the invention of the guitar included (a) stretching the strings over a sounding board, (b) adding a neck to allow for longer strings (hence deeper sounds), and (c) greater variability in the string length (hence wider range).

The pandoura, a lute-like instrument, was common throughout the ancient Near East at least a thousand years before the Common Era. If to the definition of the guitar one adds the hourglass shape and the frets, then the earliest such instruments seem to have appeared in Turkey—in bas-relief sculptures in Alaca Höyük—and in Coptic Egypt five hundred years later.

The Moors are credited with bringing the *guitarra* to Spain (from North Africa by way of Italy) in the sixteenth century. The earliest treatise on playing the guitar is a Spanish work dated 1586. The instrument flourished in Iberia as nowhere else from the Middle Ages on.

Now the banjo—constructed like a guitar but with a closed, skin-like (vellum or parchment) sounding board and often an open back—is often believed to have originated in the South, yet Thomas Jefferson noted in his *Notes on Virginia* in 1784 that "the instrument proper to them [Africans] is the Banjar, which they brought hither from Africa …" The diaries of many seventeenth-century British explorers describe banjars (also called "banza," "banshaw," and other variations) throughout Africa and the Middle East.

Joel Sweeney, a white Southern peanut farmer who claimed he had learned to play the instrument by watching slaves on his Virginia plantation, developed the modern five-string banjo. Sweeney performed the melodies he had learned, and soon others were performing in blackface. The early blackface concerts were developed to re-create an authentic African cultural experience—it was not until after the Civil War that they degenerated into the mean-spirited, racist minstrel shows of the 1890s.

The ukulele was brought to the Hawaiian Islands by Portuguese sailors who had come to work on the plantations being developed there. The instrument, known in Portuguese as a *cavanquinho* or *bragha*, was easy to pack and provided perfect accompaniment for folk songs the sailors sang—especially a song known as *machete* (also the word for a long saber-like knife). The instrument itself then became known as a machete (which could spell a dangerous source of confusion) but was later known as a ukulele. The word "ukulele" comes from the nickname of Englishman Edward Purvis (the word means, roughly, "the jumping flea or runt"), who popularized the instrument in the Islands in the late nineteenth century. The instrument became a favorite of flappers in the 1920s.

The Gutenberg Bible Was the First Printed Book

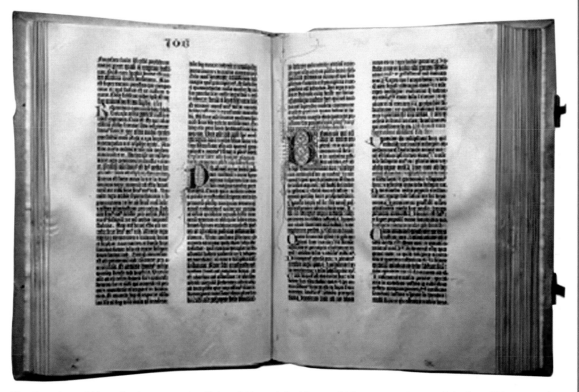

The Gutenberg Bible—also known as the 42-line Bible and the Mazarin Bible—is a rendering of the Latin Vulgate translation of the Bible. The printing took place on February 23, 1455, marking the beginning of the age of print in the West.

Gutenberg produced the first printed book, right? Nope, books were printed in China during the sixth century using a block printing technique. Okay, then Gutenberg was the first to print a book using movable type, right? Nope, the Chinese were using movable type by the twelfth century. Okay, then the Gutenberg Bible was the first book printed (in the 1400s) with movable type in Europe, right? Nope, Gutenberg's first book was not the Bible but a schoolbook on Latin grammar called *Ars Minor*. Then why is the Gutenberg Bible such a big deal? Because it was the first practical, mass-produced, widely distributed book of its kind, and the methods of production developed by Gutenberg marked a media milestone that changed the world.

Then when exactly *was* the first printed book created? Well, in the early twentieth century, a British adventurer named Sir Aurel Stein excavating in the city of Dunhuang, China, for the British Museum uncovered a library that barbarians had walled up a thousand years earlier. The library contained Buddhist works of all kinds, but among them was a Chinese edition of the *Diamond Sutra*, printed in 868 CE—the oldest printed book yet found. (The technique of using movable type for printing arrived a bit later.)

This singular volume is attributed to Bi Sheng, a Sung (Song) Dynasty scribe who perfected the technique in the 1040s—four centuries before Gutenberg.

Joseph Heller Titled His Novel *Catch-22*

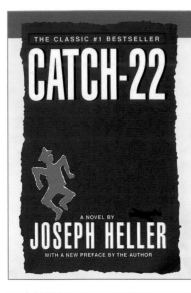

The well-known novel about World War II, published in 1961 and followed by a movie in 1970, was not given the title that its author, Joseph Heller, intended. He had titled the book *Catch-18*, because eighteen begins with a vowel and, when pronounced, eighteen follows more smoothly after the word "catch." At about the same time, however, Leon Uris was coming out with a book called *Mila 18*. To avoid confusion between the two books, Heller's publisher suggested he change the title to *Catch-22*, and Heller agreed.

(*Publisher's Note:* If any reader knows—really knows—why *Catch-22* was chosen and not, say, *Catch-21* or *Catch-23*, we'd love to hear from you. The editorial meeting during which the number was arrived at is potentially one of the most interesting—and at the same time possibly one of the funniest—of all time.)

Hollywood Became America's Film Capital because of Its Weather

Sure, the weather was one factor—Hollywood's warm climate made it easy for filmmakers to shoot outdoors year-round. And Southern California's diverse topography (mountains, beaches, lakes, and ocean) meant that they had a variety of landscapes at their disposal to film movies whose plots and settings called for varying geographic features.

But thrift probably trumped weather. Hollywood at the time wasn't exactly the wealthy enclave it is today, and the area was a vast desert of cheap real estate. Cheap labor too—then, as now, California was home to large numbers of Asian immigrants.

Perhaps most alluring, though, was Hollywood's proximity to Mexico. What did that have to do with anything? Well, Mexico is a handy destination for someone on the lam—which a lot of filmmakers were at the time. They were illegally using technology patented by Thomas Edison, and Edison's Motion Picture Patents Company, formed in 1909, took a very hard line against those who challenged its monopoly.

Today, most of the major studios that once dominated the area's economy have relocated elsewhere. The famous "Hollywood" sign remains, though. The sign, by the way, was never meant to be an emblem of the movie industry or even the town. Originally built in 1928, it was not even intended to be permanent. It originally read "Hollywoodland" and was an oversize novelty ad for Hollywoodland Realty; the "land" part eventually fell off, and the sign was never removed.

The original "Hollywoodland" sign had nothing to do with the film industry.

The Harlem Globetrotters Are from Harlem in New York City

This most famous of exhibition basketball teams did not originate in Harlem, nor were any of the team's original members from New York. The team started in the Negro American Legion League as the Giles Post. Abe Saperstein, a Chicago-based promoter, bought the team and renamed it the Savoy Big Five, named after their sponsor, Chicago's famous Savoy Ballroom. The deal with the Savoy eventually fell apart. The team went through another name change, becoming Saperstein's New York Globetrotters and, later, the Harlem Globetrotters. So, where did the name Harlem Globetrotters come from? Saperstein, ever the promoter, wanted to capitalize on having a traveling team of black ballplayers. Harlem, being the center of African-American culture, provided an instant signal as to the makeup of the team. Additionally, Saperstein wanted potential audiences to think that his team had traveled the world—hence, Globetrotters.

Although the team initially played the game seriously, it languished for competitors when the Globetrotters began beating their opponents by fifty or one hundred points. As a result, the team began playing in a more theatrical fashion, becoming the clown princes of basketball. This mix of comedy and athleticism won the team international fame … and new teams to play.

Eugene "Killer" Edgerson of the Harlem Globetrotters goes for the slam-dunk over the heads of the Nationals at the San Diego Sports Arena.

Ice Hockey Is the Official Sport of Canada

Although hockey is one of Canada's most popular sports, its players are among the best in all the world, and the sport's official museum is located in Toronto, lacrosse was named the national game of Canada in 1867.

A form of lacrosse was played by native North Americans and went by a variety of names: *dehuntshigwa'es* in Onondaga ("men hit a rounded

Toronto Maple Leafs playing against Detroit Red Wings, Stanley Cup Playoffs, 1942.

object"), *Tewaarathon* in Mohawk language ("little brother of war"), and *baaga'adowe* in Ojibwa ("bump hips"). Noting the similarity between the sticks used to play the game and the crosier (a hooked staff carried by Catholic bishops), French traders named the game *la crosse*. A final note: even if Hockey isn't the official sport of Canada, it might as well be.

The Olympic Gold Medal Is Made of Gold

Nope. The last time Olympic gold medals were made of pure gold was in 1912. These days the "gold" medals are made of silver and plated with gold. (The silver ones are also plated—with silver, naturally.)

Gold medals, clockwise from top left: 2002 (Salt Lake City), 1998 (Nagano), 1992 (Albertville), 1994 (Lillehammer).

Mister Rogers Was a Navy SEAL

You would never have suspected that gentle Mister Rogers was a Navy SEAL. Or that our lovable "neighbor" was a sniper who chalked up forty-two confirmed kills while serving in Vietnam. Or that he wore a long-sleeved sweater on his television show to cover up the dozens of racy tattoos he got while in the service. Well, you would never have suspected all this for good reason: he never was or did any of those things (and he definitely didn't look the part). With Mister Rogers, there were no big surprises. What you saw was what you got. Trivia tidbit: "McFeely" was Fred Rogers' middle name.

Lassie Was a Female Dog

Beginning with Pal in 1943, all the dogs that played Lassie in the movies or on TV were female impersonators—i.e., males. Hence Pal and his successors helped keep alive a venerable theatrical tradition stretching from the days of Shakespeare to the days of drag queens.

But seriously, male collies were used to play Lassie for good reason. Before spaying became commonplace, female collies tended to "blow coat" when in heat—that is, they would shed profusely and quite noticeably, making for a shabby appearance on the tube or silver screen. Male collies don't blow coat, or don't do so nearly as much, so they had a more well-groomed look. Also, male collies outweigh females by at least ten pounds, lending them a more commanding presence on screen.

Lassie filming on location in Florida.

Marisa Tomei Won the Academy Award Because Jack Palance Announced the Wrong Name

After the 1993 Academy Awards ceremony, a rumor began to circulate that Marisa Tomei (below), who won the Oscar for her role as Mona Lisa Vito in the comedy *My Cousin Vinny*, received the award erroneously. Different versions of the story assert that Palance either was unable to read the printing on the card, became confused, or was too intoxicated to announce the correct name. He then either arbitrarily announced Tomei as the winner or called out her name because it fell last in the list of nominees and thus had not yet scrolled off the teleprompter screen.

However, there are several safeguards in place to ensure that such a mistake is virtually impossible. The people from Price Waterhouse, who are the official tabulators of the Academy Award ballots, are present at every award ceremony. If a wrong name were ever read, one of the officials from Price Waterhouse would come to the podium and announce the correct winner.

Further, Palance could not have read the wrong name from the teleprompter screen, because the winners' names are never displayed there. Every time the phrase "and the Oscar goes to …" is spoken during the ceremony, the teleprompter displays only the stage directions, namely (envelope) and (announce winner), to the presenters in order to keep the winner's identity a secret.

So why was Marisa Tomei the focus of such a bizarre tale? Although the source of the rumor has never been unearthed, the most likely reason for the rumor's formulation was the belief by some that Tomei and her role were too slight to merit her winning an Academy Award over the other nominees (Joan Plowright, Miranda Richardson, Vanessa Redgrave, and Judy Davis), who were established performers appearing in more dramatically substantial films.

The Polka Originated in Poland

The name "polka," which embraces both the dance style and the musical genre, did not originate in Poland. The dance first arose among peasants of eastern Bohemia. "Polka" is derived from the Czech word for "half," *pulka*, referring to the half-step or the abbreviated, lively footwork characteristic of the dance. A number of dance historians attribute the polka's creation to Anna Slezak, who formulated the dance while listening to the song *Strycek Nimra Koupil Simla* ("Uncle Nimra Brought a White Horse"). Joseph Neruda, upon first seeing the

dance, asked the young woman to repeat it. Impressed with both the song and the footwork, Neruda introduced the dance to Prague in 1835, where it became a sensation.

The polka continued on its world tour during the 1840s, reaching Paris and then sweeping across the dance floors of Europe and the United States. It was in post–World War II America that Poland and polka became intimately linked, because Polish immigrants adopted the polka as their "national" dance.

Richard III Was an Evil Hunchback

The Richard III depicted in Shakespeare's play of the same name was a vile fellow who happened to be a hunchback; he was so ugly that dogs barked at him as he passed. Historically speaking, no one knows just how vile he was, but Richard III was definitely not a hunchback—the hump appears to be purely a Shakespearean invention.

In fact, contemporary portraits of the monarch reveal a guy who was not that bad looking. Predictably, a British society dedicated to rescuing Richard III's reputation from Tudor calumnies was founded in 1924. It was known as The Fellowship of the White Boar (Richard's emblem was a white boar). An American branch was founded in 1969.

Stan Was Dumber than Ollie

In all their movies, Stan Laurel played the dumb one and Oliver Hardy played the . . . less-dumb one. Off-screen, however, Stan was anything but intellectually challenged.

Early in his career, Stan was an understudy to comic genius Charlie Chaplin, and he excelled as a writer, director, and actor both before and after teaming up with Hardy.

Unlike Stan, Ollie was not a writer or director, but he was a talented singer. Early in life he avoided formal education by repeatedly running away from school. So who was the dumber of the pair? Probably no one really cares. But one of Stan's lines on the subject, directed at Ollie (perhaps even written by Stan), is unforgettable: After Ollie harangues him, Stan says defiantly, "I'm not as dumb as you look."

Edison Invented the Phonograph to Bring Music to the Masses

Contrary to popular belief, Thomas Alva Edison, the father of the lightbulb, did not invent the phonograph as a means of listening to music. Edison was actually partially deaf and had no use for music. The phonograph was invented in 1877 in order to facilitate the use of the newly invented telephone. Edison had helped Alexander Graham Bell in perfecting the telephone with his invention of the transmitter. But Edison was convinced that the telephone would be too expensive to be put into the homes of average Americans.

Thomas Edison with early version of phonograph.

So Edison invented the phonograph, or what he called the "telephone repeater," by shouting verses from "Mary Had a Little Lamb" into the machine, which he was then able to play back and hear.

Even though the phonograph wasn't useful in conjunction with the telephone, the American public still enthusiastically embraced it—and the telephone turned out to be affordable after all.

The *Titanic* Accident Was a Complete Surprise and Could Never Have Been Anticipated

Few people know about the book written by American novelist Morgan Robertson called *Futility*. The book was about a ship called the *Titan*, the largest ship in the world and supposedly unsinkable. One would assume that Robertson was simply (not so subtly) alluding to the *Titanic* disaster of 1912, except for the fact that the book was written fourteen years prior to the accident.

The ship in Robertson's story was similar to the actual *Titanic* in almost every way. They were both triple-screw and could reach about twenty-five knots. The fictitious ship was 882.5 feet long, while the real one was 800 feet long. Fully weighted, the *Titanic* weighed about 66,000 tons; the *Titan* weighed 70,000 tons. Both had a maximum capacity of 3,000 passengers and were not equipped with enough lifeboats because they were reputedly unsinkable.

The sinking of the *Titanic* stunned the world for many reasons, including the loss of life and because most of the passengers on board had been rich and famous. But because experts had declared the ship unsinkable, none believed that such an accident could occur. The ship, both in real life and in Robertson's novel, represented the best of modern society, and both shocked the world when they sank on a cold April night after hitting an iceberg in the Atlantic Ocean.

The Keys on a Typewriter Keyboard Are Arranged Specifically for More Efficient Typing

The odd arrangement of letters on a typewriter keyboard is actually intended to slow down typing. Original typewriters couldn't keep up with the speed of typists, and typewriters would constantly jam as a result. So the letters had to be arranged in such a way that people would be forced to slow down when they typed. This is known as the QWERTY keyboard after the first six letters on the upper left. According to research, any other keyboard arrangement would actually be easier for typing than the QWERTY arrangement.

Originally, the inventor of the typewriter, Christopher Latham Sholes, laid out the keys in alphabetical order. He soon realized that the keys would jam if typing occurred at a great speed because too many frequently used letters were placed too close together. So the QWERTY system was developed to place the most frequently used letters as far apart on the keyboard as possible. Sholes publicly (and falsely) claimed that the QWERTY system was scientifically devised to promote efficient typing.

In 1936, August Dvorak invented a more efficient keyboard, but by then the QWERTY keyboard had been so widely accepted, it was too popular to be replaced.

Washington Crossed the Delaware as Depicted in the Famous Painting

The famous painting *Washington Crossing the Delaware,* by German-born American painter Emanuel Leutze, was painted in the 1850s and contains many historical errors. The painting was actually completed in Düsseldorf, Germany, and Leutze used the Rhine as a model for the river.

The first error involves the flag flying in the front of the boat. The flag in the painting has thirteen stars and stripes, a design that wasn't adopted by Congress until 1777, even though the depicted event took place in 1776. Second, the small and filled-to-capacity boat in which the future president of the United States is riding probably would not have been so small or crowded. Washington had actually collected many Durham boats from the Pennsylvania side, and these were about forty to sixty feet long, much larger than the one in the painting. The boats wouldn't have been crowded because there were more than enough boats to go around, just not enough soldiers to fill them. Also, Washington wouldn't have been standing, and certainly not in the bow of the boat holding such a dramatic pose. Leutze painted the soldiers holding their guns with barrels pointed upward, which would not have been smart because of the precipitation in the form of sleet that had been falling from the sky that morning.

The purpose of the painting was probably to stir up the Germans during their own revolution in the nineteenth century. Historians agree that Leutze hoped that celebrating a victorious and inspiring moment of the American Revolution would help bring about revolution against the conservative government in Germany. Unfortunately, the painting didn't have such inspiring results.

Uncle Tom of *Uncle Tom's Cabin* Was an "Uncle Tom"

Used less often these days than it was back in the sixties and seventies, the term "Uncle Tom" was derogatorily applied to African-Americans who sucked up to white folks. Far from the obsequious stereotype, the Tom of Harriet Beecher Stowe's novel is a figure of great compassion, patience, and dignity—even nobility. Although he is always polite to his masters, he will not obey orders he considers to be wrong. He is downright insubordinate on some occasions, though perhaps more in the manner of Gandhi than of a reckless mutineer. Even so, the Uncle Tom character in the novel is a far cry from the kind of fawning sycophant to whom his name was later applied.

"Webster's" Dictionaries Are the Most Authentic

Noah Webster, who died in 1843, was the American lexicographer par excellence. But because names and titles can't be copyrighted, lots of dictionary publishers since Webster's time have appropriated his name without any direct connection to the man or his work. After all, if it's got Webster in the title, it must be the real thing, right? Not necessarily. The closest thing to the real McCoy is produced by the Merriam-Webster Company, which bought the rights from Webster's heirs to create revised editions of the original classic. Oddly enough, Webster had called his magnum opus *An American Dictionary of the English Language*—a title that did not include the word "Webster's."

James Whistler's Most Famous Work Is Entitled *Whistler's Mother*

This American-born artist's most famous painting is not, nor has it ever been, titled *Whistler's Mother*. True, the 1871 work *was* of his mother, Anna McNeill Whistler, but it was titled *Arrangement in Grey and Black, No. 1: Portrait of the Painter's Mother*. (*Arrangement in Grey and Black, No. 2* was a portrait of Scottish philosopher and historian Thomas Carlyle.) However, once the painting of his mother achieved a level of fame, Whistler renamed it *Portrait of My Mother*. Although the work seems somewhat conservative in its design, Whistler experimented throughout his career with impressionistic styles and colors, and was much less interested in classic draftsmanship.

Van Gogh Cut Off His Ear

The popular myth about painter Vincent van Gogh is that he was a raving maniac who sliced off his own ear. Like the severed ear itself, however, the amount of truth to this legend is only partial. When his close friendship with painter Paul Gauguin had begun to sour, the two argued a lot, usually after they drank a lot. At one particularly tense moment, on Christmas Eve, 1888, Van Gogh grabbed a razor and went after Gauguin. Of course he ended up using the razor on himself instead—by his account, as a sign of remorse but possibly to relieve the constant ringing in his ear (tinnitus) caused by Ménière's disease—but he didn't slash off his entire ear, just the lobe and a little extra. Van Gogh then wrapped the bloody thing in newspaper and presented it to Rachel, a local prostitute he loved, imploring her to take good care of it (excuse me?). Understandably, Gauguin made himself scarce and never spoke to Van Gogh again. The authorities failed to see either the humor or the romance of it all and promptly placed Van Gogh in an asylum.

"Woodstock" Happened in Woodstock

The famous music festival that took place in 1969 and which has become known as "Woodstock" never took place in Woodstock, New York. Not that the promoters of the festival didn't try. Woodstock was where two prominent participants in the event, Bob Dylan and members of The Band, owned homes, and the company that was formed to stage the concert was called Woodstock Ventures. But the town wouldn't grant the necessary permits, and the organizers had to look elsewhere. After looking in neighboring towns without any luck, they arranged to hold the event on a farm owned by Max Yasgur in Bethel, forty miles away. Yasgur claimed the organizers had kept the enormous scope of the event from him and tried to back out, but last-minute "negotiations" saved the day. Two twenty-fifth-anniversary concerts were staged in 1994—one on Yasgur's farm, called "Bethel '94," and the other in the town of Saugerties (about fifteen miles away). It was called "Woodstock '94."

The Body of an Actor Who Hanged Himself Can Be Seen in the Background of *The Wizard of Oz*

This amazing falsehood has persisted for years but came into its own as a legendary slice of film trivia during the rise of the VHS tape. The story has undergone a metamorphosis over the years. Originally, it was attributed to a stagehand being caught on the set after the cameras started rolling (or, more spectacularly, a stagehand's falling out of a prop tree into the scene). With the advent of home video, viewing audiences were able to rewind and replay the scene in question, view it in slow motion, and look at individual frames in the sequence. The focus of the rumor shifted from a hapless stagehand to a lovelorn Munchkin driven to suicide.

So, what is it that viewers see in the background? According to Stephen Cox's book *The Munchkins of Oz* (1996), a creature of the feathered variety is the most likely culprit. To give the indoor set used in this sequence a more rustic feel, several birds were borrowed from the Los Angeles Zoo and allowed to roam the set. At the very end of this sequence, as the three main characters move down the road and away from the camera, one of the larger birds (often said to be an emu but more probably a crane) standing at the back of the set moves around and spreads its wings. No Munchkin, no hanging—just a big bird.

Additionally, the forest scenes in *The Wizard of Oz* were filmed before the Munchkinland scenes, so none of the Munchkin actors—including the one who is supposed to have died—would have been present on the set.

The Song "White Christmas" Was Introduced to Audiences by Bing Crosby in the Movie *White Christmas*

This song—inextricably associated with Christmas, patriotism, and nostalgia for a simpler era—is among the best-selling singles of all time. The origins of the song date back to early 1940, when Irving Berlin (who had never celebrated the holiday himself) wrote it for the film *Holiday Inn*, released in 1942 and starring Bing Crosby and Marjorie Reynolds. The first version was Bing Crosby's December 1941 recording— which, serendipitously enough, was released at the perfect time to be embraced as a kind of holiday anthem for U.S. soldiers dreaming of returning to the comforts of home and family (the song was invariably requested whenever Bing sang for troops). He recorded the song again in 1947, as the master had by then been damaged by overplaying. The new version far surpassed the original in sales and is the one most often played today.

In 1954, *White Christmas*, essentially a remake of *Holiday Inn*, was released, capitalizing on the song's unprecedented success and the popularity of the earlier film. *White Christmas* eventually became the more well-known movie, thus cementing its association with the song in the public memory.

"White Christmas" isn't the only song whose origin is incorrectly attributed to a popular movie. "As Time Goes By," of *Casablanca* fame, was actually written in 1931 by Herman Hupfeld for the

Promotional poster for the 1942 film *Holiday Inn*, starring Bing Crosby and Fred Astaire.

Broadway musical *Everybody's Welcome*. A 1931 Rudy Vallee recording of the song enjoyed some popular success, but Dooley Wilson recorded the version immortalized in *Casablanca*.

"Yada Yada Yada" Was Coined on *Seinfeld*

As used on the *Seinfeld* TV show by Jerry, Elaine, George, and other characters, the phrase is uttered at the end of a statement that the speaker is mercifully trying to cut short so as not to bore the listener. "Yada, yada, yada" simply means "and you know the rest" or "and so on and so forth" or "you don't want to know the details" or "blah, blah, blah."

So was the phrase used for the first time on *Seinfeld*? Some sources are confident that comic Lenny Bruce used the expression in the 1960s and that he probably picked it up from other Jewish comedians. They in turn inherited the phrase—or similar variants thereof—from the early days of vaudeville. Yada, yada, yada …

Places

The Arctic Is Always Cold

Usually, but not all the time and not everywhere. Summer temperatures within the Arctic Circle may reach into the high eighties Fahrenheit, but that's pretty rare. With recent global warming, creatures from more southern climes, such as mosquitoes and small birds, have been seen for the first time in Arctic territory. And polar bears, which need hefty chunks of surface ice in order to survive, are literally drowning as the ice melts. Climatologists warn that, within a few lifetimes, melting ice caused by global warming could raise the sea level by up to twenty feet, putting many islands—and even some large coastal cities—under water.

Antarctica, the fifth largest continent, is also the subject of misconceptions. People generally believe that Antarctica is a desolate, flat land covered with a thick layer of ice, but it has mountainous regions, exposed land, and forested areas on the coast. Also, Antarctica is colder than the Arctic by some twenty degrees Fahrenheit. Scientists believe this is because the watery foundation under the Arctic ice shelf keeps the Arctic warmer than Antarctica's frigid land base (for the same reason coastal areas have warmer climates). It's also the case that Antarctica is largely a plateau, so that the surface land is elevated by a few hundred feet. And the higher the elevation, the colder the air.

The Canary Islands Were Named for Canaries

Nope, it's the other way around. The yellow songbirds that live there were named for the islands. Okay, then how did the Canary Islands get their name? Ancient explorers discovered a breed of large, nasty dogs roaming the islands, and they came up with the Latin name *Insularia Canaria*, or "Island of Dogs." Later, people noticed that the island was home to a beautiful and distinctive breed of bird, so they named the bird after the island. To make a long story short (if it's not too late for that), the birds got their name from the islands, and the islands were named after the dogs.

A wild canary is about 4 to 5 inches long with yellow-green feathers and streaking on its back.

If You Dig Straight Down, You'll End Up in China

TRUE!   *by Daryl Cagle*

©Daryl Cagle; http://www.cagle.com

Source: L.A. Times quoting calculations by Lewis Carroll.

If kids could really dig a backyard hole to China (assuming that there is no friction) a kid could jump in and pop up on the other side 42 minutes later, 42 minutes after that he'll be back where he started.

The place that is located at the exact opposite side of the globe from another place is called its antipode. For example, the antipode for the North Pole is the South Pole. The antipode for most of the United States is not China but somewhere in the middle of the Indian Ocean. The antipode for China is the southern part of South America. Now that you know where you'll end up, you can start digging.

The cartoon at left, while slightly amusing, is incorrect on two counts: First, dropping straight down toward the center of the earth will not land you in China at the other end but in a much wetter place, namely the Indian Ocean. But even if you did hit some dry land at the other end, the trip would take much longer than forty-two minutes, because the force of gravity being exerted on you as you fall varies as you travel down the hole. As you fall, you are being acted on by less and less of the earth's bulk, or mass, which determines the degree of gravity you are subject to. Then, once you pass the center, or halfway point, the force keeps increasing until you reach the other end. But unless you have an antigravity machine, you won't get very far past the center of the earth.

The Sierra Nevadas Are in (Where Else?) Nevada

It may seem strange, but the four-hundred-mile-long Sierra Nevada mountain range is not located in the state of Nevada—not even a small part of it. It's entirely in California. Three of the nation's great natural attractions are located in this splendid area: Yosemite National Park, Lake Tahoe, and Sequoia National Park.

So why is it called that? Probably because Nevada was the last state the pioneers recognized before they tackled the mountains that stood between them and California, their destination.

Timbuktu Is a Fictitious Place

The name is used jokingly as the ultimate far-away-place-in-the-middle-of-nowhere. But the town is quite real, and it's not an inconsequential one at that. Also spelled Timbouctou, the city is located at the southern edge of the Sahara, about eight miles north of the Niger River in the nation of Mali. It was founded in 1100 and today is the home of three prestigious universities.

Another town that keeps being consigned to the realm of the mythical is Chelm—no doubt because of all the stories in Jewish folklore about the town's "wise men." The town is real, located in the southeast corner of Poland, just southeast of Lublin.

The Grand Canyon Is the Deepest Gorge in the United States

The Grand Canyon is the largest but not the deepest. That honor goes to Hells Canyon (also known as the Snake River Canyon and the Grand Canyon of the Snake), located on the border of Idaho and Oregon. At its lowest point, the Grand Canyon is about a mile deep, while Hells Canyon is about a mile and a half.

Above: The Grand Canyon is a steep-sided gorge carved by the Colorado River and is located in the state of Arizona. It runs about 277 miles long and ranges in width from 0.25 to 15 miles. At points along the way, it reaches a depth of 1 mile.
Left: Snake River Canyon is famous for Evel Knievel's 1974 attempt to jump it in his Skycycle X-2.

England and Britain Are Interchangeable Names for the Same Place

England is actually just one of the three countries, in addition to Scotland and Wales, that make up the island of Great Britain, often referred to as just Britain. The British Isles comprise Great Britain, Ireland, the Isle of Man, and the Channel Islands, Great Britain being the largest of the bunch. The United Kingdom is the kingdom of the British Isles, consisting of Great Britain, Northern Ireland, the Isle of Man, and the Channel Islands.

The term "English" applies only to England and its citizens, while "British" is used when referring to Great Britain and the United Kingdom (popularly dubbed "the UK").

The emerald-hued British Isles as seen from satellite.

The Great Wall of China Can Be Seen from the Moon— or at Least from Space

People who have been there (on the moon or in space) will confirm that the Great Wall can't be seen from up there. From the moon it is barely possible to make out continents, let alone a wall.

An associated myth is that the Great Wall is the only man-made object that can be seen from space—meaning from a low orbit. Not so. From a low orbit one can make out a number of things on the earth's surface, including highways, cities, railroads, ships, farm fields, and even a few large buildings. It is also possible to discern the V-shaped wakes of large ships—but not the ships themselves.

From the same vantage point, the Great Wall of China is impossible to see, because it is nearly the same color as the surrounding earth.

Below, the Great Wall of China; and at right, as seen from space via a NASA satellite (see arrow). The (unmagnified) false-color image is what makes the Wall visible; otherwise, it would not be possible to see.

The Word "Dixie" Comes from the Mason-Dixon Line

The origin of the word "Dixie," meaning the South, has never been determined for sure. But the theory that it stems from Jeremiah Dixon, one of the two surveyors who gave their names to the Mason-Dixon Line, is given the least credence by historians and lexicographers. Two other theories are regarded as more likely.

One is that Dixie originated with ten-dollar notes issued by a bank in antebellum Louisiana. The notes contained the word *dix* (French for "ten") and were known as "dixies." The surrounding area became known as Dixieland, a name that broadened to include the entire South.

The second theory has to do with a Manhattan slave owner named Johan Dixy. When slavery was abolished in the North in 1867, he relocated his slaves to the South. Dixy was unusually kind toward slaves, so "Dixy's Land" became synonymous with a kind of eden.

Whatever its true origin, the word "Dixie" was not popularized until the song "I Wish I Was in Dixie" (published in 1859) was performed repeatedly in minstrel shows. The song was written by an African-American

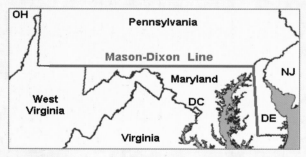

The original Mason-Dixon line.

man named Daniel Emmett. Ironically, he was a Northerner who was born and died in Mount Vernon, Ohio.

A popular misconception about the Mason-Dixon Line is that it extends across the entire continental United States, dividing North from South. In fact, however, the line was created to settle a series of land disputes between Pennsylvanians and Marylanders and was later extended to a distance of only 233 miles across the lower border of Pennsylvania.

Hong Kong Is a City

Officially, Hong Kong is not a city but a "special administrative region" of the People's Republic of China. As such, it contains a number of islands and a number of cities within it, including Kowloon, Tsuen Wan New Town, Sha Tin New Town, and Victoria City, which is located on Hong Kong Island. On the north shore of Hong Kong Island is "Central" (or Central District), where the tall buildings

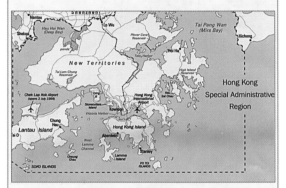

Above: Map of the islands that make up the special administrative region of Hong Kong.
Below: The city skyline of Hong Kong at night.

are located. Central is the historical, political, economic, and cultural heart of both the island and the special administrative region. Confused? You're not the only one. Depending on the context, "Hong Kong" can refer to a number of places: the city that is part of an island, the island itself, or the entire special administrative region.

Iran Is the Modern Name for Persia

Just the opposite: "Iran" is a name that goes back to antiquity, but "Persia" is of Greek coinage. The Greeks called the land Persia after the largest of Iran's provinces, Pars. "Persia" survived into the Middle Ages and right through modern times, when many Iranians felt the name "Persia" promoted the unwelcome westernization of their country.

Ironically, "Persia" took on an antiquated, neocolonial quality during the rule of the Shah, and "Iran" was perceived as the radically new name for the country once the Shah was deposed. But it is, in fact, the name by which the land was known since ancient times.

The World's Biggest Pyramid Is in Egypt

The world's largest pyramid is much closer to us than Egypt—it's just south of the border in Cholula, Mexico, near Mexico City. Now overgrown with vegetation, the pyramid appears to be a natural hill and is topped by a church built in the 1500s.

It took nearly eighteen centuries to build this Great Pyramid. Construction began in the second century BCE and ended in the early sixteenth century CE. It was dedicated to Quetzalcoatl, the feathered-serpent deity and one of the principal gods of many Mexican and northern Central American civilizations. The

Aztecs believed that Xelhua, one of the seven giants in Aztec mythology who escaped the flood by ascending the mountain of Tlaloc in the terrestrial paradise, built the Great Pyramid of Cholula.

So just how large is this structure? It has a base of 450 by 450 meters, a height of sixty-six meters, and a total volume estimated at 4.45 million cubic meters. Not only is it the world's largest pyramid, but it is the largest monument ever constructed anywhere in the world—almost one-third larger than the Great Pyramid of Giza in Egypt.

The Colossus of Rhodes Straddled the Ancient Harbor

One of the Seven Wonders of the Ancient World, this giant bronze statue of the god Helios was built in the third century BCE on the Greek island of Rhodes. About two-thirds the size of the Statue of Liberty, the Colossus was often depicted with one foot on either side of the entrance to the harbor. Supposedly, ships entering and leaving the harbor would pass between its "colossal" legs. However spectacular, the image is purely imaginary. The statue was real enough, but it was situated near the harbor entrance, not astride it.

We don't know exactly what the Colossus looked like, but we do know how it was built, because the builder, Chares of Lindos, left a record kept throughout the twelve years it took to build (292–280 BCE). First the feet were built—together or at least close to one another. Then dirt was placed around the feet so they were buried in the center of a mound. As each section was finished, the mound grew higher, burying the portion of the statue most recently completed. The figure apparently had a raised hand, perhaps holding a torch, because the head had also been buried in the

process (and this would have been unnecessary if the head were the top of the statue). When the structure was complete (almost entirely buried in the middle of a 110-foot hill of dirt), the dirt was removed, exposing the majestic Colossus.

Unfortunately, the Colossus stood for only a few decades before an earthquake reduced the wobbly wonder to a pile of rubble. Local citizens and tourists alike gawked over the ruins for centuries until the pieces were carted off, according to legend, on the backs of 900 camels by invading Arabs in the seventh century.

Above, left: Engraving of the statue of Helios.
Right: The statue as imagined in a sixteenth-century hand-colored engraving by Martin Heemskerck.

When You Use the Panama Canal to Travel from the Atlantic to the Pacific, You Travel East to West

That certainly makes sense—after all, the Atlantic Ocean is east of the Pacific Ocean, right? Not in this case, because the isthmus of Panama resembles a duodenum and turns, like a sideways *S*, so that at the Canal Zone, the Atlantic entrance to the canal is above and to the west of the Pacific entrance. That is, when you travel from the Atlantic to the Pacific, you travel southeast, and when you travel from the Pacific to the Atlantic, you travel northwest.

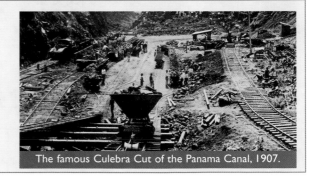

The famous Culebra Cut of the Panama Canal, 1907.

The Statue of Liberty Is in New York

Liberty Enlightening the World, more commonly referred to as the Statue of Liberty, has kept the torch of enlightenment raised in New York Harbor since its dedication by President Grover Cleveland on October 28, 1886. However, the true address of this iconic figure has been a matter of much debate.

The Statue of Liberty is located on Liberty Island, approximately a mile and a half southwest of the southern tip of the borough of Manhattan (in New York, New York) and 2,000 feet from Liberty State Park (in Jersey City, New Jersey). Based on proximity alone, New Jersey could lay claim to the Lady in the Harbor. However, one thing stands in the way—namely, the federal government, because Liberty Island is owned and operated by the National Parks Service.

Proponents for New Jersey as the statue's home turf cite Liberty Island's location on the New Jersey side on maps delineating the boundary between the two states. While the island's location in New Jersey is a geographical fact, the U.S. Supreme Court (in *State of New Jersey v. State of New York*, 1998) held that New Jersey retains only the rights to all the *submerged* land surrounding the statue, extending eastward to the boundary line between New York and New Jersey. But New Jersey does not have a legal claim on the land of Liberty Island above the water line.

While the island is geographically within the borders of New Jersey (check any map and you'll find it is closer to New Jersey than other islands that are indisputably within New Jersey), New York has several points on its side. According to the United States Geological Survey, Liberty Island is located in New York's Eighth Congressional District. If one wanted to call the Statue office, the number is (212) 363-2000 (with a Manhattan area code). And the mailing address is Liberty Island, New York, NY 10004.

So, on which state's land does the statue rest her pedestal? The argument may rage on, but, in the end, her heart belongs to Washington, D.C.

Red Square Is So Named Because "Red" Means "Communist"

Russia didn't become "red" in the Communist sense until 1918, but the name Red Square has been around since the 1600s. Its Russian name includes the word *krasnaya*, which can be translated as either "beautiful" or "red." It originally meant beautiful, referring to nearby Saint Basil's Cathedral—an ornate and colorful architectural wonder commissioned by Ivan the Terrible. Supposedly, after the cathedral was completed, Ivan blinded the architect, just to be sure he would never build anything as beautiful again. You've got to admit, Ivan had a pretty strange way of showing gratitude.

Red Square, Moscow, Russia, USSR, 1989.

Pennsylvania Was Named after William Penn

Actually, Pennsylvania was named after William Penn's father, Sir William Penn, who died in 1670. Penn senior had lent Charles II 16,000 pounds, and Penn the younger asked that the debt be repaid with land north of Maryland.

Pennsylvania, by the way, means "the woodlands of Penn." On the Liberty Bell, Pennsylvania was erroneously spelled "Pensylvania" (with one *n*) and then again misspelled when the Liberty Bell was recast—this time deliberately to make it as close to the original as possible.

Treaty of Penn with the Indians, by Benjamin West.

Mount Everest Is the World's Tallest Mountain

If the distinction of "world's highest mountain" were decided based on how far its peak protrudes upward from the center of the earth, then technically the prize would go to Chimborazo. Located in the Ecuadorian Andes, Chimborazo tops off at 20,561 feet above sea level. Everest ranks first—but only if height above sea level is the criterion.

Because the earth is not perfectly round and bulges at the equator, sea level at the equator is about fourteen miles farther from the center of the earth than at the North Pole. Located only two degrees from the equator, Chimborazo can add considerable distance to its "true" elevation and becomes the world's highest mountain—about two miles higher than Everest.

Mount Everest is located on the border between Nepal and China. It is called Sagarmatha in Nepalese.

Mount Chimborazo is a stratovolcano in the Cordillera Occidental of the Andes in Ecuador. Its last eruption is believed to have occurred sometime during the first millennium CE.

Famous Misquotations and Misusages

"OK" Originated with Andrew Jackson

Theories abound as to the etymology of this term, and its ultimate origin is still in question. What is certain, though, is that it did not originate with Andrew Jackson.

Martin Van Buren, during his campaign for the presidency, used the expression "OK" as a rallying cry; it was an abbreviation of his nickname, "Old Kinderhook" (the town he was born in). OK didn't originate with Van Buren, though. It was probably coined sometime in the 1830s as a joke—an abbreviation for "oll kurrect," an intentionally humorous misspelling of "all correct."

That OK was used ignorantly by Jackson was a slanderous rumor begun by Martin Van Buren's political enemies (Van Buren was a friend of Jackson's and a fellow Democrat). The rumor went that Jackson, while working as a court clerk, marked legal papers with "OK"—implying that by alluding to the "oll kurrect" misspelling, Jackson was borderline illiterate.

Not only was Jackson quite literate, he was also an attorney, a judge, a congressman, and a U.S. senator before he became president—but he was never a court clerk.

Attorneys Are the Same as Lawyers

The two terms don't neatly overlap in meaning. Strictly speaking, an attorney is a person legally empowered to act on behalf of another, as in "power of attorney." That person doesn't have to be a lawyer. A lawyer is someone professionally trained in the law—usually a law school graduate—who is authorized to give legal advice or represent another in court. An attorney who also happens to be a lawyer is formally known as an attorney-at-law.

"Cannes" Is Pronounced "Cahn"

The famed resort city on the French Riviera, home to the celebrated annual Cannes Film Festival, is often mispronounced "cahn," especially by Americans who are trying to pronounce the name in a way that sounds classy and educated. The fact is, in France and in most other places in the world, Cannes is pronounced "can," as in can of peas.

"Alibi" Means "Excuse"

Not exactly. *Alibi* is a Latin word meaning "in another place." In a court of law an alibi amounts to a claim that the person accused of a crime is innocent because he or she was in a different place at the time the crime was committed, and so could not have committed the crime. It does not mean that the person is simply excused from blame.

"Biannual" Means "Every Two Years"

Nope, biannual means twice a year, as does semiannual. Biennial means once every two years. While we're at it, biweekly means twice a week, as does semiweekly. But bimonthly means once every two months, and semimonthly means twice a month, as does fortnightly. Got that straight? Logic seems not to play much of a role here, and dictionaries will often list both, with one under "nonstandard" usage.

"Comprised of" Means "Composed Of"

The phrase is heard a lot, and there's no doubt about the intended meaning, but "comprised of" sounds ignorant and is simply bad English. The word "comprise" means "contain or include," as in "Her repertoire comprises a number of different dance styles." To say "comprised of" in this sentence is the same as saying "Her repertoire is included of a number of different dance styles." Ewww.

"Decimate" Means "Completely Destroy"

The original meaning of "decimate" was "to kill every tenth one." Over the years the word has come to mean something much more inflated, such as "to destroy a major part of," as in "Famine decimated the population."

This meaning has become acceptable, but when the word is used to mean "completely destroy or eliminate," as in "The dinosaurs were decimated by a meteor," it's just plain wrong.

It's Okay to Say "Different Than"

Mostly, it's not okay. In the vast majority of cases "different than" is wrong and "different from" is right. What's the reasoning behind this? "Than" is more at home in a comparative phrase: "Jim is bigger than Jeff," or "I can do anything better than you can." Since "different" is not ordinarily a comparative word like "bigger" or "better," "different than" sounds awkward to the seasoned ear. Case in point: "Apples are different than oranges" sounds ignorant. "Apples are different from oranges" sounds educated.

In the rare instances where "different than" is used in a comparative phrase, it's perfectly respectable. For example: "Venice is more *different than* any other city," or "Her eccentricity had always made her seem different, but after the sex-change operation she was even more *different than* before."

The grammar police won't arrest you if you say "different than," because lots of people do it these days. But usage snobs and others who know better may wince.

It's Always Wrong to Use a Double Negative

Mostly, but not always. So when is it wrong and when is it okay? Statements like "I didn't say nothing" or "It was so stuffy I couldn't barely breathe" sound ignorant. But a double negative is perfectly respectable in other kinds of statements, such as "The dog is not unfriendly" or "The puzzle is not unsolvable." This typically British way of speaking is known as "litotes"—for example, one might say that an experience was "not altogether unpleasant" or, more simply, "not bad."

The Drawing Room Was a Place to Draw Pictures

Primarily a British term that is no longer widely used, a "drawing room" in its original form was known as a "withdrawing room." It refers to the room in a household to which the owner, his wife, or guests could "withdraw" after dinner, say, for private conversation and relaxation—and perhaps to view works of art. Who knows—the collection may, coincidentally, include a few drawings.

FDR Coined the Phrase "The Only Thing We Have to Fear Is Fear Itself"

Sadly, we of the twenty-first century have come to expect very little book-knowledge of our elected officials—we automatically assume that any spark of eloquence or erudition has been provided by a speechwriter or advisor who toiled away while the candidate was off developing the social, negotiating, and argumentative skills necessary to win elected office. In earlier times, more was expected of office holders, and presidents were often judged on their education as well as their baby-kissing and blintz-eating. FDR was a particularly well-read president, having been educated at Groton, Harvard, and Columbia Law School. While FDR availed himself of an excellent team of speechwriters (such as Samuel Rosenman and playwright Robert Sherwood), he also had the literary tools to lend some savoir faire to his speeches.

The electrifying phrase that FDR uttered in his first inaugural address, on March 4, 1933, "The only thing we have to fear is fear itself," was indeed lifted—but precisely from whom is a question. Thoreau wrote in his *Journal* back in 1851, "Nothing is so much to be feared as fear," and similar statements can be found in the writings of Bacon, Montaigne, Wellington, and others. But what made FDR's delivery of the line unique and memorable was his timing—the slight pause after the first "fear." That pause conveyed the speaker's mastery and confidence, implying that whatever the object of our fear might be, it was well under control. When that object of fear turned out to be fear itself, the effect was dramatic: it managed to mitigate the collective worries of a desperate and depressed nation.

Above: Portrait of FDR.
Opposite page: FDR addressing Congress in 1938.

By FDR's day, misquotation became a bit more difficult. Virtually every speech a president made would be recorded for posterity, but speeches made before ascending to the presidency were another matter. Three famous Rooseveltian quotations uttered before he was elected have come under scrutiny and may have either never been uttered or been lifted from another source. The first is the phrase that signaled the coming of the New Deal and the federal government's determination to address the deprivations of the Great Depression: "One third of our nation is ill-fed, ill-housed, ill-clad." The phrase was taken from H. G. Wells (with "ill-clothed" for the last word), who used it in *In the Days of the Comet* in

1906. In fact, "New Deal" was hardly original with Roosevelt. The term was uttered by Lloyd George in 1919 and became his campaign slogan. Oddly enough, another speaker at the Democratic Convention in Chicago that summer of 1932, John McDuffie of Alabama, used the term in a speech just hours before FDR's acceptance speech—but no one seemed to be paying much attention.

Finally, FDR was reputed to have opened a speech to the Daughters of the American Revolution, an organization that at the time urged that the U.S. borders be closed, with the words, "Fellow immigrants." The story was widely circulated and fostered the public perception of Roosevelt as pro-immigrant in spite of his patrician upbringing. Only later did the reporter who first filed the story admit that, while FDR did speak eloquently to the DAR of the need to recognize that all Americans are immigrants of one sort or another, he did not open his address with these words.

Dwarfs Are the Same as Midgets

According to the traditional differentiation, dwarfs have shortened arms and legs but the rest of their bodies are normal size. Midgets differ from dwarfs in that their bodies are proportional throughout. These days, the word "midget" is considered offensive. The term "dwarf" is okay, but "little person" is preferred. There are some two hundred causes of dwarfism. Some are genetic, some are hormonal, and some are a combination of both. In the canine world, dachshunds and basset hounds were created by breeding selectively for dwarfism.

Emerson Said, "Consistency Is the Hobgoblin of Little Minds"

Quoted sneeringly by high-minded types who like to focus on the larger picture at the expense of the boring details, this phrase misquotes Emerson by leaving out one key word.

What Emerson said was, "A *foolish* consistency is the hobgoblin of little minds." Consistency itself is not the culprit. Without it, our lives would be so chaotic we'd still be living in the Stone Age. A "foolish" consistency—as practiced by anal schoolmarms, authoritarian personalities, grammar police, by-the-book municipal servants, and others who get off on a mindless preoccupation with nit-picking—is another matter entirely.

George Gipp's Dying Words Were "Win One for the Gipper"

George Gipp was a star football player for Notre Dame from 1916 to 1920, scoring an amazing eighty-three touchdowns during a stretch when the Fighting Irish amassed a record of twenty-seven wins, two losses, and three ties (19-0-1 during Gipp's final twenty games). Gipp was Notre Dame's first All-American and was just as outstanding a star on defense, where he played defensive back; in four years, not a single pass was completed to his zone. The élan of the Notre Dame team was legendary as were the leadership qualities and character-building qualities of its coach, Knute Rockne.

Gipp—nicknamed "the Gipper"—was something less than an exemplary student: in 1919, he was expelled from the school, either for cutting classes or for being spotted leaving a dance hall that doubled as a brothel. The outcry on and off campus was so great—a mob of locals threatened to storm the administration building—that Gipp was readmitted. Gipp also had a weakness for gambling and was a habitué of the local pool halls, where he was deemed an expert player (and too well known to be any good as a hustler). During one game (against Northwestern), with Notre Dame down at halftime, Rockne was urging the team when he noticed Gipp off to the side, leaning against a locker and staring absently into space. "I don't suppose you have any interest in this game," Rockne is said to have snarled. "You're wrong there, Coach," Gipp is reported to have said. "I have $500 bet on it, and I don't intend to blow my money."

It was during the November 20, 1920, game against Illinois that Gipp contracted a throat infection. Before the advent of penicillin, such infections had to be taken seriously, and Gipp was advised to be hospitalized, which he refused. (Gipp had been told the previous summer that his tonsils were infected and that they should be removed, but he was afraid the operation would prevent him from playing that fall and so refused to go through with it.) In the final game of the season, Gipp was sidelined with a bruised shoulder and a high fever, but he insisted on going in. Rockne reluctantly sent Gipp in, and he promptly scored the winning touchdown. Soon after the game, however, Gipp was admitted to the hospital. His condition steadily worsened, and he died on December 14. On his deathbed, he supposedly told Rockne, "Sometime, Rock, when the team's up against it, when things are wrong, when the breaks are beating the boys, tell them to go in there with all they've got and win one for the Gipper. I don't know where I'll be then, but I'll know about it and I'll be happy."

How do we know he said this? Because it was in an obituary for Gipp or in any of the tributes and services that closed down the state of Indiana as it mourned Gipp's passing? Because it appeared in all the stories about and bios of Gipp and memorial plaques honoring him in the years following his death? No, we know he said it because eight years after Gipp's death, during Notre Dame's worst season under Coach Rockne, Rockne used the story to inspire the team to beat Army and "win one for the Gipper." Rockne was as famous for his locker-room pep talks as for his strategy on the gridiron. He once sat silently in the locker room during halftime when the team was behind and then, just as the halftime was drawing to a close, turned to the players and said, "All right, ladies …" The team went out onto the field breathing fire and creamed their opponent. So Rockne was not above concocting a bit of fiction if it would help him win a game.

The story would probably have died right there except for the fact that a radio sports announcer who had heard the story would tell it often during lulls in the action. Upon hearing that Warner Brothers was making a movie about Rockne, that sportscaster, who had by now turned to acting, lobbied vigorously for the role and won it. (The studio reportedly believed that the publicity to be derived from the actor's close association with the story would help the film, and anyway, the star role wasn't Gipp, it was Rockne, played by Pat O'Brien.)

Ronald Reagan as George Gipp in the 1940 film *Knute Rockne, All American.*

The movie was not a smash at the box office—except that the actor who played Gipp continued using the story to make all sorts of political points. He even took on the nickname "the Gipper"and was known by that nickname right through his unpredictably exalted political career. Of course, that particular announcer-actor-politician was Ronald Reagan. Reagan acknowledged throughout his life (as did Pat O'Brien) that the Gipper story was probably apocryphal—but that didn't deter him from telling it.

It's Okay to Say "For All Intensive Purposes"

One hears this from time to time, sometimes accompanied by raised eyebrows or suppressed laughter. As you probably already know, the cliché is correctly phrased "for all intents and purposes."

"Halley's Comet" Is Pronounced "Hay-Lee's Comet"

The name of eighteenth-century British astronomer Edmund Halley is correctly pronounced like Halle in Halle Berry (rhyming with "alley"). The mispronunciation "hay-lee" was probably perpetuated by Bill Haley and the Comets (who some say ushered in the era of rock and roll). While we're at it, Halley's Comet is more properly known as Comet Halley or 1P/Halley (1 for first-documented and P for periodic).

Henry Ford Said, "A Car Can Be Any Color, as Long as It's Black"

He may or may not have made that statement, but the implication is that black was the most appropriate color for a car, or at least Ford's personal predilection. The fact is that the first Model T's came in other colors. But since Ford wanted to build his cars as quickly as possible, and black paint dried faster than any other color, he could rush them off the assembly line at a pace that added up to less time per car and more cars to sell. And he managed to sell some fifteen million.

"Humble" in Humble Pie Means "Humiliated"

This is one of those cases where two words of the same spelling but with entirely different roots end up working well together. To "eat humble pie" means, of course, to be humiliated, especially when having to admit error or make an apology. But the origin of "humble" in "humble pie" has more to do with, well, deer guts. It comes from "umble" or "numble," which means the internal organs (heart, liver, kidneys, intestines) of an animal such as a deer—parts less likely to make for a sumptuous dinner. In the old days, umbles were consumed reluctantly by servants, while their masters dined on venison. So if you ask someone the origin of the phrase "eat humble pie" and he tells you it's from "humble" as in "not proud," you can gloat as he eats humble pie—or you can take it one step further and have him eat crow, which I've heard is worse than deer guts.

Infinitives Should Not Be Split

"To boldly go where no man has gone before" (via *Star Trek*) is to boldly split an infinitive. But this "wrong" phraseology sounds a lot better than "To go boldly" or "Boldly to go." The rule that claims it is wrong to split an infinitive has persisted in English classes and among the grammar police for an inordinate period of time. But the rule has no real grammatical basis or practical purpose. Its main appeal has been to know-it-alls who get a charge out of correcting other people's usage. So where did the rule come from? Some say it began with Latin scholars or pedantic grammarians sometime in the mid-nineteenth century, but who knows. The "rule" is no longer something to *seriously obey*.

James Cagney Said, "You Dirty Rat" in His Movies

Not even once—but everyone is convinced he did. Cagney himself hated being tagged with the line, nor did he care for its being repeated by the many impressionists who used it to evoke the Cagney persona.

Most people don't realize that James Cagney was a very cultured individual. He was also, of course, a phenomenal dancer (as demonstrated in his film portrayal of George M. Cohan) and starred in over seventy films, only a handful of which were gangster films. Cagney's failure to live down this stereotype was one of the great disappointments of his life.

JFK Originated the Line "Ask Not What Your Country Can Do for You; Ask What You Can Do for Your Country"

There's no question that John F. Kennedy uttered these words in his 1961 Inaugural Address and that the sentence inspired a nation and set the tone for his administration—but the phrase did not originate with JFK. The sentiment was voiced by Khalil Gibran, who asked, "Are you a politician asking what your country can do for you, or a zealous one who asks what you can do for your country?" Similar sentiments can be found in American political rhetoric: Oliver Wendell Holmes and Warren G. Harding both exhorted the citizenry to be (in Harding's words) "less concerned about what the government can do for it and more anxious about what it can do for the nation." Leo Rosten traced the quote (or a rough approximation of it) to an inaugural address delivered by Cicero in 63 BCE, when he became a consul in the Roman Senate. But, as some have pointed out, the rhetorical device of inverting the "ask" and the "not"—"ask not" instead of "do not ask," with a dramatic emphasis on the "not"—was Kennedy's, and Kennedy's alone.

"Libel" and "Slander" Are Synonymous

Libel and slander are the same in that each is a kind of "defamation," which consists of making false statements that harm someone else's reputation. Slander is oral defamation, and libel is written (or recorded) defamation. Why add "recorded"? In the old days the difference between libel and slander was clear. But with the invention of the electronic media (radio, television, movies, computers, CDs, etc.), libel has in some cases been expanded to include not only written material but recorded oral communication. In many jurisdictions, libel is considered a more serious offense than slander; presumably, the fact that the defamation will be available for others to read for all time makes the insult that much greater—and the harm that much more grievous.

Lenin said, "The Capitalists Will Sell Us the Rope with Which We Will Hang Them"

Arguably the most widely quoted remark of Vladimir Ilyich Lenin was almost certainly never said. Experts on the Soviet Union reject the quote as spurious because they have never found any evidence of the famous observation in any of his writings or in any record of his remarks. Lenin was said to have spoken the words to Grigori Zinoviev, one of his close associates, shortly after a meeting of the Politburo in the early 1920s.

The closest experts have come to the misquote was: "They will furnish credits which will serve us for the support of the Communist Party in their countries and, by supplying us materials and technical equipment which we lack, will restore our military industry necessary for our future attacks against our suppliers. To put it in other words, they will work on the preparation of their own suicide."

Americans never really liked Lenin, and because the Bolshevik leader spoke a foreign language, it was easy to misquote him and literally put words in his mouth. There were many alleged quotes spread around the United States that Lenin never said.

Lenin was claimed to have referred to liberal Americans as "useful idiots of the West," a phrase that has been used by anti-communists to describe Soviet sympathizers in the West. But,

A mosaic of Lenin from a Moscow metro station.

once again, the expression can't be found in any of Lenin's writings.

Anti-communist Republican Senator Joseph R. McCarthy claimed in 1953 that Lenin said, "The world cannot exist half slave and half free; it must all be slave." McCarthy used Lenin's alleged quote to compare it with Abraham Lincoln's views in his attack on the communist party. But the misquote was entirely fabricated by McCarthy, possibly just a paraphrase of what McCarthy thought Lenin's position was.

Leo Durocher Said, "Nice Guys Finish Last"

The great manager of the Brooklyn Dodgers, Leo "the Lip" Durocher, became famous for this remark and even used it as the title of his autobiography. But in that autobiography, Durocher explains that he was misquoted—actually "mispunctuated." It was 1948 and Durocher was being interviewed by a newspaper reporter on the steps of the dugout. During the interview, the New York Giants took the field for practice and the reporter asked Durocher what he thought of them. He looked and said, "Nice guys." Then he paused and added, "Finish last," by which he meant "They'll finish last." The line appeared in print as "Nice guys finish last," but a more accurate rendering would have been: "Nice guys; finish last" or "Nice guys, [but they'll] finish last." *New York Journal American* sportswriter Jimmy Cannon picked up the line and used it to build for Durocher an entire philosophy of life and baseball. But, of course, that's not what Durocher actually said.

Lincoln Said, "God Must Have Loved the Common People; He Made So Many of Them"

The quote is a slightly more eloquent version of something Lincoln dreamed he said. In *Our Presidents*, a book by James Morgan published in 1928, Lincoln is supposed to have dreamed he was in a crowd and someone was heard saying (about Lincoln), "He is a very common-looking man." Lincoln dreamed that he answered, "Friend, the Lord prefers common-looking people. That is the reason he makes so many of them."

Clever, but there's no evidence Lincoln ever had such a dream—and certainly none that he ever uttered either the old or the new, improved version.

General MacArthur Originated the Phrase "Old Soldiers Never Die; They Just Fade Away"

MacArthur quoted a popular barracks song from World War I in his valedictory address to Congress in 1951 and people have associated him with the phrase ever since.

But what MacArthur said was, "I still remember the refrain of one of the most popular barracks ballads of that day, which proclaimed most proudly that old soldiers never die; they just fade away. I now close my military career and just fade away." He cited the words as coming from an outside source, but he is the one who will always be remembered for them.

The other famous quote from MacArthur, "I shall return," is probably original. MacArthur uttered those words in 1942 when he was forced by the Japanese to leave the Philippines for Australia.

Marie Antoinette Said, "Let Them Eat Cake"

This remark, supposedly spoken on the eve of the French Revolution, is alleged to be the queen's less-than-compassionate response to peasants complaining that they didn't have enough bread to eat. But "Let them eat cake" was never uttered by Marie Antoinette. Regardless, some might say, the quote still reflects her ignorant and insensitive mind-set toward a starving populace, so she might as well have said it. Wrong again. Marie Antoinette was not perfect, but she got a bum rap in more ways than one.

Marie Antoinette (1755–1793), Queen of France and Archduchess of Austria.

The daughter of Austrian royalty, Marie Antoinette was sent to France for an arranged marriage aimed at cementing relations between France and Austria. Her groom, Louis XVI, was heir to the French throne. He was also awkward, obese, and genitally challenged, so the blushing bride was blushing for all the wrong reasons. Early in the mar-

riage, the queen managed to find male company on the side, and she sometimes behaved in a manner that was immature and rebellious. But she cleaned up her act after Louis ascended to the throne and after the king's member, repaired by some deft surgery, was finally able to stand at attention and salute. Children followed, and thereafter the queen became a devoted mother and took on a degree of grace and dignity worthy of a queen.

Even so, due to exaggerated rumors and vicious innuendo passed along by her ill-wishers over a period of years, an impression of the queen as a spoiled, uncaring, ignorant slut became etched in the minds of the populace and laid the groundwork for her undoing. Years later, after being tried, convicted, and sentenced to death by the guillotine (largely due to her case having been tried in the court of public opinion), the queen was wheeled through Paris in a dung cart and spat upon by the crowds. Her grace and dignity remained, however. As she mounted the scaffold, she accidentally stepped on the executioner's foot. Her last words were, "Monsieur, I beg your pardon. I didn't do it on purpose."

According to biographer Antonia Fraser, "Let them eat cake" actually did spring from the mouth of a real person, but it wasn't Marie Antoinette. The callous sentiment was uttered by Marie-Thérèse, the wife of Louis XIV, a century before Marie Antoinette was born.

Nathan Hale's Dying Words Were "I Only Regret That I Have But One Life to Lose for My Country"

It's a nice story, but is it true? Let's take a closer look at this celebrated icon of American history.

Nathan Hale was born on June 6, 1755, in Coventry, Connecticut, the sixth of Richard and Elizabeth Strong Hale's twelve children. Ten of the Hale children survived into adulthood, but Elizabeth died a few months after the birth of her twelfth child, leaving Nathan motherless at age twelve. Richard got remarried two years later to a wealthy widow. The Hale farm was successful, and by all accounts, the Hales were active in the church and supportive of the cause of American independence. Nathan appears to have been athletic and studious, distinguishing himself at Yale in both sports and academics. He was a member of the secret Linonia literary fraternity, a group that met regularly to discuss philosophy and literature; by his senior year he was the society's president. He was active in dramatics and oratory—and judging from the bills he accumulated, not above occasional mischief and campus mayhem. A highlight of the Yale graduation ceremonies in September 1773 was a debate over the education of women. Nathan argued for women's admittance to all institutions of higher education—and won the debate.

Hale became headmaster of the Latin School of New London, Connecticut, in 1774 and promptly opened the school to young women. A wealth of correspondences between Nathan and his old classmates, as well as written testimony from the people of New London referring to Nathan, all paint a portrait of Hale as a robust, handsome, high-spirited young man, eager to avoid the conventional path his father and older brother Enoch had taken, leading from teaching into the ministry. When news of Lexington and Concord reached New London in 1775, Nathan joined the revolutionary army, inspiring many townspeople to join as well.

Nathan was stationed outside Boston and spent most of 1775 in a standoff against the British occupying the city. When the British left for Halifax and New York, Nathan, by now a captain, decided to go to New York and join Knowlton's Rangers, a group formed by Lt. Col. Thomas Knowlton after the British victory at the Battle of Long Island in September of 1776. Knowlton's group (clearly a guerrilla and espionage unit) set out to prevent a British invasion of Manhattan, at least until the winter, in hopes of giving Washington time to regroup. It was thought that several raids would convince the British to remain on Long Island and protect their flank, but such raids required detailed information on British troop deployment on Long Island. This prompted the need for a reconnaissance mission, which seems to be what Hale volunteered for.

Hale was ferried onto Long Island from Norwalk, Connecticut, on about September 10 and proceeded to contact sympathetic residents among the heavily Loyalist population. He masqueraded as a Dutch schoolteacher, carrying his Yale diploma with him to support his cover, and began his survey of the island. Inside of a week, however, the British left Long Island and landed on the south shore of Manhattan, and Washington and his troops retreated north to Morningside Heights. This made Hale's mission unnecessary. Instead of returning to Connecticut, however, he went to Manhattan to continue his reconnaissance—and this was a fatal mistake. Many more people would know him in Manhattan and his cover story would be difficult to support there. Hale was identified and arrested on September 21. He had maps and documents on his person that made it clear that he was a spy—historians wonder whether this was a result of his espionage experience or evidence of a betrayal. According to one report, Hale was betrayed by his Loyalist cousin, Samuel Hale, visiting Manhattan from Newburyport, Massachusetts; another has Hale arrested while still on Long Island by Major Robert Rogers, a hero of the French and Indian Wars who had turned Loyalist. In any case, he was brought before General Howe at his Manhattan headquarters and quickly sentenced to hanging the next day.

September 22, 1776, was a tumultuous and eventful day in American history. The British occupied lower Manhattan and the Great Fire of 1776 was raging—some believe it was started by the revolutionaries in an effort to slow the British advance; others believe it was set by the British, attempting to smoke out any rearguard patriots and intent on punishing the city for its support of the revolution. On that morning, Nathan Hale was taken out to the gallows next to Dove Tavern on the corner of what is now Third Avenue and 66th Street. He was given the opportunity to say his last words and then he was hung—his body was left hanging for several days (as a warning to other revolutionaries) and then buried in an unmarked grave.

What Hale's last words were, exactly, has become the stuff of legend. No eyewitness accounts exist, but several contemporaneous accounts refer to the event. One is a diary entry by a British soldier, Robert Mackenzie, who reports that Hale died with great dignity and heroism, though he does not record what he said. Another diary entry by a British officer, a Capt. Frederick Mackenzie, records Hale's last words as, "It is the duty of every good officer to obey any orders given him by his commander-in-chief." This makes sense only as a way for Hale to graciously forgive his executioner for carrying out his orders. The familiar story of Hale's heroic final oration began with a British officer, John Montressor, who claimed to witness the hanging and related the story to an American friend and officer, William Hull. Hull's is the earliest record we have of the quote, but it is not an eyewitness account, only a secondhand one via Montressor (from whom no record has survived).

Much of what we know about Hale's final days is due to the efforts of his brother Enoch Hale, who came down from Connecticut to investigate Nathan's fate. Enoch kept a diary and recorded many speculations regarding Nathan's betrayal, arrest, and death. His diary does not contain the famous quote. But its absence is not proof Hale never said it. And the reason is that these words are a close paraphrase of a line from a play that was very popular in the Colonies at the time, especially among the patriots of the revolution. It's from Joseph Addison's *Cato*, a tragedy in five acts written in 1712 and performed throughout the Colonies in the years prior to the Revolution. (Washington even had the play performed for the Continental Army in Valley Forge during the winter of 1777.) The play is about the suicide of a young pretender to the crown of Rome during the days of Julius Caesar when he realizes he must forfeit his liberty to the victorious emperor. Several notable quotations derived from the play, including Patrick Henry's famous declaration, "Give me liberty, or give me death." Hale would have been very familiar with the play; he would very likely have even been part of a performance of it at some point during his years at Yale or as a schoolmaster.

The relevant line appears in act IV: "What pity is it, that we can die but once to serve our country." Now, had Hale uttered the words he is supposed to have uttered, he would have been paraphrasing Addison and not saying anything original (whereas the remark about following orders would have been his own). Even Enoch would not have recorded the Addison words as being Nathan's last words. He would have regarded them not merely as a quote lifted from a famous and popular play, but as rhetorical enhancements of what Hale really had to say. But others hearing Hale's paraphrase, even if they were aware of the Addison source (and remember that the British officer would very likely not be aware of the play or the quote), would have recognized the rhetorical and aphoristic power that Hale's rendition had given these thoughts—and deemed these words his.

Abraham Lincoln Coined the Phrase "of the People, by the People, for the People" at Gettysburg

The famous last line from Lincoln's Gettysburg Address was actually used first by Unitarian minister and abolitionist Theodore Parker in 1850 when he was addressing the New England Anti-Slavery Society in Boston, Massachusetts. Parker said, "Democracy is direct self-government, over all the people, by all the people, for all the people." Lincoln dropped the "all" repetition from his speech to enhance the flow of the sentence.

Parker probably borrowed the phrase from Daniel Webster, who in January of 1830 told the Senate that the government was "made for the people, made by the people, and [is] answerable to the people." John Marshall also used the expression: "Government over all, by all and for the sake of all." Other men, such as William Wirt and Thomas Cooper, had also previously used similar words to express the same idea. John Wyclif is said to have written "This Bible is for the government of the people, by the people, and for the people" in the fourteenth century. Cleon of Athens expressed the same idea way back in 400 BCE.

The only image of Lincoln at the battlefield of Gettysburg.

Incidentally, the exact sentence in the Gettysburg Address is often misquoted when people put "and" in front of "for" in the last section of the triad.

Mark Twain Quipped, "Everybody Talks about the Weather, but Nobody Does Anything about It"

The line has become a classic American witticism, and Twain tried to give credit where credit was due—to his friend and sometime collaborator, Charles Dudley Warner. But the line became associated with Twain from the very start, and finally even Twain gave in and took credit. Warner used the line in an editorial in the *Hartford Courant* in 1897, attributing it to an unidentified "well-known American writer." At the time, everyone assumed Warner meant Twain, but why wouldn't he mention his friend by name? Some thought the allusion to a "well-known American writer" was Warner's polite way of referring to himself.

The line was used with great effect by Hal Holbrook in his one-man show, *Mark Twain Tonight*; he placed extra emphasis on the word "does," which is essential for the full comedic effect. In interviews, Holbrook said he never ceased to be amazed by how many people really didn't get the joke.

Neil Armstrong Said, "That's One Small Step for Man, One Giant Leap for Mankind"

On July 20, 1969, astronaut Neil Armstrong stood on the landing pad at the bottom of the ladder of the lunar excursion module and prepared to hop onto the surface of the moon. Now, much thought had been given to what Armstrong would say with the entire world listening and watching—just as considerable thought went into the selection of Armstrong as the American who would be the first man to walk on the moon. (NASA thought he had the name they wanted to be remembered throughout all of history as the first American on the moon.)

Many people still remember listening to Armstrong as he set foot on the moon, and many remember thinking, "That doesn't make sense. Shouldn't that be, 'That's one small step for a man …'?" When Armstrong returned, he was aghast to discover what millions of people around the world heard him say. Armstrong swore he did not omit the "a" when he intoned the line—and, indeed, it seems that a bit of static interrupted the transmission at just the moment when Armstrong would have been uttering the "a."

Portrait of Neil Armstrong (born August 5, 1930), commander of the *Apollo 11* mission, in his space suit. Photograph taken on July 1, 1969.

He was asked why he paused after the word "man"—it seemed he was wondering if he had said the phrase correctly (and many viewers no doubt remember thinking that as well while watching in 1969). But Armstrong insisted he got it right (the pause was caused by him tensing up for the hop onto the lunar surface, he said) and the word "a" was lost in the static.

Oddly enough, history books that record Armstrong's words consistently record them as they were heard and not what he claims to have said—sense or no sense. Also, many viewers did not know that when Armstrong landed on the moon, he had only seventeen seconds of fuel left. Had he not found a flat surface in time, he would have crash-landed, and the mission (along with the entire U.S. space program) would have ended in disaster.

"Presently" Means "Right Now"

It's routinely misused as a synonym for "currently," but "presently" does not mean "at present." The word refers not to what's happening now but to what's about to happen. "Presently" is synonymous with "pretty soon," "any minute now," "before too long," "shortly," etc. It's tempting to use "presently" to mean "at present," because it sounds more logical and less awkward. But to people who know better, it sounds ignorant.

"Reticent" Means "Reluctant"

You hear it all the time: "Bob was reticent to join the party" or "I am reticent to swim in a river full of piranhas," etc. But "reticent" means "quiet," not "unwilling." Undiscriminating types constantly seem to mix up the two words, probably because they sound vaguely alike and both begin with an *R*. But that's no excuse. You should always be reluctant to use "reticent" to mean reluctant—and if you're tempted, you'd be better off remaining reticent.

Ronald Reagan Said, "There Is Nothing Better for the Inside of a Man than the Outside of a Horse"

Though Reagan was fond of saying it, the line didn't originate with him, nor did he ever claim it did. Many orators said the same or very similar things about the "outside of a horse" and the "inside of a man." The earliest may well have been Lord Palmerston, a nineteenth-century British statesman.

"Whence" Means "Where," as in "From Whence He Came"

"Whence" is actually two, two, two words in one—namely, "from where." For example, if you say, "Renee is returning to France, *from whence* she came," it's like saying, "Renee is returning to France, *from from where* she came." So if you don't want to sound like an ignoramus, you'd better say "Renee is returning to France, whence she came." Even better, avoid the word entirely. It's about as *au courant* as your great-grandmother's lace curtains.

Patrick Henry Said, "Give Me Liberty or Give Me Death"

This famous phrase supposedly concluded Patrick Henry's fiery speech delivered at the second Virginia Convention in March of 1775 and inspired American troops to march off to war. But did he really utter those celebrated words? Probably not. Washington and Jefferson were both present at the convention but made no mention of the speech in their writings. Also, the quote may have been lifted, at least in part, from a line in a play by Joseph Addison that was popular at the time ("It is not now time to talk of aught/ But chains or conquest, liberty or death"). Hale's famous last words may have tapped the same source (See Nathan Hale, page 210.)

Sam Goldwyn Said, "Gentlemen, Include Me Out"

Nope. Although Goldwyn's gift for malapropisms seems to have inspired the genre, this and a whole slew of other gems were made up by others (Hollywood scriptwriters and journalists) and attributed to the Tinseltown mogul. Here are a few more popular Goldwynisms that Goldwyn himself never uttered:

"It makes the hair stand on the edge of my seat."

"It rolls off my back like a duck."

"I'll give you a blanket check right now."

"Anyone who would go to a psychiatrist ought to have his head examined."

"I was on the brink of a great abscess" (for "great abyss").

"You've got to take the bull by the teeth."

"To hell with the cost" (in response to a colleague who said a certain project would be too caustic).

"Our comedies are not to be laughed at."

"Quick as a flashlight."

"We can get all the Indians we need at the reservoir."

"The next time I send a damn fool for something, I go myself."

"I read part of it all the way through."

Spiro Agnew Coined the Phrase "Nattering Nabobs of Negativism"

Spiro Agnew, Richard Nixon's vice president, is usually credited with this sneeringly dismissive piece of alliteration directed at journalists. Actually, the phrase was the work of wordsmith William Safire, who worked as a White House speechwriter at the time. Other famous derogatory phrases (which Agnew applied to journalists, intellectuals, Vietnam War protesters, and others he considered nemeses) were written by either Safire or Pat Buchanan, another Nixon speechwriter. Among them: "pusillanimous pussyfoots," "hopeless, hysterical hypochondriacs of history," and "an effete corps of impudent snobs." Ironically, both Safire and Buchanan made their mark as journalists.

"Sensuous" Means the Same as "Sensual"

These two words are often used interchangeably, but they have slightly different shades of meaning. In the eyes of the usage police, however, mixing up "sensuous" and "sensual" is a minor offense compared with mixing up such words as "reluctant" and "reticent," or "flout" and "flaunt." Anyway, to get back to the point: "sensuous" refers to the senses (sight, sound, touch, smell, taste) and often to the aesthetic pleasures they offer (as from a sunset, concert, summer breeze, cologne, or gourmet meal). "Sensual" also refers to the senses, but the word is charged with erotic overtones (as in "sensual pleasure," "sensual massage," "sensual lips," and the noun "sensuality"). Now, will anyone notice if you mix them up? Probably not.

Voltaire Said, "I Disapprove of What You Say, but I Will Defend to the Death Your Right to Say It"

It was really Evelyn B. Hall, a British biographer writing under the name S. G. Tallentyre, who wrote the famous saying in 1906. In Hall's book, *The Friends of Voltaire,* she used the phrase when quoting Voltaire's "Essay on Tolerance," but the sentence never appears in the essay. In 1935, Hall wrote a letter to the *New York Times* admitting that she had only tried to "paraphrase" Voltaire's ideas.

She wrote, "I did not intend to imply that Voltaire used these words verbatim, and should be much surprised if they are found in any of his works." What Voltaire actually wrote was, "Think for yourselves and let others enjoy the privilege to do so too."

According to Hall, the phrase was in reference to a book published by Claude Adrien Helvetius in 1758, *De l'Esprit (On the Mind),* which Voltaire was not impressed with, but which was condemned by the government. The book was banned and burned, and Helvetius was exiled from France. At this, Voltaire exclaimed, "What a fuss about an omelette!" (i.e., "What a tempest in a teapot!"). Hall's famous misquotation was simply meant to represent a summarization of Voltaire's attitude toward the entire episode.

Regardless of the origin of the phrase, it has become one of the most famous quotations from Voltaire and is popular among American civil libertarians. It was used for many years by the *New York Herald-Tribune* as the motto of the "Letters to the Editor" column.

You Shouldn't Say "Who" When You Should Say "Whom"

It all depends on the circumstances. Assuming you know when to use and when not to use each word correctly ("who" is usually the subject and "whom" the object), aren't there occasions when being correct just sounds silly? And aren't there occasions when being "wrong" sounds better than being right? The answer to both is yes. In casual conversation, for example, the who-whom rules are more relaxed. Suppose your friend gets a postcard. You wouldn't say, "Whom is it from?" Or even worse, "From whom is it?" You'd say, "Who is it from?"—even though *whom* is "correct" and *who* is not.

The written word, on the other hand, often calls for a bow in the direction of formality. So it may be best to mind one's grammatical manners, depending on how much formality seems appropriate. You'd expect a legal document to say "the parties to whom payment was made," not "the parties who payment was made to." And you've got to admit that "for whom the bell tolls" has a catchier ring than "who the bell tolls for."

W. C. Fields Said, "Any Man Who Hates Dogs and Babies Can't Be All Bad"

First of all, Fields did not originate the quip—but he liked it so much that he often quoted it. Second of all, the line is often misquoted as "Anybody who hates children and dogs can't be all bad." The difference is subtle, but it's the difference between a finely wrought comic line and a pedestrian one.

But the most frustrating thing about this line is that it was not said *by* W. C. Fields but *about* W. C. Fields. It was first uttered by Leo Rosten at the opening of a roasting of Fields at a 1939 Masquers' Club dinner.

Rosten was, for reasons that were unknown to him, invited to the dinner and informed only upon arriving that he was to be seated on the dais and was expected to be the first to address the crowd, which consisted of the biggest stars and moguls in Hollywood. Rosten stood at the podium for a moment, tongue-tied and petrified. He heard George Burns mutter to him, "Say somethin'!" with (as Rosten puts it) "unmistakable disgust." Rosten continues:

> "Someone who was hiding in my throat uttered these words: 'The only thing I can say about Mr. W. C. Fields is this: Any man who hates dogs and babies can't be all bad.' …The next morning, the local papers led off their stories about the banquet with my ad lib. Overnight, I was an international wit."

After the remark became credited to Fields, Rotsen felt a bit cheated. "Hardly a week passes," he lamented, "in which I do not run across some reference to 'Fields's immortal crack.' But it was mine, I tell you, *mine*!" (Steady there, Leo.)

W. C. Fields playing pool, circa 1934.

"Wherefore Art Thou, Romeo?" Means "Where the Heck Are You, Romeo?"

"Wherefore" means "why," not "where." It's a word that isn't used much anymore (probably for good reason), except in legalese and in such clichés as "the whys and the wherefores." From the balcony scene in *Romeo and Juliet*, the famous line is spoken by the heroine. She is lamenting the unfortunate fact that, because their families (the Montagues and the Capulets) are engaged in a bitter feud, her romance with Romeo has no future. In this context, the line roughly translates as "Why did you have to be *that* Romeo?" or "Why did you have to be a Montague?" or "Dammit, just my luck, wouldn't you know I had to fall in love with Mr. Wrong!"

It Is Wrong to Begin a Sentence with "And" or "But"

This is another of those seemingly inviolable rules of grammar we were taught in grade school. *But* if the rule is so important, then why have the giants of English and American literature been breaking it since day one? *And* who really cares one way or the other?

Truman Coined the Phrase "If You Can't Stand the Heat, Get Out of the Kitchen"

Although credited with coming up with the phrase, Harry Truman simply popularized it. In the 1930s, Truman had heard the line used by E. T. "Buck" Purcell, a politician from Truman's home state of Missouri. Truman's folksy language was a change of pace from FDR's patrician oratory.

Winston Churchill Coined the Phrases "Blood, Sweat, and Tears" and "Iron Curtain"

Well, *he* certainly thought he did, but each phrase has its own history. First, let's take a closer look at "blood, sweat, and tears." When Churchill took office as prime minister in May of 1940, he said, "I have nothing to offer but blood and toil, tears and sweat." Someone pointed out to him that a similar phrase was used by Henry James in his novel *The Bostonians*, published in 1886. Churchill was unfazed and continued using the phrase throughout the war, though the public seemed to edit it down to the more economical and less redundant "blood, sweat, and tears." Eventually, Churchill also adopted the pithier version and even used it as the title of his war memoirs.

The case of "iron curtain" is more problematic. In a memorable speech Churchill delivered in Fulton, Missouri, on May 5, 1946, he warned: "From Stettin in the Baltic to Trieste in the Adriatic an iron curtain has descended across the continent." The phrase "iron curtain" became the West's way of referring to the nations in the Soviet Bloc, and Churchill was credited with coining the term. But the phrase—even its application to Russia—predated Churchill's speech. Leo Rosten documents many uses of the term "iron curtain" dating back to the Talmud and cites an early modern use by the Queen of Belgium, who, in August 1914, complained that "Between the Germans and me there is now a bloody iron curtain—which has fallen forever." The phrase was also applied to France by a political theoretician in 1915, who called it "a nation with an iron curtain at its frontier."

H. G. Wells seemed to be the first to apply the image to Russia (without the distinctive reference to iron), but he did so some ten years before the Russian Revolution. After the Revolution, the phrase "iron curtain" was used by several writers to refer to what was taking place vis-à-vis Russia. But the first one to use the term in the sense meant by Churchill—that made it a part of the Cold War lexicon—was, of all people, the Nazi Minister of Propaganda, Joseph Goebbels. In February 1945, the *Manchester Guardian* quoted Goebbels as warning (in *Das Reich*) that "the whole of east and southeastern Europe…[might] come under Russian occupation. Behind an iron curtain, mass butcheries would begin…." Rosten's comment: "If Goebbels had anything it was *chutzpah*."

After the war, top-secret dispatches from Churchill to President Truman showed that Churchill was warning about the iron curtain descending on Eastern Europe a year before his Fulton speech. Within a week of the German surrender, Churchill wired Truman in May 1945: "An iron curtain is drawn over their [the Russian] front. We do not know what is going on behind…The whole of the region east of the line Lubeck-Trieste-Corfu will soon be completely in their hands…and then the curtain will descend." By October of 1945, the phrase was appearing in many British reports from Russian-held territories; the London *Sunday Empire News* said simply, "There is an iron curtain across Europe." So although Churchill did not invent the expression, his 1946 speech etched it into the public consciousness and made it a key catchphrase of the twentieth century.

"Flaccid" Is Pronounced "Flassid"

Nope, it's pronounced "flak-sid." But since people say it wrong all the time, the wimpier dictionaries have caved and now accept "flassid" as a second pronunciation. At least they've held their ground when it comes to such bizarre mispronunciations as "sussess" for "success."

"Not Up to Par" Means "Second-Rate"

In golf, of course, par is a first-rate score, and below par is even better. If you shoot "par for the course," you are probably ready to go pro, if you haven't already. Ordinary "par-lance," however, seems to have gotten it backward: "par for the course" means typical, and "not up to par" means below average, mediocre, or worse. Go figure.

The Official Motto of the United States Postal Service Is "Neither Snow nor Rain nor Heat nor Gloom of Night Stays These Couriers from the Swift Completion of Their Appointed Rounds"

Officially, the United States Postal Service has no motto. Most people think that "Neither snow nor rain nor heat nor gloom of night stays these couriers from the swift completion of their appointed rounds" is the motto because it is inscribed on the façade of the General Post Office in New York City (below). A quote from Herodotus, the lines were chosen by the architect of the building, William Mitchell Kendall of McKim, Mead & White. It refers to a highly esteemed group of mounted Persian postal couriers who remained steadfast while under attack by the Greeks around 500 BCE.

Other postal buildings display a variety of sayings, none of which are considered official mottos. On the Washington, D.C., City Post Office, an inscription appears, written by Dr. Charles W. Eliot, president of Harvard from 1869 to 1909. Before it was carved into the building, the original text was apparently edited slightly by none other than President Woodrow Wilson. It reads as follows:

Messenger of Sympathy and Love
Servant of Parted Friends
Consoler of the Lonely
Bond of the Scattered Family
Enlarger of the Common Life

Carrier of News and Knowledge
Instrument of Trade and Industry
Promoter of Mutual Acquaintance
Of Peace and Goodwill
Among Men and Nations.

Alexander Woollcott Joked, "I Must Get out of These Wet Clothes and into a Dry Martini"

As Paul E. Boller and John George point out in their classic collection *They Never Said It*, the line certainly sounds like something Woollcott might have said. But not only didn't he come up with the line, it wasn't original with the fellow who used it in one of his films, humorist Robert Benchley, who first heard it from a press agent.

The line seemed to have too urbane a flavor for the nebbishy character Benchley made himself out to be, so the remark became attached to Benchley's fellow Algonquin Round Tabler, Alexander Woollcott (right).

Willie Sutton Said He Robbed Banks "Because That's Where the Money Is"; Sir Edmund Hillary Claimed He Climbed Mount Everest "Because It's There"

A clever line, and Sutton was the sort of artless fellow who might have said such a thing in response to what he thought was a foolish question. But the line was invented (expediently) by a reporter who interviewed Willie in the slammer and came away with only a few dull, one-word responses.

A similar line—and similarly misattributed—is that of Sir Edmund Hillary, first successful climber of Mount Everest. In response to the question of why he climbed the mountain, Hillary is supposed to have said, "Because it's there." But the fact is that another intrepid mountain climber, George Mallory, uttered the line over thirty years before Hillary's famous 1953 climb. Mallory and his partner, Andrew Irving, had made two climbs up Everest and were in the midst of what appeared to be a successful third climb that would take them to the top—but they disappeared. The line became attributed to Hillary, partly out of confusion stemming from the similarity between their names and partly because Mallory was no longer around to get credit for it.

"Forte" Is Correctly Pronounced "Fortay"

Many people pronounce "forte" "fortay" when referring to a person's area of strength, as in "ballroom dancing is not my forte." But, technically speaking, "fort" is more legitimate because the word is French and that's how they pronounce it in France. "Fortay" has become so common, however, that you may be pegged as ignorant if you say "fort," when you are anything but. Because language is democratic, "wrong" pronunciations acquire legitimacy through popular usage. Hence "fortay" is now accepted by dictionaries as an alternate pronunciation. To make things even more complicated, the Italian word *forte* (a musical term meaning loud) is correctly pronounced "fortay." So what to do? Why not skirt the issue entirely by saying "ballroom dancing is not my strong suit."

Odds and Ends

Big Ben Is a Clock

Big Ben is heard but not ordinarily seen. Named after London's first commissioner of works (Sir Benjamin Hall), Big Ben refers not to the clock or the clock tower but the huge, thirteen-ton, nine-foot-diameter bell inside the tower walls. Though rarely uttered, the clock's official name is the Great Clock of Westminster. Great it is, with a minute hand that is some fourteen feet in length.

The Great Clock of Westminster.

The Crown Jewels Belong to the British Government

That sounds logical, but it's not the case. The crown jewels are privately owned by Queen Elizabeth II, as are Buckingham Palace, Windsor Castle, Balmoral Castle, Hampton Court, the Tower of London, the royal yacht, London's royal parks—and while we're at it: all the sturgeons, whales, and dolphins in the waters surrounding the British Isles.

If You Are Arrested, You Are Allowed Only One Phone Call

You hear that a lot in movies and on TV. So is it true that you are allowed to make only one phone call after the police haul you down to the station? Suppose you dial and get a wrong number. Or suppose the line is busy. Or suppose you reach your lawyer and he says, "I'm on another line, I'll have to get back to you." What then? Not to worry. You are permitted by law to make as many phone calls as necessary in order to speak to an attorney and to obtain the money needed to post bail. If the police say you are allowed only one phone call, either they don't know any better or they are lying.

Alcatraz, or "The Rock," as viewed from San Francisco.

An Airplane's Black Box Is Black

Most large airplanes carry a "black box," which records what goes on inside the cockpit and throughout the plane during a flight. In the event of a crash, the black box is located and used to find out what went wrong. If its color were really black, the box would be too hard to find in the wreckage. So the "black" box is actually a bright, eye-catching shade of orange.

The term "black box" is often used by journalists. In the aviation industry the boxes are known as flight recorders, and in automobiles they are called event data recorders.

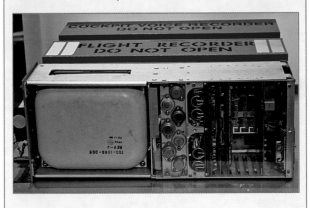

Dry Cleaning Is Dry

Dry cleaning is dry only in the sense that no water is used in the cleaning process. But it is decidedly wet because liquids are used in the process. The purpose of dry cleaning is, of course, to clean clothing that can't stand up to soap and water and to remove stains that are not soluble in soap and water.

Dry cleaning was invented by accident. A French businessman noticed that stains were magically removed from his tablecloth when his maid spilled kerosene on it. The first dry-cleaning services used kerosene or gasoline to clean clothes, but not surprisingly this approach led to some unpleasantness (fires and explosions for one thing; an unpleasant odor for another).

In the 1930s the dry-cleaning industry adopted a cleanser called perchlorethylene ("perc"), which is still used today. The substance gets out stains, doesn't catch fire or explode, and is gentle on clothes. Even so, it is somewhat toxic, and it definitely won't win any awards for its fragrance.

Lead Pencils Contain Lead

Writing and drawing were done with lead styluses until 1564. Then something better came along, prompted by the discovery of a mother lode of graphite in Borrowdale, England. Graphite made a darker mark than lead, but sticks of graphite were too soft and breakable to write with. Someone then thought of putting the graphite into wooden holders that were carved and hollowed out by hand. Hence the so-called "lead pencil" was born—but the name never got the "lead"out.

Inuits Have More than a Hundred Words for Snow, and They Live in Igloos

The word "Eskimo" is now politically incorrect (or at least borderline so) and is considered offensive by some Inuit people living in North America and parts of Siberia. But the Inuits were once referred to as Eskimos (just as a point of reference).

Although *igloo* is the Inuit word for a house of any kind, the Inuits of the past did not "live" in the domelike structures made of snow blocks that we call igloos. They lived in sod houses in the winter and tents (made of wood and skins) in the summer. Igloos (snow houses) were used as temporary shelters (they could be constructed in about two hours) when men were out hunting game.

In the famous 1922 documentary *Nanook of the North*, a man desperately builds such a shelter when he's caught in a dangerous blizzard. The film did much to perpetuate the idea that people of the North lived in such structures all the time. These days most Inuit families live in heated homes made of wood, stone, or cement, just like everyone else.

The notion that the Inuits have multiple (and presumably superfluous) words to describe snow may stem from anthropologists, linguists, and playwrights of the past, who claimed the Inuits have between four and fifty words for snow. Later, the *New York Times* upped the count to one hundred.

It seems reasonable, in that the Inuits (also known as the Yupik peoples) have lots more snow to deal with than the rest of us, hence they must have more words for it than we do—and probably more poetic ones at that.

So how many do they really have? Let's cut to the chase and avoid a long discussion about multiple and polysynthetic languages. The bottom line is that the Inuits have about the same number of words for snow as we do, and we have quite a list: slush, sleet, powder, hardpack, dusting, flurries, flakes, drifts, blizzards, to name a few. And this list doesn't even begin to hint at the litany of meteorological terms for snow. So the words for snow are many—whether in our culture or that of the Inuits—but in either case they don't add up to one hundred.

The same may be said of other cultures that have an abundance of one natural phenomenon or another: Sahara peoples don't have appreciably more words for sand than we do; Londoners don't have inordinately many words for fog; Russians don't have a noticeable overabundance of words for vodka … you get the idea.

Kilts Must Be Worn without Underwear

It's true that some Highland traditionalists insist that kilts must be worn with no underwear. And some Scottish regiments dictate that underwear has no place in a proper military uniform. (As a result, going without is often euphemistically labeled "going regimental.")

But circumstances may have an influence on the option. For instance, marching on a very windy day without underwear may reveal more than the colors of one's tartan. And athletic competitions generally demand something be worn under the kilt. Ultimately, however, there is no absolute mandate one way or the other. The consensus is that whatever one chooses to wear under his kilt is his own business.

The Federal Reserve Is a Part of the Federal Government

The Federal Reserve System (the Fed, informally) is not a part of the federal government, but the government does have its hand on a few of the controls. The Fed is the central banking system of the United States. Ironically, it is both centralized and decentralized, in that it is run by a board of governors in Washington, D.C., but is made up of twelve privately owned regional banks (called Federal Reserve Banks) located in big cities across the country. Created by the Federal Reserve Act of 1913, the Fed was "designed to add both flexibility and strength to the nation's financial system." Among its tasks are regulating banks, setting interest rates, and controlling the money supply. So where does the federal government come in? The board and its often high-profile chairman are appointed by the president and must be approved by Congress. Although the president may try to influence the decisions of the Fed chairman, the chairman acts independently and need not comply.

Federal Reserve headquarters in the Eccles Building on Constitution Avenue in Washington, D.C.

CIA Agents Routinely Perform Daredevil Feats of Espionage

Most of the men and women who work for the CIA are not spies but technicians, analysts, and academics. Their task is to deal with the intelligence information gathered from satellite photography and imaging and electronic data—they also read a lot of foreign newspapers and other publications. The CIA employs more PhDs (from a variety of fields) than any other agency.

You would never suspect it from the legions of movie and television melodramas depicting secretive spies and duplicitous double agents, but less than 5 percent of CIA agents are involved in exciting stuff like espionage or covert operations. Even so, in keeping with the agency's penchant for secrecy, the public is not allowed to know the exact number of CIA employees or its operating budget. Petitions have been brought to Congress suggesting that funding be cut for covert ops, because the resources needed for field work can cost the government—and the taxpayers—a pretty penny.

Below is a picture of CIA headquarters in McLean, Virginia (only the headquarters, mind you—they've got offices all around the country and all over the world). It's a rather imposing building filled with cubicles and meeting rooms. Despite its appearance, it is not equipped with a huge indoor hockey rink. (Then again, who knows? Maybe it is.)

The likes of Harrison Ford and Kiefer Sutherland play suave and exhilarating characters in movies and on TV, but recent scandals and news stories have brought to light the mundane work that most CIA agents really do. When agent Valerie Plame was allegedly outed by one or another member of the Bush administration, it was revealed that she was merely an analyst, not some secret government super-spy.

Guess it just goes to show you, not even the most awe-inspiring government agencies are as captivating and compelling in real life as they seem on the silver screen.

Entrance to new CIA headquarters in McLean, Virginia. The agency has at times permitted filmmakers inside its venerable halls so that they could reproduce the ambience of the workplace on film.

Everyone's Fingerprints Are Unique; So Are Snowflakes

Using fingerprints as a forensic tool has a number of uncertainties associated with it, but for the most part it is still a valid and useful tool in police work. The notion that everyone's fingerprints are unique is centuries old, but not until 1892, when Sir Francis Galton proposed using that concept to identify wrongdoers, did criminologists start to take notice. Galton investigated the various forms of fingerprints. He also established criteria for identifying them, and for determining when two fingerprints came from the same person.

The act of imparting a fingerprint to a surface is subject to so many variables (material, temperature, pressure, etc.), that finding two fingerprints that are truly identical (even two from the same person) would strike experts as very unlikely—nearly as unlikely as finding  two people whose fingerprints were identical. Galton estimated that the process by which a fingerprint is formed is so random and unpredictable that the odds of two people having the same fingerprint are astronomically against—some 64 billion to one. He devised a system for describing and "matching" fingerprints that, when expanded, formed the basis of the method used in modern law inforcement.

In the 1990s, several court cases successfully challenged fingerprint evidence, showing the criteria for matching fingerprints to be highly subjective and susceptible to tampering and evidence planting. But assuming everything is on the up-and-up, that the fingerprints are clearly lifted and examined under controlled conditions, does the old adage about no two fingerprints being alike hold?

Here is one way of looking at it: in forming a fingerprint, which consists of a complex configuration of "ridges," growing skin comes to many forks in the developmental road, at each of which its evolving pattern can turn in one direction or another. After a series of fifteen such forks in the road, the number of possible outcomes amounts to more than 32,000, each equally likely. After thirty such forks, the number of outcomes is over 120 million; after fifty, the number explodes into the billions. Hence, under ideal circumstances and eliminating any subjectivity or possibility of fraud (both huge conditions), the

Ordinary hexagonal dendrite snowflake. Captured by the Beltsville Electron Microscopy Unit, part of the USDA.

likelihood of two people having the same fingerprint is minuscule—even smaller than Galton's 64 billion to one. But it's still not zero—so it remains theoretically possible.

The same question (and the same principle) would seem to apply to snowflakes: are there two snowflakes that are identical? For centuries, no one thought it was remotely possible—until 1988, when scientist Nancy Knight, of the National Center of Atmospheric Research, found two identical snow crystals in a Wisconsin snowstorm. Could the same be true of fingerprints? No one knows. But given what happened with snowflakes, it just goes to show that you can't rule out the possibility, however unlikely the odds.

A Life Sentence Costs More than an Execution

Nope, it's just the opposite. By some estimates, the death penalty is three to six times more costly to the taxpayer than life in prison. Why? For one thing, death penalty trials are different from regular murder trials. The defendants are less likely to plead guilty, no matter how much evidence is stacked up against them, so the trials may be up to five times longer. The trials require more lawyers, more preparation time, longer jury selections, and more expert witnesses. Many questions have arisen as to whether the cost is worth it. For one thing, a very small percentage of capital cases ever result in a death sentence; hence few victims are avenged (which is arguably the chief purpose of the death penalty in the first place). To pay for the cost of death penalty prosecutions, some jurisdictions have had to cut back on public crime-reduction plans. Others have had to reduce the size of their police forces, and still others have gone bankrupt.

Lloyd's of London Is an Insurance Company

You may have heard that the legs of certain celebrities—among them Betty Grable, Fred Astaire, and Mariah Carey—were insured by Lloyd's of London. True. But Lloyd's of London is not an insurance company. It is an "insurance market" consisting of multiple members that function as an association of separate underwriters. Lloyd's began in the 1600s, mainly for the purpose of insuring ships. It was named after Edward Lloyd, the owner of a coffeehouse where the members (merchants, ship owners, and underwriters) met.

A Manuscript Is Not Protected Until It Is Copyrighted

Many people think that until a book is actually published, with the circled letter *C* on the copyright page, it is not protected by copyright. Not so. A book or manuscript is protected by copyright from the moment it is created. The same goes for other creations, such as photographs,  musical recordings, and videos. This holds true even if the work has not been registered with the copyright office and regardless of whether or not the work displays a copyright notice. One thing you can't copyright is the title of a book.

Murder Has Always Been Against the Law in the U.S.

A Texas law passed in 1837 allowed a husband to kill his wife's lover if the two were caught *in flagrante delicto*—i.e., with his (or their) pants down (or skirt up). Seemingly to allow Texas husbands to keep their options open, the law was not repealed by the state legislature until 1974.

Prison Costs Less than a College Education

Just the opposite, and the difference in cost to the taxpayer is rather dramatic. For example, a 2002 study of fifteen western states found the average cost of a year in college to be about $9,500 per student and the average cost of a year in prison to be about $25,000 per inmate.

The Pennsylvania Dutch Came from Holland

Their ancestry is German, and their language is Pennsylvania German (as well as regular German and English). "Dutch" comes from *Deutsch*, which means German. Many, but not all, are Amish (pronounced "Ahm-ish," not "Aim-ish"). For the most part, the group's ancestors emigrated from Germany in the 1700s. But other of their forebears were English, Welsh, Scottish, French, and Swiss—not Dutch.

Boys Are Better at Math than Girls

In the early nineties, talking Barbie dolls were produced that said—among other phrases relating to clothes, shopping, and boys—"Math class is tough!" Far from offering evidence that girls are bad at math, Barbie's words gave us a glimpse into the reasons why this myth has been so difficult to discredit. Maybe girls find math tough not because they aren't as good at it as boys, but because their environment, even down to the toys they play with, discourages them from excelling at math.

The controversy over this issue has been stirring for decades. Obviously, the vast majority of mathematicians have been male. And boys have always scored better in math on standardized tests like the SAT. But these tests are often taken

when kids are in their teens, long after socialization has set it.

What's less often publicized is the fact that before the age of about twelve, girls score consistently higher than boys in math tests and get higher grades in math classes than boys. It's only in middle school—with all its attendant gender stereotypes and pressures—that this begins to change. By the twelfth grade, boys are scoring about 1.5 percent higher than girls. But that's hardly a major discrepancy.

The question remains, then: why don't more women choose to study math in college and go into math-related fields after graduation? Whatever the reason, it's not because they aren't good in math.

A Sailboat Cannot Sail Faster than the Wind That Propels It

Seems logical—but wrong! The mistake arises from a misunderstanding of the way sails and wind interact. The wind imparts a momentum to the sails that propels the boat connected to the sails. As long as the wind keeps imparting this momentum, the boat will speed up. This happens when the wind strikes the sail obliquely (at an angle) and then bounces off. A conventional sailboat (in the hands of a capable seaman) can easily sail at twice the speed of the prevailing wind; specially designed catamarans, which have low hull-weight to sail-weight ratios, can sail at eight times the wind speed.

Sailboats under the Menai Bridge in Wales.

Bullets Shot into the Air Are Harmless

No siree. A bullet shot into the air—even with the joyful exuberance of a partying bandito—leaves the gun barrel at anywhere from 500 to 1,500 miles per hour. At a weight of about five grams, the bullet would be as lethal coming down as it is going up, except for the air resistance, which might slow it down slightly. While the effect of being struck by such a bullet on its return to earth is not *as* deadly, it can still be deadly. Every year, dozens of people are severely injured and sometimes killed by bullets that were shot into the air (in celebration or warning) from, say, a quarter mile away.

A Bullet Can Knock Down a Man and Blow Up a Car

According to Newton's third law of motion, for every action, there is an equal and opposite reaction. This means that if a bullet is fired from a gun, the force imparted on a human being can be no greater than the amount of force the shooter feels as recoil. If the guy being shot is knocked backward by the force of the bullet, the shooter must also be knocked down when he fires the gun. A muscular reaction will most likely cause the body to lurch a bit, due to the shock to the nervous system caused by the bullet.

Bullets don't seem to be able to cause as much damage to certain objects in real life as they do in the movies. When cars instantly burst into flames when shot by one bullet in the movies, this is an extreme exaggeration. The only way this could happen would be if gas were to leak from a punctured gas tank onto a hot manifold. But according to tests, an ordinary bullet would not cause such a fire.

The Rickshaw Was Invented in China

While most people think of the rickshaw as quintessentially Chinese, it was invented in Japan by an American Baptist missionary named Jonathan Scobie in the 1860s. Based on the French *brouette*, the contraption was used to transport Scobie's invalid wife around Yokohama. Scobie later manufactured hundreds of rickshaws and used them to provide work for his converts. The word "rickshaw" comes from the Japanese words for "strength" and "vehicle."

Plaque and Tartar Are the Same Thing

"Plaque" is the sticky stuff that accumulates on your teeth. Bacteria in plaque secrete acidic toxins that erode the enamel of your teeth and can lead to gum disease. Brushing and/or flossing after each meal removes plaque.

"Tartar" is plaque that has not been removed and has hardened into rocklike deposits. It generally collects at the base of the tooth and under the gumline. Only a dentist can remove tartar.

George Reeves, TV's Superman, Committed Suicide

When George Reeves died, the man who played TV's Superman was no longer flying, but the rumors were. Various reports claimed that he committed suicide by jumping out a window because he had gone crazy and believed he really could fly—or that he simply shot himself in the head because his career was paralyzed due to typecasting. The coroner's report confirmed that he was shot in the head, but the suicide angle has been subject to much scrutiny and doubt.

Reeves had been dating the wife of a mob-tied Hollywood executive, who had been harassing Reeves for months, even after the wife and the actor broke up. When Reeves was found dead in his bedroom after a party, the evidence for suicide was not all that convincing: no fingerprints were found on the gun; no powder burns were found on his head; his hands were never tested for gunpowder residue; the empty shell was found not near his body but *under* it; and even though he was lying across the top of the bed, the gun was found between his feet.

Furthermore, Reeves was scheduled to do another season of shows, was engaged to be married, and was said to have been in jolly spirits. So does something smell fishy here? You bet.

Footnote: some say the Superman role is cursed, given the tragedy that befell Reeves' successor, who

George Reeves (1914–1959) was declared dead by gunshot wound, and his death was officially ruled a suicide.

coincidentally was, of course, named Christopher Reeve. (Keanu Reeves should probably choose his roles very carefully.)

Truth Serum Makes You Tell the Truth

It usually doesn't, except in the movies—and that's the truth. Various sedative substances (among them sodium pentothal, ethanol, and scopolamine) have been used by law enforcement personnel to coax the truth out of those unwilling to tell it, but most of the time it does not work.

Truth serum is probably even less reliable than the notoriously fallible polygraph (lie detector) test, the results of which in most jurisdictions are not admissible in court. In both instances, it's too easy to give a false positive—indicate one is lying about something known to be true.

Teachers with Tenure Can't Be Fired

After a probationary period, teachers may be granted tenure, which means they are allowed to keep their job indefinitely. Contrary to popular belief, however, this does not mean they can never be fired or laid off. It just means they can't be fired arbitrarily or without cause. For example, teachers with tenure may be fired for incompetence or serious misconduct but not for holding unpopular political views. People often believe tenure policy has changed in recent times. Not so.

You Can Stand an Egg on End Only on the Vernal Equinox

During the spring (vernal) equinox—which falls on March 20th or 21st—the earth's axis is 90 degrees away from the sun and the sun is exactly parallel to the equator, resulting in day and night being of equal length. (This particular balancing act is repeated at the fall [autumnal] equinox.) Since it occurs on the first day of spring, this event has long been associated with renewal, rebirth, and the dawning of a new natural cycle. Some religions even celebrate New Year's on this day.

The egg, of course, is a potent symbol of rebirth—hence the Christian tradition of

coloring and hiding eggs at Easter. Perhaps this is how the idea arose that on the spring equinox, raw eggs can be stood on their ends, supposedly denoting a kind of natural harmony that occurs on this day (special "gravitational forces" are often cited as the scientific explanation).

The truth is that you can perform this feat on the day of the vernal equinox—just as you can on any other day of the year. All you need is a perfectly level surface, the roundest egg you can find, a steady hand—and a lot of patience.

Wills Must Be Read Out Loud to the Family

Amid an atmosphere of uncertainty and suspense, the family gathers in the lawyer's office for the reading of Grandfather's will. With plodding solemnity, the bespectacled lawyer reads the document, and of course it contains a few surprises. To the greedy, good-for-nothing grandson, the black sheep of the family, "I leave the sum of one dollar." And to Oscar, the family's loyal servant of many decades, "I leave the sum of one million dollars." Or so it goes in the movies and mystery novels.

In real life (or real death), a will is rarely read out loud. Copies are sent from the lawyer to the beneficiaries, and the will is filed with the county clerk's office. Once filed, the will becomes a public document that can be viewed by anyone who shows up at the Hall of Records and asks to see it.

Umbrellas Were Designed to Keep the Rain Off

Umbrellas, which have appeared in ancient Egyptian, Greek, and Chinese art, have been around for thousands of years. But they were first used as parasols—designed not to keep the rain off but to provide shade from the sun. The Chinese, by waxing or lacquering their paper parasols, were first to use them as rain protection.

Above right: Umbrellas in trees at Seattle's Bumbershoot festival, 2005.

Jayne Mansfield Was Decapitated When She Died

In the early morning hours of June 29, 1967, on a stretch of Highway 90 outside of the New Orleans suburb of Slidell, Louisiana, the life of Jayne Mansfield, one of Hollywood's most iconic sex symbols, came to an end.

Mansfield, traveling with her boyfriend, Sam Brody, and three of her five children (Mariska, Zoltan, and Miklós), was being driven to an engagement in New Orleans on that fateful night. The road that they traveled was obscured by the haze from a distant mosquito fogger that prevented the car's driver from seeing the tractor-trailer ahead of him. The obstructed view resulted in the car crashing into the truck and then sliding under it. Mansfield, Brody, and the car's driver, Ronnie Harrison, were killed instantly. The three children seated in the back escaped serious injury.

Due to the catastrophic nature of the accident and the larger-than-life status of one of its victims, rumors began to circulate that Mansfield was decapitated in the accident—but is that how she really died?

Although Mansfield's death was gruesome, she was not beheaded. According to her New Orleans Certificate of Death, the immediate cause of death is listed as a "crushed skull with avulsion of cranium and brain." Scalping, not beheading, is perhaps a closer description of Mansfield's injury: "avulsion of cranium and brain" means that the top of her skull and brain were torn or sliced away.

So, where did the decapitation myth begin? The source is likely Kenneth Anger's 1975 book *Holly-wood Babylon*. The work features a photo

Jayne Mansfield (1933–1967).

of the mangled car and what appears to be a blonde wig (or, possibly, the top of Mansfield's head) nearby.

Similar urban legends surround the death of many Hollywood celebrities—from James Dean to Princess Diana. There just seems to be something compelling about a celebrity with a widely recognizable face losing it in the process of his or her demise.

An Epilogue
in Fifteen Dedications

Harold Rabinowitz is the "packager" of Amazing … But False! *The role of a book packager (in this case The Reference Works, where Harold is at the helm) is to assemble a book, including all the text and illustrations, and then present it in its final form to a publisher, who prints and distributes it. Harold is much more than the book's packager, however. Gradually, over a period of many decades, he was instrumental in developing the concept of* Amazing … But False! *In the engaging account that follows, he traces his many-faceted sentimental journey and the intriguing stops he made along the way.*

Dave, our author/editor of this tome, observes in his "Author's Note" at the very start of the book that people don't usually read prefaces (which is what his Author's Note really is). Well, how many of the few people who read prefaces do you think bother to also read epilogues? Not many, I'll wager, so it looks like it's just us, dear reader.

Now, as the "packager" (the one who assembles a book and presents it to a publisher in its final form) of *Amazing … But False!*, and as one who played a key role in developing the concept for the book, I think I may have a few interesting points to make; at least I hope they will be informative… perhaps even entertaining. I've chosen a somewhat idiosyncratic way of doing this: I'm going to lay out a series of dedications we didn't select for this book and annotate them with a commentary. Like people who collect mugs or ashtrays from all the places they've been to, these dedications chart a rivulet that courses through my life, lining one particular strain that forms a recurring theme.

Right about now, you're probably turning back to the beginning of the book to learn to whom we did dedicate the book; let me save you the trouble: after much discussion and debate, we dedicated the book to the fictional character Cliff Clavin, the lovably irascible mailman who graced the barstool in the TV sitcom *Cheers*, played pitch-perfect by John Ratzenberger. I'm happy with this choice; Cliff Clavin is the poster child for misinformation, and I am frankly surprised he didn't have more of a presence on *Frasier*, the successful spin-off of *Cheers*.

But there were other candidates—some generally known, who would have been appropriate; and some wholly personal, making some explanation necessary (if not useful). In the end, the dedication in the front of the book was determined by Dave, and that was as it should be; the dedication is properly the author's province. But we're alone now, you and I, and here are the people I would choose—some well known, some barely known, some known only to me. In the course of this, you'll discover many of the sources that led me to undertake this particular book project, both in terms of hard information and in terms of inspiration and spiritual encouragement.

DEDICATION

To Jimmy Wales, Founder of Wikipedia.com, and to Michael and Helen Selzer, Founders of Bibliofind.com

The first, the man who has done more than anyone else in history to expose just how much misinformation abounds, and whose work assures people like me an inexhaustible supply of material and a virtually never-ending source of income; and the second, who ended the need to comb through the dusty back rooms of countless used book stores … but not the pleasure of it.

This was the dedication I had wanted in the front of the book, but Dave spoke so eloquently of the contribution Wikipedia had made to the advancement of knowledge that I relented. But just think for a moment about the task of this book—not simply to list facts but to correct misapprehensions that are commonly held.

In the early days of Wikipedia, all sorts of things were appearing. The *Onion* ran a front-page story a while back under the headline: "Wikipedia Celebrates 750 Years of American Independence" with a subhead that read, "Founding Fathers, Patriots, Mr. T Honored." Now even though this headline ran just this past summer, it is way out of date. Wikipedia has taken steps to ensure some editorial oversight over the content (so that American Independence Day is not celebrated on July 25th).

The Selzers, who created Bibliofind, will never know the effect they have had on my life. Before Bibliofind, I had to pore through the dusty back rooms and basements of used book stores to find the old books I needed —and those I might one day need. Now I can find any book in any store around the world and can get any book I need whenever I need it. If I rummage in used book stores these days, I do so just for the pleasure of poring through old tomes (which I someday hope to understand and explain). Every now and then, however, I am gripped with the fear that something terrible will happen and the phenomenon of Bibliofind.com (or the other large service of that kind, AbeBooks.com) will cease to be available. What a dark day that will be.

DEDICATION

To My Uncle Laybl

The man to whom I will always be grateful for the phrase "Amazing … But False!"

My mother's brother, Laybl, was only a year or two younger than her, but she always treated him with great respect. Why? Because he was educated. And what he was educated in was optometry. He was an optometrist. I would discover later that he was able to get a license to "practice" optometry by being able to sign his name. Nevertheless, my mother called him "Dr. Roth," explaining that he was, after all, the boss of an optometrist who was himself a doctor.

Uncle Laybl was a fount of misinformation and is probably responsible for a variety of misconceptions that I still harbor. As I grew older, I would listen to his pronouncements with an amused smile. He would say, "Isn't that amazing, Hershel?" and I would say (still smiling), "Yes, Uncle Laybl—amazing … but false!" I would then try to correct my uncle (in that smart-aleck way Brooklyn whippersnappers excel in), much to my parents' disapproval. I would repeat these exchanges to my classmates and sometimes to my teachers, and by the time I got to college, this phrase would become my signature phrase. I would often say that one day I would write a book with that title.

A few months ago, I was in a hotel lobby in Jerusalem and saw a man walking toward me whom I recognized as someone I knew in college over thirty years ago. He recognized me too, and when we were both finished joyfully greeting each other, the first thing he asked me was, "So, did you ever get to do *Amazing … But False!*?" I have Uncle Laybl to thank for that—for the phrase and for the obsession.

DEDICATION

To H. Allen Smith and Paul Tabori

Two childhood heroes—whose voices still ring in my ears so many years later.

Twice in my younger years I was hospitalized due to accidents, both times for several weeks, and both times in Beth Israel Hospital in Manhattan. Aside from the injury, I was perfectly fine and alert, which means that I was soon incredibly bored. The library cart that came around had virtually nothing but romance novels and a few westerns, but it had two other books that were well worn, though the volunteer told me it had been years since anyone had read them: one was a book by H. Allen Smith entitled *Low Man on the Totem Pole;* the other was a book by Paul Tabori, *The Art of Folly.*

I had been a voracious reader before, but these books captured me as none others before—was it something in them that was different, or in me, or was it just that I was able to lavish much more attention on these as the hours passed? There was a familiar, urbane sophistication that somehow spoke to me with a voice I recognized as congenial with the one I already had inside my head.

I have since devoured and enjoyed many books by these two: among my all-time favorites is Smith's *Buskin' with H. Allen Smith,* his compendium of tall tales and home-spun wisdom; and Tabori's *The Natural Science of Stupidity* (republished recently under the title *The Natural History of Stupidity*). Tabori emphasized the role pure and sober knowledge plays in a free and humane society. Someday I'm going to find a reason to anthologize his "Martian Memo," in which a Martian comments on the foibles of us Earthlings.

I'm convinced that everyone for whom the written word is important has books like these—books that, though minor, still left a lasting impression on a young mind about the power of words and the presence of voice. These were mine, and they have stayed with me my entire life; in some ways, I have spent a lifetime trying to emulate these two writers or become an odd amalgam of the two of them.

DEDICATION

To A. S. E. Ackerman

The man who wrote his books so I wouldn't have to go out and acquire many other books—my God, was he wrong!

On a bright fall day as I was nearing my twelfth birthday, I took the Metropolitan Avenue Bus down Grand Street in the Williamsburg section of Brooklyn to visit a sick friend in the Greenpoint Projects. When I got off the bus, there was a thrift shop in front of me and among the bric-a-brac on the stands on the sidewalk were a few books, above which was a sign that read, "Books 25 cents." Twenty-five cents!—not bad, I thought. So I looked, and among the flotsam and jetsam in the bin (mainly Reader's Digest condensed books, as I remember) I found a hefty volume entitled *Popular Fallacies Explained and Corrected,* by A. S. E. Ackerman, published by Lippincott in 1924.

Though buying it meant I would not have enough money for the bus and would have to walk home, I sprang for it—and spent the next month poring through it. What incredible things I found in that volume: "That Archimedes destroyed the Fleet of Marcellus of Syracuse in 212 BCE by means of Mirrors reflecting the Sun's rays." That wasn't true, but who knew you could even imagine that could be done? "That Marriage usually takes place between Persons having opposite Characteristics, e.g., Tall with Short, Dark with Fair, etc." You mean that's not true? You mean it's not true that people who like it cold in the bedroom wind up invariably with people who like it hot? "That Increasing the Weight of the Bob of a Pendulum makes the Clock go more slowly." It doesn't? I don't believe it; I gotta see this for myself. And so I did—and that was my introduction to physics.

That simple encounter got me hooked on books; started me on the road to physics; and into the fine art of debunking. Having spent half my bus fare on the Ackerman book, I figured I might as well buy another.

Ironically, Ackerman writes in the preface to his book that his motivation was to save the reader the trouble of having to acquire all the books necessary to research all the subjects he covered. But what's this? In small letters at the bottom of the sign: "Paperbacks 10 cents?" Why, I could buy another and still have some left over for a Chunky! So I looked through the paperbacks for something that "looked Jewish," thinking I might need it to defend this purchase with my parents. What was that second book that I bought? I'll tell you later.

DEDICATION

To Rabbi D.

Who presented me with the two great mysteries of my young life.

After spending an entire summer desperately trying to "save" me from a life without piety, Rabbi D. forced upon me a decision: would I allow him to throw color war (the grand competitive games that mark the end of the summer camp season) for the sake of a young man who would be distraught if one team did not win? I was on a stretcher at the time, wincing with pain as I was being carried to a waiting makeshift ambulance. I said yes as I was driven away—but I have never been able to be certain whether or not this was only a test of Rabbi D.'s devising.

Why is this important? Because it was during those weeks in the hospital, with these questions buzzing around my head, during the time I encountered Smith and Tabori, that I discovered something remarkable: writing about what happened that summer actually helped me make sense and, more importantly, make peace with the remarkable events that had transpired. I filled pages and pages in my barely legible yeshiva-boy scrawl, all on the back of Beth Israel Hospital stationery. There was Zorch the lifeguard, Fish the canteen owner, Bobby the counselor, and Mordy the … Oh, what I wouldn't give to have some of those pages today.

But why did writing about what happened help? I don't know, but I then became a writing fool, filling pages and pages of my own private blatherings, even as I went on to become an editor of (I hope) reliable, rock-solid reference books.

Rabbi D. never visited me in the hospital; I have not, in fact, had any contact with him since, though I've been told that he has gone on to become a respected Talmudist in the yeshiva community. But here I am thanking him for making me … the sorry, pathetic, obsessive wordsmith I am today (just kidding about the "sorry, pathetic" part).

DEDICATION

To Martin Gardner

The man who first showed me that criticism is as much a part of science as it is a part of literature.

In a spring of the early eighties, I spent several weeks at my father's bedside as he recuperated from being run over by a car. It was touch and go for some time, but he eventually recovered well enough to walk with a cane. During those weeks in the hospital (again Beth Israel, as it turned out—must be the food), I needed a book to read to distract me from the unending worry about and attention to my dad, and what I found was a book by Martin Gardner entitled *Science: Good, Bad and Bogus*.

Using an inimitable style that is at the same time engrossing and yet unadorned, Gardner does a number on all manner of pseudoscience and folderol with humor, and even a little kindness. In those difficult days, he became my companion and my solace. I quickly found another title he had done earlier (but not so much earlier as to warrant reprinting by Dover, which is what it was) called *In the Name of Science*. These two titles are what saw me through those difficult times, and I'll always be grateful to Martin for them.

Now we are seeing a time when a critical approach to science has been downplayed and physics is in a pickle that it doesn't quite know how to get out of (see the Dedication after the next one). That spirit of criticism—one that science was no stranger to in times past, but which the current economic tyrannies of tenure and career have made a thing of the past—is one that modern science would do well to learn, and it could find no better teacher than Martin.

DEDICATION

To Irving Agus and Meir Feldblum

Who showed that beneath the shifting sands that lay at the foundations of Jewish history and the Talmud lies a rock even firmer than the most devout can imagine.

During a brief graduate career in Judaica, I made the acquaintance of two scholars who gave me so much, and I have never had the right opportunity to thank them: Irving Agus was a professor of Jewish History and Rabbi Meir Feldblum was a professor of Talmud. In addition to teaching in fields of Judaica, they had something else in common: they were both considered contrarians and unorthodox (or should I say unconventional) by both colleagues and students— even as they were respected for the depth of their learning and the breadth of their knowledge.

They had something else in common: they both taught—one in the corridors of medieval European Jewish history; the other in the corridors of Near Eastern Talmudic textual analysis—that an uncompromising look at the foundations of faith, and the historical underpinnings of its texts, cannot be a wasted and trivial enterprise—nor can it be dangerous or blasphemous. Whatever happened, happened—and it was up to us to make sense of it and to understand it.

Both men had difficult lives, alternately being considered cranks or upstarts. But I knew them both as warm, kind men who cared about their students and about their work—who took that work as seriously as they took their own existence on this planet. What more could one ask of a scholar? I would dedicate this work to them because I could hear both of them saying, "That's *all* that's not true?"

DEDICATION

To Leonard Susskind and David Finkelstein

One who taught me enough string theory to let me pass on it—early; and the other who taught me enough physics to make it a pleasurable obsession for life.

In a winter of the early seventies, I found myself in a graduate physics program being run under the auspices of a Jewish university. Many of the faculty were Jewish (though I believe only one professor was observant), and many had admitted to me at one point or another that they were there to perform some service to their Jewishness. Whatever.

I took one course in Mathematical Methods, a requirement, with Susskind, but he decided that he wasn't going to waste time lecturing on that. Instead, he taught us about a burgeoning new theory, string theory, and left us to learn the math from the available textbooks. The other course was in quantum theory with a great practitioner of the field, David Finkelstein.

So here's how it worked: we'd hear lectures from Susskind in the late morning, then trot over to Finkelstein and discuss what we had learned with him. Professors in those days didn't do much conversing (now they do even less), so in many ways, this was an extended conversation the two physicists were having through us.

At the end of the course, the five of us in the class had hopes that Professor Susskind would simply forget about a final exam; the fact is we had had a rollicking time working with him on the niceties of this new theory, and (you remember the sixties) physics professors were known to do things like that.

On the last day, Susskind turned to me and asked me, "So, Harold, what do you think?" In what has become an expensive and annoying habit, I answered honestly; "What do I think? I think you're full of s—!" He smiled, turned to the entire class, and said, "I hope you gentlemen have been studying Arfken carefully; the final will be based on that book."

I aced that final, but the experience convinced me that physics was not a career I could embark on. Though the "string theory mafia" had not yet taken control, it was obvious that if you didn't believe in the theory, and didn't actually work in it, you were not going to be able to get very far in physics. Now I read in many quarters physicists bemoaning what a sorry and fruitless spectacle string theory has made of the discipline and of modern science. Well, let me tell you that that was clear back then. And that experience—with those two scientists—saved me thirty years of pointless, misguided work in the cushy environs of the physics academe.

DEDICATION

To Claudia de Lys and Vilhjalmur Stefansson

Whose books opened a world worth knowing beyond the streets of Williamsburg.

Except for Flohr's Hebrew Book Store on Division Avenue, there were no bookstores in Williamsburg while I was growing up (notwithstanding that thrift shop on Grand Street), so the Williamsburg Public Library was, for me, a very important place. Two books that I found there left a very lasting impression, and I have since acquired several copies of them: Claudia de Lys' *Treasury of American Superstitions* and *Adventures in Error* by Vilhjalmur Stefansson. They are both dedicated to correcting popular misconceptions, but they do it in unique and admirable ways.

The first through an uncompromising erudition of the scientific literature—showing a fairness and thoroughness of which I believe ol' A. S. E. Ackerman would approve, and a fat-free and trim prose that a marathon-runner would envy; and the second by actually going there and checking it out.

Stefansson was a Harvard-trained anthropologist whose explorations of the Arctic were models of serious, scientific research—he coined the phrase "adventure is a sign of incompetence." By the time I found Barry Lopez and Farley Mowat on wolves, I was already well aware that most of what we know about the animal was wrong. I have turned to these books again and again; de Lys has been republished many times, but Stefansson has sadly been forgotten.

DEDICATION

To Gershon

My weekly companion for eight years—keeper of secrets.

Having to walk a mile and a half to synagogue every Saturday for eight years, and then back again, I had as my companion a junk man who was also our Torah reader. His name was Gershon and he was a man with a great white beard (neighborhood kids were convinced he was Santa in disguise), huge hands, and a pleasant smile.

I discovered that a junk man knows more about what's going on in a community than just about anybody. And being a stalwart member of the synagogue, he knew even a bit more. Junk knows no religious denomination, so Gershon dealt with all sorts of people in the area, and he and his truck covered the entire North Shore.

As far as I'm concerned, Gershon was the first person in the community—an area north of Boston near the Fells Reservation—who noticed that so many people were succumbing to cancer. He noticed this well before the people in Woburn brought their lawsuit, and maybe even before those people noticed something was amiss, for there were similar outbreaks in other communities in the area, and only a junk man would know that.

Gershon tried to alert me to this—as a member of the Burial Society, he had attended to many of the congregation who had passed on, and so he was painfully aware of how many people in the community had been struck down by cancer. I began asking other clergy in the area if they noticed anything unusual among their flock.

I was just coming to the conclusion that something was amiss and had taken steps to gather some leaders from different faiths to discuss this when I (as my colleagues put it) got "bounced out of the pulpit." I know Gershon tried to alert others, but few people took him seriously. And that's the lesson in all this, isn't it? At any given moment, someone, somewhere is thinking something that everyone else thinks is wrong or has overlooked, and that someone could be anyone—a clerk in the Swiss Patent Office or a junk man in Massachusetts.

DEDICATION

To Tom Burnam and J. Allen Varasdi

For my money, inventors of the genre.
And to all their fellow debunkers.

Burnam and Varasdi authored books that could very well be looked upon as the model for what we are doing in this book, but as Alan Garner, the British fantasy writer, once said, "every generation has to create its own *Iliad*." Burnam did one classic volume—*The Dictionary of Misinformation*—and then followed it up with an even more interesting sequel—*More Misinformation*. Varasdi authored a book entitled *Myth-Information*. Both are alphabetically arranged and contain mountains of material on the subject—all engagingly written, with an admirable care for detail and precision.

There have been others deserving of mention and acknowledgment: Richard Shenkman produced a series of books, all entertaining and all rock solid in their scholarship. The most famous one is *One-Night Stands with American History*, but you'll get just as much joy from *Legends, Lies and Cherished Myths of American History; Legends, Lies and Myths of World History;* and the inimitable *I Love Paul Revere Whether He Rode or Not*.

The field has its practitioners, many of whom have made contributions to our enlightenment—I salute them all. Beginning with James Randi (who was kind enough to contribute a foreword to this volume); Ian Wilson, whose books on religious subjects, and Colin Wilson, whose books on the occult, have all been real eye-openers. Being able to see beyond the borders of the conventional has always been deemed a valuable talent—and sharing that a valuable gift, at least until recently. It's frankly amazing how conventional people have become, fearing anything really new or avant-garde.

One toiler in these fields deserves special mention, because he has taken the enterprise to a new level of seriousness. That's Michael Shermer. I had read six books by this man before I realized they were all by the same author. Each one—*How We Believe; The Borderlands of Science; Science Friction;* and *Why People Believe Weird Things*—and many others all deserve to be read and studied. I for one can't wait to see what he comes up with next.

Of course, we musn't forget about the hooey-mongers of the past—the "experts" who predicted that people would never fly or reach the moon, or that the stock market would never break 1,000. Many of these "expert" pronouncements have been collected by Christopher Cerf and Victor S. Navsky in an entertaining volume entitled, *The Experts Speak*. Seeing how wrong the intellectual leaders of bygone eras have, in fact, been, would, one would suppose, instill a little humility in the leaders of today. Fat chance!

Finally, authors of such books all owe a debt to the Wallechinsky family (and it's leader, Irving Wallace) for the many books issued over the years under the rubric of *The People's Almanac*. In addition to being enormously entertaining, these volumes celebrated the enterprise of fact-finding and brought style and humor to what was previously a dreary field.

DEDICATION

To Shirley

Who proved that no one knows what's best for you better than you.

This is a sort of left-handed dedication, because this person and I were once related. I seriously doubt whether the lesson I learned from Shirley has been learned by Shirley herself, but that lesson is simply this: for better or for worse, no one can know what's best for another person better than the person himself (or herself). Life is just too complicated and too personal to allow anyone to make up another person's mind. I really like (and have often used) a line attributed to Adlai Stevenson: "If two people think exactly the same thing, you can be sure only one of them is doing the thinking."

How many times have I heard people say about others (or even about me), if only he could do this, or if only he would do that. But the truth is, we really never know the full situation a person faces.

I've watched people ruin the lives of others because they thought they knew what was best for them. Parents do it to children; governments do it to citizens—even doctors do it to patients. If this book does anything, I hope it instills in readers a modicum of humility—if you can be wrong about such trivialities, might you not be wrong about things that really matter?

I dedicate this to Shirley for another reason: because the time has come for me to decide whether the price I paid to pursue the dream I had some thirty years ago was worth it. It would be easy to say it was were I basking in the aura of success—but I'm not. I'm struggling like just about everybody else in the publishing game. And that's when saying it means the most: yes, it's been worth it ... so there, Shirley.

DEDICATION

To Leo Rosten

Whose books on error brought intelligence and style to a subject that could have languished on the promotional shelves forever.

As a child, I was a great fan of Rosten; we would stage dramatizations of his Hyman Kaplan stories for assemblies, to an audience that was appreciative if somewhat fatigued in the late afternoon after a long day in the classroom—or maybe that's why they were appreciative. Rosten's style was as clear as it was infectious, and I often have to catch myself from lapsing into that style.

Rosten was comfortable in virtually any field he tackled, and his reference books—mainly on Jewish subjects—are classics for their humor and their authority. In the late seventies, he authored a volume entitled *The Power of Positive Nonsense* that contained his take on the subject of popular misconceptions. Many of the pieces that appear in this book began as thoughts voiced by Rosten; we hope we did him proud.

He also authored several other volumes about people famous and near-famous, always writing about them with warmth, reverence, and honesty.

Rosten was (I've heard) attached to the Navy as a cryptologist during World War II and was known in cryptology circles as an expert in the field. That makes his influence all the more authoritative in this book; ferreting out the truth from a coded message is a fit metaphor for what we are doing here ... in fact, one might say, for what life is all about.

Anyway, we single out L*E*O R*O*S*T*E*N, not because he needs any endorsement from the likes of me. His was a writing style marked with both humanity and knowledge, passion and compassion, wit, charm, and seriousness of purpose. To him go our thanks for many hours of reading and thinking pleasure.

DEDICATION

To Nancy Burns-Silver

A Woman of Valor, Courage, and Mercy—and possessor of the most finely tuned BS detector I've ever known.

Nancy came to me after producing a self-published guide for cancer patients entitled *Cancer Made Easier*. As a seasoned reference editor, I was amazed at what a good job she had done; she was, after all, an amateur in reference publishing. But Nancy had a need to help others, and she came to us hoping we would ply our craft and create a more useful book. I'm glad we were able to complete the production of the book in time for her to see it; that we have not been successful disseminating it is a continuing disappointment.

I would dedicate this book to Nancy for another reason. She had as well developed a sense for detecting BS as I've ever come across. She had heard every promise a physician could make and had come to the realization that—they really don't know. In a race against the clock, Nancy knew, the clock always wins, and nothing you know today will seem as solid tomorrow. That's why, in contrast to all the buckaroo heart surgeons, the only doctors I've ever known who could be described as humble are all oncologists.

DEDICATION

To Walter M. Miller, Jr.

For showing us a glimpse of a future—hopefully not ours.

That other book I found on the stands in front of that thrift shop on Grand Street was a paperback novel: *A Canticle for Liebowitz*, by Walter Miller. In a way, everything I've done since has been a conscious or unconscious effort to reproduce that work and pay homage to it. Now I realize that Miller was not a great stylist; he can't hold a candle to Vonnegut, for example. But, as they say, you never forget the love of your youth, and *Liebowitz* was a book that stayed with me for many years—it still haunts me.

I kept waiting for Miller to write something else, but the only things that I ever saw were occassional short stories. I had heard that he had become a recluse, and when the same thing seemed to have happened to another literary hero of mine, Henry Roth, I began to wonder if I had become a jinx.

Miller shot himself in 1996 (at the age of seventy-two), just months after his wife of nearly five decades passed away, succumbing to cancer. He was even more

of a recluse during his final years, and I imagine (though I have no hard information on this) that he was a very tortured soul. The book is often considered a pessimistic, apocalyptic work; I couldn't sleep for a week after reading the section on Francis' death.

But today I see it as hopeful. If *something* can endure so bleak an end to the world, then maybe we can endure fates less … final. One passage that appears toward the end of the book has particular meaning to me these days and is worth thinking about—and I end this experiment in epilogue with it:

"Listen, are we helpless? Are we doomed to do it again and again and again? Have we no choice but to play the Phoenix, in an unending sequence of rise and fall? Assyria, Babylon, Egypt, Greece, Carthage, Rome, the Empires of Charlemagne and the Turk. Ground to dust and plowed with salt. Spain, France, Britain, America—burned into the oblivion of the centuries. And again and again and again."

Index

Image Credits

Pamela Adler – pp. 48, 186, 196, 224, 231

Rene Baur/Cleft Cartoons – p. 109

Bildarchiv Preußischer Kulturbesitz – p. 72

Bureau of Land Management – p. 94

Daryl Cagle/Cagle Cartoons, Inc. – p. 189

California Institute of Technology – p. 72

Central Intelligence Agency – p. 228

Denkrahm – p. 159

Fall River Police Department – p. 68

Jeffrey Frole – pp. 166, 222, 235

General Mills – p. 140

Craig M. Groshek – p. 116

Dr. Samuel D. Harris National Museum of Dentistry – p. 82

Illinois Historic Preservation Agency – p. 77

istockphoto.com – pp. 96, 111, 156, 157, 166, 232, 235

John F. Kennedy Presidential Library – p. 75

Library and Archives Canada – p. 218

Library of Congress – pp. 23, 25, 28, 29, 34, 39, 44, 64, 67, 70, 73, 74, 76, 77, 78, 79, 165, 194, 203, 210, 217, 219

The Mariner's Museum Collection – p. 78

Missouri Department of Conservation – p. 107

National Aeronautics and Space Administration – pp. 71, 84, 86, 88, 99, 190, 191, 213

National Archives and Records Administration – pp. 21, 35, 145, 208, 212

National Atlas of the United States – p. 192

National Biological Information Infrastructure – p. 108

National Cancer Institute – pp. 138, 139, 141, 147, 152, 157

National Gallery of Canada – p. 38

National Human Genome Research Institution – p. 152

National Institutes of Health – pp. 138, 148, 152

National Oceanic and Atmospheric Administration – pp. 19, 93, 102

Ronald Reagan Presidential Library – p. 205

Franklin D. Roosevelt Presidential Library – p. 202

Dan Smith – p. 227

Harry S. Truman Presidential Library – p. 81

United States Army – p. 110

United States Census Bureau – p. 234

United States Department of Agriculture – pp. 133, 135, 229

United States Department of Energy – pp. 33, 104

United States Department of Health and Human Services – p. 158

United States Department of the Interior – p. 20

United States Department of the Navy – pp. 37, 42

United States Fish & Wildlife Service – pp. 112, 120, 126, 129, 135

United States Geological Survey – pp. 97, 123

United States National Park Service – pp. 113, 195

University of California Cooperative Extension – p. 110

University of California, San Francisco – p. 155

The Reference Works, Inc. would like to thank the following for their hard work in bringing this volume to publication: Editors Pamela Adler and Harold Rabinowitz, Photo Editor Elizabeth O'Sullivan, Editorial Interns Cynthia Hamilton and Briana Lugo, Copy Editor Jean Rogers, and Indexer Jack Donner.

1	4	3	5	9	8	7	6	2
9	6	8	7	3	2	4	1	5
7	5	2	1	4	6	3	9	8
5	2	7	6	8	4	1	3	9
8	9	1	3	7	5	2	4	6
4	3	6	2	1	9	5	8	7
6	1	9	4	2	7	8	5	3
2	8	4	9	5	3	6	7	1
3	7	5	8	6	1	9	2	4

Sudoku solution from page 27.